Leninism

Leninism

ALFRED G. MEYER

FREDERICK A. PRAEGER, *Publisher*
New York

BOOKS THAT MATTER

Published in the United States of America in 1962 by
Frederick A. Praeger, Inc., Publisher
64 University Place, New York 3, N.Y.

The original clothbound edition of this book
was published in 1957 by Harvard University Press,
Cambridge, Mass.

Library of Congress Catalog Card Number: 62-10312

Manufactured in the United States of America

For Eva

Preface

In publishing this work, I am repaying part of a debt I owe to the Russian Research Center, Harvard University, with which I was associated for five years. Under the center's auspices I wrote my doctoral dissertation, "Lenin's Theory of Revolution" (completed in 1949), on which the present work is based to some extent. I owe gratitude also to Professor Harold H. Fisher and the entire staff of the Hoover Institute, Stanford University, where I began my research in the writings of Lenin, aided by a generous Fellowship in Slavic Studies. Additional leisure to put the work into its final form was provided through the generous assistance of the Research Program on the History of the Communist Party of the Soviet Union, Columbia University. Professor Robert L. Wolff helped me considerably by giving me an opportunity to teach a course on the development of communist ideology under the auspices of the Committee on International and Regional Studies, Harvard University, in 1951 and 1952. Professors Hans Apel, Robert V. Daniels, Victor Erlich, Merle Fainsod, Michael Karpovich, Clyde K. M. Kluckhohn, Herbert Marcuse, Talcott Parsons, and Nicholas N. Poppe, and Mr. Richard De Haan have read the manuscript from beginning to end and provided a great deal of valuable criticism and advice. Professor William Y. Elliott was a patient and kind adviser while I was writing my dissertation.

Columbia University
March 1956

A. G. M.

Contents

Leninism

Note

Throughout the footnotes, the titles of articles, speeches, and pamphlets by Lenin will be cited in English for the convenience of the reader. All translations of quotations are by the author, unless stated otherwise.

In the transliteration of Russian, a modification of the system adopted by the Library of Congress has been used. But, since the names of some of the leaders of the Russian revolution are familiar to American readers in different spellings, I have taken some liberties with the transliteration system in the case of family names. For instance, family names which in Russian end in ский have throughout the book been given the ending "sky" (Trotsky, Osinsky, etc.).

Introduction

The importance of an understanding of Leninism (which denotes the thought not only of Lenin himself but also of his associates) for a grasp of contemporary world affairs needs no elaboration, although the mark it will make in the development of social thought in the very long run is probably being underestimated. At the same time, even among those who consider it important to become acquainted with Leninism, there is by no means agreement about the reasons why we should study it. It is undisputable that the ideas and behavior traditions of V. I. Lenin, the leader of the Russian revolution, have caught the imagination of millions in our day and represent the official Holy Writ for the subjects of vast empires comprising over a third of the earth's population. But the task of making a broad survey of Leninism is made difficult by a number of factors. Based on a philosophy that is uncongenial to thinkers in our culture, Leninism comprises a set of uncomfortable and highly controversial ideas, the very preoccupation with which can serve, today, to compromise a writer. Since Leninism is at the same time deceptively crude and simple, at least in the way in which its advocates are wont to propound it, many students of political thought tend to consider it unworthy of serious attention. Hence, instead of inquiring what Leninism is, our social scientists have more often asked themselves why anyone might be prompted to turn to these ideas and follow them. The relevancy of any study of Leninism has been questioned. Its appeal has indeed been noted, and its official acceptance as virtual dogma in the entire communist world is acknowledged, but there is a good deal of dispute over the effectiveness of Leninist ideas even in this communist world. The extreme flexibility of Leninism makes it possible for communist leaders to justify almost any policy by pulling a set of suitable quotations from the grab bag of Lenin's pronouncements. Hence the conviction is widespread that Leninism has turned into a dead letter, in no way determining the actions of communist leaders, whether they are in command of a revolutionary party or manage an established regime. While some students derive the entire history of the communist world from Leninism, others have turned for that purpose to Russian history or to a survey of the social forces in communist society, and they give little or no relevance to the theoretical heritage of Leninism.

In presenting the reader with a survey of Leninism, I do not wish to follow either extreme. I am firmly convinced that the growth of communist parties and the history of communist regimes can not be understood without a knowledge of the social structure, the political past, and the economic problems of the societies involved, and it will be apparent to the reader that the development of Leninist ideas has been shaped decisively by just such social, economic, political, and historical conditions. I would not, however, have written this book were I not convinced that the tradition of ideas itself has had an influence on the history of communist parties and regimes. It may be true that Leninism has been reduced to a grab bag of rationalizations and justifications and that the makers of communist policy have turned into unprincipled Machiavellians, whose attitude toward Leninism is entirely manipulative. It may be true, although there is a good deal of evidence to the contrary. Even if it were true, however, it would not mean that Leninism had become entirely irrelevant for an understanding of communist policies. For, even if the leaders' attitude toward it were altogether manipulative, it would still be true that they thought in terms of Leninism. Their image of the outside world, their approach to the solution of problems — everything they see and everything they do is couched in the imagery of Lenin's ideas, so that, their manipulative attitude notwithstanding, these ideas provide the concepts which determine not only their thoughts but also their actions. Unconsciously or consciously every communist leader looks back to Lenin for guidance in solving his problems and understanding the world. Unwittingly or wittingly he lets Lenin do some of his thinking for him; and, for this reason, Leninism is the theme on which all subsequent communist thinking and acting, whether by Stalin, his opponents, or his successors, are variations.

It is my hope that this has been shown with sufficient clarity in the present work. My aim has been to make a survey and analysis of those of Lenin's ideas which have played a role in determining and in justifying the conduct of the Communist Party's work, the crucial political decisions, and also the long-range plans and aspirations of the Russian communist movement and the Soviet state. In making this survey, I have tried to explain Lenin's ideas, rather than assess their adequacy from the point of view of social science or determine their justifiability from the point of view of moral philosophy. Indeed, Leninism contains many an apt observation as well as much that is unrealistic; it combines bold new visions with stubborn, old-fashioned nonsense. Its underlying moral judgments and political attitudes will inspire some and repel others, depending on their own upbringing and on the aspects of Leninism that come to their attention most sharply. From certain points of view, however, the adequacy of Leninism as social science and its acceptability as moral philosophy are irrelevant. Whether its ideas are realistic or unrealistic, whether the actions it has inspired are just or unjust, these ideas and these actions are given facts and forces in the contemporary world and must be studied as such. Ideas are not necessarily correct even if most of mankind believes in them; actions are not necessarily moral even if they are part of universal behavior patterns. Observations concerning the scientific and moral adequacy of Leninism will be made by each reader with such readiness and such awareness that my own comments would not only be superfluous but might in fact detract from whatever merits this work may possess.

I have, therefore, tried to confine myself as much as possible to the task of exposition and analysis, even though many a personal judgment has undoubtedly managed to creep into the text. In order to give the reader a feeling for Leninist ways of thinking and arguing, I have quoted Lenin and, at times, his comrades at great length. In some instances, when it seemed that additional quotations were likely to overburden the text, those passages which I wanted to present to the reader have been relegated to footnotes.*

* To explain Lenin's style of writing, which may be exceedingly tiresome for many readers, the following remarks might be helpful: (1) Lenin's

Since this book is chiefly concerned with the grand outlines of
Leninist thought on history and politics, many interesting
problems of ideology that arise in the study of Leninism have
been neglected. They have been bypassed in an attempt to
correct the tendency of perhaps the most able writers on this
subject to take a knowledge of the outlines for granted and to
concentrate on details. I hope that I have not erred by going
too far in the opposite direction.

Some readers will miss a discussion of Leninist philosophy. By
that is meant not the underlying, unstated philosophy which
pervades Leninism, and which will be discussed, albeit in the
briefest fashion, in this Introduction, but the explicit, systematic
philosophic work done by Lenin, especially in the field of
epistemology. Orthodox communist expositions of Leninism inevitably begin with this Leninist philosophy of "dialectical
materialism" and make it the center of Leninist thought. I feel
that omission of this subject is logical in a treatment of Leninism
as a history-making ideology. Lenin's own manipulative attitude
toward philosophy has been established fairly well. Or, rather,
Lenin seems to have been torn between an attitude of disdain for
philosophic problems and one of profound interest in them.
This may be the cause of the deep inconsistencies marking
Leninist philosophy. For political reasons he could write a work
like *Materialism and Empirio-Criticism,* which is greatly at

sentence structure sometimes seems rather German, and this might be explained by his prolonged sojourns in German-speaking countries and his
constant exposure to German-language writings. (2) His tendency to use
adjectives pleonastically may be explained by his dialectical training. Hege-
lians try to give exhaustive descriptions. They approach their subject from
every conceivable angle and, in order not to omit any facet, in order to
render every nuance, throw adjectives in abandon. (3) Lenin writes
as he speaks, and he speaks like a stump speaker. His writing is political
oratory, in which the effort is to hammer arguments into the brains of a
stubborn audience. Often it also shows an awareness of the importance
of the moment: Lenin speaks and writes in the solemn drone of a party
convention orator. (4) Undoubtedly Lenin was brought up on the Old
Testament. His parents were devout, and he became an atheist only in his
teens. At the same time, he is the prophet of a new creed. He explains the
world to the faithful, exhorts them to follow the commands of History, and
brims over with scorn and indignation at heretics and sinners (Mensheviks
and capitalists).

variance with some of the ideas he put down in his private note-books. In any event, the impact of philosophical beliefs and attitudes on policy in the Leninist movement and the Soviet state has been of no more than marginal importance; hence I decided that, apart from some remarks in this Introduction, philosophy should be omitted from this survey.

All social thought is controversial, not only at the time it is written but centuries and millennia later. For this reason alone it is impossible to write definitive studies about any school of social thought; writing about a subject that has been treated well by others remains, therefore, a legitimate scholarly task. Furthermore, not only does the subject matter of an ideological study remain controversial, but any interpretation offered is itself controversial. A writer needs to develop both empathy with and detachment from his subject. Both of these attitudes are open to criticism; there is no ideal or desirable mixture. My own attitude toward the subject requires no elaboration here, since it will doubtless become clear to the reader.

A number of additional problems, intimately related to each other, trouble the student of political creeds. One of the most baffling is the question of how to interpret the creed in its totality, how to summarize it in systematic form, how to give it coherence. One source of difficulty is the possibility that the creed may not, indeed, be a coherent one, that it may be composed of contradictory elements, and that any attempt to present it as a system will do violence to it. In the case of Leninism, this problem is acute indeed, especially since Lenin was no ivory-tower philosopher but a man of political action, and his activities as the leader of a political party form a part, perhaps even the most essential part, of his theory. Many students have tended to dissociate Lenin the theorist from Lenin the strategist, claiming to discern profound contradictions between the two; others have gone so far as to say that Lenin's theories can safely be disregarded because he was foremost a man of practical decisions and unconcerned with theoretical considera-tions. The reader of this book should not expect an unambiguous answer, but should, instead, attempt to form his own opinion. In the present volume he will receive conflicting impressions: of

Lenin as a comparatively unprincipled political operator, and Lenin as a purposive political theorist; of Leninism as a masterful integration of political thought with political strategy, and Leninism as a bundle of unresolved contradictions. It is my belief that an attempt to force a resolution of these inconsistencies would do violence to the subject matter.

Another puzzling problem is that of relating Leninism to the numerous formative influences that have acted on it. It is necessary to select those features of the over-all environment within which Leninism developed that are essential to an understanding of this development. But, clearly, only a sketchy summary of them can be presented. For the "environment" of Leninism includes such broad and complex things as Russian society and its problems; the Marxist movement, its theories and its sociology; the traditions of the Russian revolutionary movement; and the personal traits of Lenin and his followers, seen both as individuals and as representatives of social, national, intellectual, or psychological types. Volumes could be written on any one of these environmental features, and additional volumes about the manner in which they are related to each other. Each student will inevitably stress some and neglect others and will thus, consciously or not, weight the scales in favor of a particular interpretation.*

* For instance, Leopold H. Haimson, in his penetrating study *The Russian Marxists & The Origins of Bolshevism* (Cambridge, Mass., 1955), discusses Leninism primarily as a function of personal character, Russian social problems, and the intellectual traditions of the Russian revolutionary movement, especially the dialectics of "consciousness" and "spontaneity." Nathan Leites, in *A Study of Bolshevism* (Glencoe, Ill., 1953), sees Leninism as a function of the Russian national character as defined by Geoffrey Gorer in his controversial *The People of Great Russia* (New York, 1950). Others have seen Leninism as a straightforward and logical application of Marxist principles, as unprincipled Machiavellian power drive, or as a response to deep religious urges of our time. I have striven to treat Leninism as the creed of communist movements everywhere. This treatment has led me to emphasize the Marxist as against the Russian origins, the rational and impersonal as against the irrational and psychological aspects. Lenin's political ideas are treated in the present work as parts of a framework of ideas, not as parts of a personality. For instance, while N. K. Krupskaia, in her *Memories of Lenin* (London, 1930), vol. 1, p. 3, derives her husband's attitude toward the liberals from a personal experience, we shall be interested in its relation to Leninism as a whole, and its evolution through the adaption of Marxism to Russian conditions.

The problem of relating Leninism to its formative influences is not a matter merely of emphasis; it involves unsolved questions concerning the precise nature of the relationships. For instance, it is obvious that Lenin's ideas must in some fashion be linked with the traditions and preconceptions of the Russian revolutionary movements preceding him. Where are the main lines of continuity and where are the major breaks? How can these features of continuity and change be explained? If they can be explained, how significant are the links between Leninism and other Russian social thought? One reason why no universally acceptable generalizations can be made on the nature of these links is the fact that no two scholars will make identical statements about the Russian revolutionary movements themselves. Therefore, rather than make vague and oversimplified generalizations, we shall skirt this issue in the present volume. This is not an arbitrary decision; it rests on the conviction that a knowledge of nineteenth-century Russian social thought is not one of the essential preconditions for an understanding of Leninism. The same conviction explains the omission here of Lenin's personality traits and their relationship to his intellectual, cultural, social, national, and childhood environment.

Such is not the case with the influence of Marxism on Lenin. I believe that a thorough understanding of Marxist thought and the history of the Marxist movement in Europe is indispensable for a discussion of Leninism. But even if everyone were agreed on this point, the nature of the relationship would, again, be a matter of controversy. Here too the present volume will not give an unambiguous answer, but can only attempt to contribute to a deeper understanding. At every step Marxism is confronted with Leninism, and both are compared with Menshevism, revisionism, and other Marxist "schools." There is no intention here of confronting Marx and Lenin dogmatically; in observing Lenin amend Marx, we do not wish to prove either one or the other right or wrong. Instead, we shall endeavor to explain the changes in doctrine by changes in circumstances. In this study we shall try to examine Lenin's theories on their own terms, relating them to their environment only in the barest essentials. We shall concentrate on a number of key problems in the application of Marxist theory to Russia, ask ourselves why they arose, and discuss the manner in which Lenin attempted to solve them.

Even while it should be recognized that the precise relationship between Marxism and Leninism is a controversial matter, the facts still remain not only that Lenin considered himself, first and last, a Marxist, if not the foremost interpreter and follower of Marx, but also that he was an erudite student of the vast literature produced by this school. Like so many other leaders of. the European social democratic movement, he went back to the writings of Marx again and again, taking voluminous notes, the quotations to be used not only in disputes with fellow Marxists but also in attempts to come to grips with this complicated structure of thought.*

The student who sees in Lenin primarily a man of political action, whose attitude to theory, and especially to philosophy, was brazenly manipulative,[1] will be surprised that the problem which puzzled Lenin more than any other and to which he returned whenever he had a chance was the meaning of "dialectics." Certainly this is an unusual preoccupation for a party leader and statesman reputed to be hard-headed and practical. Still, this rather abstract philosophic concept exerted a strange spell over him. The word itself fascinated him, and he seldom failed to notice it in the writings of the most divergent philosophers. From the voluminous reading notes of his which have been published, the reason for this almost obsessive interest is quite clear: Lenin was convinced that dialectics, at least in its "materialistic" or Marxist version, was the key to a correct understanding of reality and to expedient action, the quintessence of philosophy, and therefore the most important intellectual tool for a revolutionary leader. But, being of great intellectual subtlety, dialectics was difficult to understand and to explain. Hence Lenin's eagerness to dwell on it again and again. Unlike so many other Marxists, he did not care to use the jargon of

---

* An exhaustive treatise on the relationship between the thought of Marx and that of Lenin would have to take into consideration that a number of major works by Marx were unknown to Lenin because they were published only after his death.

dialectics in his writings or in conversation. To him it was not a plaything or a vehicle for the exploration or abstract philosophical subtleties that might be discussed with brilliant hairsplitters. It was a valuable practical tool, an *arcanum imperii* in the fullest sense of the term, which should be not talked about but acquired and unfailingly applied, as one applies his underlying, unstated philosophy.

If we wade through the notes he took on the writings of Hegel, Marx, Feuerbach, Clausewitz, and others,[2] we can pick up his scattered observations about the meaning of dialectics. He seems to have accepted the Hegelian-Engelsian view that it was both ontology and logic,* but he was really interested only in its ontological aspects; so that dialectics, for him, was a set of laws describing material reality in the most abstract terms.† Some of these terms are familiar to students of the history of social thought. They include not only the dialectical triad of thesis, antithesis, and synthesis, but also the "unity of opposites," a concept which expresses the "contradictory nature" of reality, the idea that everything includes within itself its contradiction or that everything is "composed of" contradictory, conflicting elements. They further include the idea that motion is inherent in all matter, being caused by no external agent, but being self-motion, engendered by the struggle of opposites within matter. This dynamic definition of matter leads to the conception of dialectics as a theory of inevitable change, if not progress, since the struggle of opposites leads to the emergence of new "qualities" at certain "nodal points" of development. We shall not attempt to invest these terms with meaning,[3] for the reason that they are not important to an understanding of Leninism. In post-Leninist Soviet ideology, they have been used to justify various policies and attitudes of the regime.

More important to a comprehension of Lenin is his view of

* See Alfred G. Meyer, *Marxism: The Unity of Theory and Practice* (Cambridge, Mass., 1954), pp. 32ff.

† "Thus in *any* proposition we can and must uncover, as in a 'cell' or 'nucleus,' the beginnings of *all* elements of dialectics, showing in this manner that dialectics is characteristic of all human knowledge" (Lenin, "On the question of dialectics," *Leninskii Sbornik,* Moscow, 1924–1938, vol. 12, p. 325).

dialectics as a guide to the understanding of everything's relatedness to everything else. In Hegel, relatedness is virtually equated with definition, and therefore a thing's infinite number of relationships means that there is an infinite number of aspects (*Momente*), which are part of its definition. As Hegel puts it: "The several different things stand in essential interrelationship with each other through their attributes; the attribute is this interrelationship itself, and the thing is nothing outside of it." [4] Finally, this determination of a thing by its relatedness to all other things is regarded as its negation, for things then *are* only as relations or functions of their "opposites." Spinoza's word, to the effect that *omnis determinatio est negatio,* is a favorite quotation of Hegel's, who asserts that contradiction is immediately apparent in a thing when it is defined by its relationships. "The most trivial examples, of Above and Below, Right and Left, Father and Son, and so forth ad infinitum, all contain the contradiction in the one. Above is what is not Below; Above is determined to be only this — not Below, and it is only in so far as a Below exists; and vice versa, in the one determination lies its opposite. Father is the Other of the Son, and Son the Other of the Father, and each exists only as this Other of the Other, and at the same time the one determination is only in relation to the other; . . ." [5] Lenin quoted this and many other passages from Hegel's *Wissenschaft der Logik* (Science of Logic) and summed up his impressions of Part I by writing: "If I'm not mistaken, there is much mysticism and empty pedantry in Hegel in these deductions, but the basic idea is worthy of a genius: the idea of the universal, all-sided, *living* connection of everything with everything, and of the reflection of this connection (Hegel, materialistically turned on his head) in the conceptions of man." [6]

Correlative to this notion that everything is related to everything else is the virtual abandonment of the idea of cause and effect as a meaningful or workable category of thought, and the substitution of the functional approach. [7] Functionalism applied to social science means that every society is viewed in its totality as a unified, organic whole that is larger than all its parts. [8] Every one of such social organisms, which Lenin sees in constant development and change, can be understood if one universal coefficient, one essential element, one central relationship is recognized.[9] Lenin has identified this basic inner structure of a society in various terms, at times pointing to the struggle of antagonistic classes forming the social structure,[10] at other times to the economic life, the mode of production, which, by the way, he conceived as a dialectical relationship of man with nature.[11] This functional view had certain practical implications for Lenin as a political strategist: once the central relationship around which the entire society revolved was clearly understood, the realistic possibility of changing the society opened itself. "Get hold of the 'basic link,'" wrote Lenin, "and you will be able to move the entire chain." [12]

In Hegel's writings, dialectics can be both logic and ontology because it is seen as the development, clash, relationship, and movement of ideas. In Marx and Lenin dialectics is seen as the abstract law of human history. In both conceptions of dialectics, the final goal is freedom. "The history of the world," Hegel wrote in his *Vorlesungen über die Philosophie der Geschichte* (Philosophy of History), "is progress in the consciousness of freedom, a progress which we have to recognize in its inevitability." For Marx and Lenin the goal is not the consciousness of freedom, but actual freedom — freedom from the forces of nature and society, freedom for the unhampered development of all potentialities inherent in man as an individual and as a species, most specifically, freedom of man from exploitation by his fellow men. Lenin in his first major work set himself the goal to help "the proletariat put an end to all and any exploitation as quickly and as easily as possible." [13] This end was to be achieved through, or was identical with, the abolition of all classes; and, since Marxism defines classes by the control they wield over the means of production, that is, by the type of property they possess, classes will be abolished when property (together with propertylessness, which is its dialectical Other Being) is abolished. So long as property and propertylessness, appropriating and working classes, exist, man is not free, because, as Marx has tried to show in his many volumes of economic writings, modes of production based on property alienate man from his inherent potentialities,

dehumanize him.[14] Marx thought that liberty was in sight
because, for reasons we shall summarize in Chapter One, he was
convinced that the working class was by its nature compelled
to abolish property classes and all other features of man's self-
alienation. Since this abolishment would also liberate mankind
from ignorance, the social revolution would at the same time
constitute a major philosophic achievement; the revolution
would fuse theory and practice into a synthesis.

The nature of the proletariat, epitomizing the entire capitalist
system, was thus, for Marx, the precondition for the revolution
and for liberty. I have tried to show in another work that this
image of the working class, and thus the central core of Marxist
ideas, was unrealistic. Marx and Engels themselves had to retreat
from their optimism of 1848 and admit that developments were
slower than they had expected. While maintaining that their
prediction was true in the abstract and in the long run, they realized that the concrete situation was complicated by countless
local and historical peculiarities at odds with the Marxian diagnosis. Political analysis and political strategy would have to take
these peculiar features into consideration. We shall see that
Lenin's contribution to Marxist thought took this failure of the
Marxian prognosis as a point of departure. From it, Leninism
went out in two directions that seem to be opposites of each
other, though the Leninist conception of dialectics seeks to combine them in a higher unity. One direction was toward the con-
cretization of Marxism, that is, toward its adaption to local and
temporary conditions. As should be expected, this entailed a
tendency toward dissolving the foundations of Marxism into
locally and temporarily applicable theories and strategies. It will
become apparent in following chapters that, point for point,
Lenin took liberties with Marxist ideas, preconceptions, and
practices, so that his adversaries in the movement could accuse
him of having broken with Marxism, of having transformed it
into a typically Russian revolutionary movement, alien to the
Western traditions of socialism.* And it is true that Leninism

---

* A lively discussion has raged recently in Europe over attempts by
Maurice Merleau-Ponty and others to draw a clear distinction between
Western Marxism (*marxisme occidental*) and Leninism (*marxisme dé-*

has many traits in common with the Russian movements of dissent of the nineteenth century and may be seen as a link in a specifically Russian chain of social thought. Still, Lenin defended every innovation he introduced as a thoroughly Marxist measure, claiming that Marxism was no fixed dogma but a "guide to action," that it should be regarded as an orientation, a framework of ideas and attitudes, within which the utmost concreteness of analysis and action would contribute to understanding and success, rather than to the destruction of the framework itself. Concreteness should be integrated, so that the most diverse situations, the most contradictory practices, would be part of a larger scheme of development.

Lenin was convinced that the call for concreteness did not contradict the Marxist conception of dialectics; on the contrary, since it was the recognition of the infinite interrelation of all "moments" of reality, this urge to be concrete was for him the most essential trait of the dialectician. To be sure, abstract historical schemes would tend to dissolve. Every period and every locality would develop according to inherent laws of its own. There is a famous passage in Hegel's *Vorlesungen über die Philosophie der Geschichte* that Lenin noted, copied, paraphrased, and marked with great care. It reads as follows:

> But what experience and history teach is this, that nations and governments have never learned anything from history or acted according to rules that might have been derived from it. Every period has such peculiar circumstances, is such an individual state, that decisions will have to be made and decision can only be made in it and out of it.[15]

Again, Lenin noted Hegel's statements to the effect that all laws are but approximations, and that "living life" — that undefinable reality to which he so often appealed — transcends all laws. To Hegel's statement that "the realm of laws is the *quiet* image of the existing or appearing world," he added the comment: "This is a remarkably materialistic and remarkably neat (on account of the word 'quiet') definition. He takes the law as something at rest — and therefore the law, all law, is narrow, incomplete, ap-

figuré). The relevant works are cited and the dispute discussed in Helmut Dahm, "Ist die sowjet-russische Dialektik latenter Existentialismus?" *Ostprobleme*, vol. 8, no. 43 (26 October 1956), pp. 1486–1500.

proximate." [16] And yet, Lenin regarded abstractions as the "essential" images of reality, as truths greater than concrete cases. He wrote:

Hegel is quite correct *in substance* against Kant. Thought which goes from the concrete to the abstract does not — if it is *correct* thought . . . — go away from the truth, but goes closer to it. . . . All scientific (correct, serious, nonabsurd) abstractions reflect nature more deeply, truly, and *fully*. From living contemplation to abstract thought *and from this to practice* — that is the nature of the dialectical way of recognizing *truth*, of recognizing objective reality.[17]

Here we have the other pole toward which Leninism moved in response to the disintegration of Marxism; or, rather, we have a statement linking both as a dialectical unity of opposites. A flexible adaption to local and temporary conditions might virtually dissolve Marxist traditions, yet through this dissolution the social democratic movement as a whole would be reintegrated on a theoretical level.

Lenin developed two methods of trying to accomplish this integration. Both are essential parts of Leninism, though one of them is certainly a bane rather than a blessing, a source of confusion, mistake, and strife rather than of synthesis. And the two ways seem irreconcilable. One is the imposition of a centralized bureaucratic administration on the revolutionary movement, in an effort to integrate it; the other is an attempt to define the characteristic traits of twentieth-century world society, and to derive from the analysis an entirely new theory of revolutionary trends. Lenin's efforts at transforming the revolutionary movement into a centralized bureaucracy are rightly considered a distinction between his and other Marxist schools, though we must keep in mind the extent to which the German social democratic movement encouraged the bureaucratic trend. While the administrative peculiarities of the Bolshevik movement are well known, Lenin's other method of reintegrating Marxism is not sufficiently appreciated. Yet his attempt to assess the basic features of our contemporary world is perhaps the most interesting, challenging, and lasting part of Lenin's work. We are talking about his theory of imperialism, to which two chapters will be devoted in this book. Here it need only be pointed out that in this theory, after much groping, he found a way toward a real integration of his entire life's work in its most concrete as well as in its abstract aspects. In his ideas on imperialism he began to develop one grand new theoretical scheme, designed to include all of the revolutionary developments of the twentieth century and the role of a fighting Marxist within these developments.

Although Lenin's theory of imperialism thus tends to give coherence to all his ideas and actions, we shall not discuss it until the end of the book. Lenin did not begin to formulate the theory until late in his intellectual development. Hence the integration of his thoughts and strategies also came late; one might even say that it was never fully accomplished, but can be seen only in a nascent state. We should certainly not strive to make Leninism more contradictory or confused than it is, but neither have we any cause to give it an appearance of integration it did not possess at the time various ideas were formulated. The book does not present the development of Leninism in strict historical sequence. But in this broad aspect, at least, it has been designed to recapitulate Lenin's own intellectual development. We shall therefore begin with a discussion of Lenin's attempts to impose centralized organization on the revolutionary movement, attempts which are often regarded as the one set of ideas distinguishing Leninism from other Marxist schools.

Chapter 1

Class Consciousness

It is necessary to make the actual pressure even more pressing by adding to it the consciousness of pressure; the shame even more shameful by making it public. . . . We have to make the ossified conditions dance by singing them their own melody! We have to cause the people to be frightened by their own image, in order to give them courage.

MARX

Torn from social democracy, the workers' movement flattens out and falls inevitably into bourgeois patterns: carrying on only an economic struggle, the working class loses its political independence, becomes the tail of other parties, and betrays the great advice that "the liberation of the workers must be the work of the workers themselves." In all countries there has been a period during which the workers' movement and socialism existed separately from each other and went their separate ways — and in all countries this dichotomy has led to the weakness of both socialism and the workers' movement.

LENIN

Perhaps Lenin's most conspicuous contribution to twentieth-century politics is his conception of the Communist Party as a creative history-making force and as the general staff of the world revolution. In the Bolshevik movement, he created the model on which many other modern totalitarian parties have been built. Lenin must therefore be considered a pioneer of the totalitarianism of our age.

The growth and the success of his party can partly be explained on the basis of Russian conditions. The tsarist regime throughout the nineteenth century outlawed virtually all political action and political thought, yet showed itself unable to enforce its ban on ideas. What it did achieve was to drive all political thought underground. All political groups, whether democratic or authoritarian, had to resort to conspiratorial methods of organization. All political action was suspect. Consequently, political thought acquired a highly dogmatic and irresponsible character. In democratic societies, where oppositions expect from one day to the next to have power thrust upon them, political ideas tend to be tempered by responsibility. Moreover, the need for a mass basis renders the parties, competing for members and followers, flexible in adjusting their policies to grass roots opinion. Tsarist society, on the other hand, produced inflexible, narrow, sectarian parties, whose leaders lived in the realm of ideas and could not easily establish contact with broad sections of the population.

It is thus easy to explain the circumstances which led to the growth of the totalitarian parties in Russia, and, in crediting Lenin with having given our world the model for modern totalitarian parties, we have to be aware of the pre-Marxian Russian revolutionaries who in the second half of the nineteenth century pioneered many of the ideas that were combined in Lenin's conception of the party. In the light of this political tradition, Lenin appears as a typically Russian revolutionary, and it is not surprising that at times he explained his preference for subversive, conspiratorial methods by the exigencies of the political struggle in a tsarist police state. We shall see, however, that this argument was not central to him in justifying such methods. For this reason, those of his followers and critics who thought that the disappearance of tsarism after 1917 or its transformation into a constitutional monarchy after 1905 would lead to the abandonment of Lenin's organizational principles were sorely disappointed. They had not understood the premises on which his ideas were based.

The disappointment among those of his followers who had harbored such hopes was all the sharper because the virtual apotheosis of the party and the totalitarian principles on which it was organized ran counter to a number of ideas and attitudes customarily associated with the Marxist traditions with which Lenin identified himself. Thus the party seems to negate the role attributed to the working class by Marx, that of the chosen people who would destroy the social structure of capitalism and construct a socialist commonwealth. Similarly, the importance that Leninism attaches to party doctrine seems to be opposed to original Marxist conceptions of the negligible role of ideas in history. In general, the Leninist emphasis on the party and its leaders, as well as its doctrine, seems scarcely in harmony with the Marxist view of history as a natural process in which events are determined by the interplay of forces and not by the will or the ideas of men, be they individuals or groups: in short, Marxism seems to oppose the idea of a party as the guiding force or the general staff of social progress. Hence, in order to appreciate the Leninist position concerning the party and its function in the historical process, we shall have to introduce a few pertinent ideas from the Marxist theory.[1]

Marxism constitutes a curious synthesis of determinism and voluntarism. It holds that history is made by man, but that man makes history not as he wishes, but as circumstances, particularly his position in the social structure, force him to make it. Moreover, the Marxist believes that history is made not by individuals but by classes, for even great individuals act only as exponents or representatives of specific social classes. History is thus man-made, but men's actions are determined by circumstances. Men may labor under the illusion that they have ideas and a will of their own; they may consider themselves the sovereign masters of their fate, and exalt the history-making power of the human mind. The Marxist, indeed, would admit that men's ideas and will do play a role, but he relegates this role to a position of minor importance. According to his view, the ideas and the intentions of men are not prime movers of history, because they are themselves determined; they are instead but transmission belts of historical forces.

Here we have a paradox: man makes history, but he does not

master it. Underlying this ambiguous view is the double, and contradictory, conception of human nature that characterizes Marxism. On the one hand, Marxism accepts what we might call a Promethean image of man as a "conscious and purposive" animal, that is, as an intelligent being who through reason can understand himself and his environment, and, again through reason, devise means by which to make himself the master of his environment. This is the most basic Marxist definition of human nature. An opposite conception is revealed, however, in the Marxist theory of history. The development of mankind from primitive to higher stages is seen as cumulative progress in man's mastery over the forces of nature. This mastery is achieved through improvements in the means of production. Cumulative technological progress is intimately tied with the development of a more and more complex social structure. This structure not only entails the development of the class struggle, including the growth of ruling classes and the appearance of exploitation; it also brings with it the alienation of man both from his natural environment and from his own human nature. Modern civilization, despite its progressive character, includes cumulative evil, in that it deprives the individual of the fullness of life. As the division of labor is perfected, men turn into specialized cogs within a vast social machinery that defies their understanding and control. Stuck in the idiocy of specialization, they cannot develop their innate physical and rational faculties. Harried and frightened by the class struggle, overawed by the social leviathan of which they are but a tiny part, they fashion themselves consoling and reassuring images of benign forces working in their favor. Their reason turns into false ideology, their knowledge into self-deception, their purpose into utopia. Promethean man becomes a pitiful caricature of his real self.

Marxism considered capitalist society to be the highest stage of human development reached so far. No age had witnessed such mastery by man over the forces of nature. But industrial civilization had brought with it the ultimate dehumanization of man. According to the Marxist view, man had finally turned into a commodity, to be bought and sold on the market. He had become a piece of equipment to be attached to machines, toiling with the speed and rhythm imparted to him by the machine, and being discarded onto the scrap heap when he was worn out. In the eyes of Marx, capitalist society was one huge market in which circulated not only dead commodities but also human labor power, ideas, and emotions, friendship, love, and beauty. It was a society in which everything that had once "been communicated but never exchanged, given but never sold, acquired but never bought — virtue, love, conviction, knowledge, conscience — passed into commerce. It is a time of general corruption, of universal venality, or, to speak in terms of political economy, a time when everything, moral or physical, having become a marketable commodity, is brought to the market to be assessed at its truest value." [2]

This is a gloomy appraisal of modern civilization and its effect on mankind. It seems to offer no hope for improvement, for what reforms could be expected of men so utterly alienated from their own true nature as Marx describes them? At this point, however, Marxist theory turns a dialectic somersault in which one development, at its very peak, reverses its direction. Man's alienation, having reached the point of absurdity, drives man to return to his innate sanity and rationality, and the class that has borne the brunt of exploitation and dehumanization turns into the Chosen People who will lead mankind out of the desert of alienation into a Promised Land of blissful humanism. This is the Marxian image of the modern industrial working class, the proletariat. It is pictured as a class of people so utterly degraded and oppressed that their misery forces upon them revolutionary indignation and as awareness of the system that keeps them in their miserable state. The workingman is seen as so alienated from everything human that his most primitive ties are corroded. He has become entirely rootless, cosmopolitan, devoid of loyalties, beliefs, and illusions. But this disenchantment means the loss of everything that caused false ideologies to linger in his mind. Deprived of all human ties, alienated from human society itself, the Marxian proletarian emerges as a newborn Prometheus, fully conscious of himself as a workingman within a capitalist world, and hence

equipped with deep understanding of the very secrets of that
world, its strengths, its weaknesses, its inherent downfall, and
the seeds of progress it carries in its loins.*

Marx believed, thus, that the conditions under which capitalism compelled the working class to live were reawakening full
rationality, consciousness, and purposiveness, in that class. Moreover, he thought that the factory itself contributed toward weld-
ing the proletariat into a major force. Work in the machine shop
is collective work, and Mark saw in the modern industrial enter-

* Marx and Engels expressed this idea in one of their joint works, written
in 1845, as follows:

"True, private property in its economic development propels itself in the
direction of its own dissolution, but only through a turn of events which
is independent from it, unconscious, takes place against its will, and is
conditioned by the nature of things — only by producing the proletariat
qua proletariat, misery conscious of its spiritual and physical misery, dehumanization conscious of its dehumanization and hence doing away with
and transcending itself. The proletariat carries out the sentence which private property by producing the proletariat has pronounced on itself, just
as it carries out the sentence which wage labor has pronounced on itself
by producing wealth for others and misery for itself. When the proletariat
comes out victorious, it will not thereby have turned into the absolute side
of society; for it will be victorious only by abolishing itself and its opposite.
Then both the proletariat and its conditioned opposite, private property,
will have disappeared.

"When the socialist writers ascribe this historical world role to the proletariat, they do not do this . . . because they hold the proletarians to be
gods. Rather the other way around. Because the abstraction from all human
characteristics, even from the *semblance* of human characteristics, has been
practically completed in the fully developed proletariat, because the life
conditions of the proletariat contain all the life conditions of contemporary
society in their most inhuman acuteness, because in the proletariat man has
lost himself, but at the same time has not only won the theoretical consciousness of this loss, but is also forced immediately into rebellion against
this inhumanity by the absolutely compelling *need* (practical expression of
necessity) which can no longer be held off, no longer be circumscribed —
for all these reasons the proletariat can and must liberate itself. But it
cannot liberate itself without abolishing its own living conditions. It cannot
abolish its own living conditions without abolishing *all* the inhuman living
conditions of contemporary society which are comprised in its own situation.
Not in vain does it go through the hard but steeling school of *labor.* It
does not matter what this or that proletarian or even the entire proletariat
at the present time *imagines* its aim to be. What matters is *what* it is and
what according to this *being* it will be compelled by history to do. Its aim
and its historic action is irrevocably blueprinted in its own life situation,
as in the entire organization of contemporary bourgeois society" (quoted
in *Leninskii Sbornik,* Moscow, 1924–1938, vol. 12, pp. 36–38).

prise a school for collectivism that was uniting the working class. Finally, the ruling classes had trained their own successors by teaching the workers how to read and write, by making them run the machines, and by drafting them into their standing armies. Thus the working class was acquiring the skills and equipment necessary to fight the property owners and to run modern industrial society. The time was drawing close, thought Marx, when the workers would rise in revolt and expropriate the ruling classes. In this very act of rising they would learn the final lessons of history and would thus emerge, out of revolution, as the Chosen People to lead mankind into a truly human future.

Marxism, in its original conception, constitutes a synthesis of conflicting theories because it obliterates a number of important distinctions: it dissolves all differences between irrational instinct and rational consciousness, between historical determinism and bold human action, between man's acts and man's ideas. All these distinctions would disappear in the proletarian revolution, in which the working class, by merely following its instincts, would gain rational insight and engage in rational action; in which historical forces working themselves out spontaneously and in a determined course would bring about the progress and salvation of mankind. The final paradox is that the revolution, by destroying the old shell of capitalist relationships and institutions, would liberate men's minds and therefore be of philosophical significance. Action, in the end, is seen to be the precondition of knowledge. In this unification of theory and practice, hitherto baffling philosophical problems would be solved by the proletariat.

Important among the implications of this optimistic assessment of proletarian consciousness was the democratism of the Marxist movement, which Engels summed up by writing that "the emancipation of the proletariat can never be anything else than the work of the proletariat itself." Throughout his political life Lenin subscribed to this proposition and indicated his agreement with the rationalist optimism of the founding fathers.[3] "The main thing in the doctrine of Marx," he wrote in 1913, "is that it brings out the historic role of the proletariat as the builder of socialist society." [4] Earlier he asserted that it was "the flower of the work-

ing class" which had "created" the social democratic movement.[5]
Starting with his very first writings, he criticized the Narodniks
(see Chapter Six) for their feeling of intellectual superiority,
their "bureaucratic thinking," their "distrust of, or disdain for, the
autonomous tendencies of the various social classes who make
history according to their interests." He scored them for treating
the masses as objects of the makers of history; and, to clinch the
argument, quoted Marx's statement that the importance of the
masses as the makers of history grows in proportion to the significance of the historic action.[6] To anyone familiar with Leninism these are strange accusations. For precisely those attitudes of
the Narodniks which he criticized are usually attributed to him,
and with reason. Yet we should realize that Lenin never completely abandoned the original Marxist vision of the proletariat
and its revolution.

The utopian character of this vision need hardly be pointed
out. At the time it was conceived, the working classes of Europe
were barely coming into existence, and in the Revolution of 1848,
which Marx and Engels hailed in advance as the millenial act
of deliverance, the proletariat played a very negligible role. In
the following decades, labor movements slowly emerged on the
Continent and gradually began to rally around the banner of
Marxist ideas. But even as they grew into formidable political
parties, thoroughly indoctrinated with Marxist slogans, the conditions that were supposed to convert them into the Chosen Class
were changing. No signs appeared of an impending breakdown
of the capitalist system; on the contrary, there were many indications that it was strengthening itself more and more. The increasing misery of the working masses foreseen by Marx did not
appear; instead, the growing general prosperity raised the standard of living of even the proletariat. Moreover, the workingman
was making his voice felt politically. The franchise was extended.
Working-class parties began to speak in European parliaments.
Socialists were even beginning to discuss the possibility of enter-
ing coalition cabinets. Along with all this, the proletariat manifested a growing interest in democratic constitutional processes,
and its revolutionary sentiments grew weak. The new faith in

constitutional democracy, in gradual reform, in compromise, and in the reasonableness of the ruling classes, which developed among the workers, was accompanied by a growing tendency to put the interests of their country ahead of those of their class. The international solidarity of the labor movement gave way to patriotic sentiments and loyalties. In short, the working-class parties of Europe were turning into legal constitutional parties, pressing for social legislation within the framework of the existing social system. They dissolved their underground organizations and began to lose interest in violent revolutionary activity.

These developments had theoretical implications. Given these changed trends, the Marxist vision of the socialist society achieved through the proletarian revolution could not but appear unrealistic. With conditions growing less propitious for revolution, and the working class turning away from revolutionary activities, actual trends were in conflict with the Marxist theory of historical development and with the professed aim of the movement. Both the aim and the prognosis of trends might have to be revised. Indeed, Marxist theory as a whole might be challenged and discarded. Most certainly, the synthesis of thought and action, idea and reality, reason and historical development, had collapsed.

A decided dualism began to creep into Marxist ideas. Conflicting schools of thought developed, which picked up divergent strands of the Marxist fabric. The so-called "revisionists" redefined the very idea of socialism and openly abandoned the goal toward which, according to Marx, the working class was striving. Social democrats of a more orthodox cast continued to speak of revolutionary socialism, but they thoroughly redefined the road that should be traveled toward this goal, excluding from it all violence and illegality. Their revolution was to be accomplished by the ballot. Radical leaders steadfastly held to Marxist doctrine concerning the goal and the method of revolutionary socialism, and professed continued faith in the working class as the Chosen People who would fulfill the mission Marx had attributed to them. And finally there was the Leninist solution, which we shall now discuss in some detail.

Karl Kautsky, who, as one of the leading theoreticians of German socialism, had a lasting influence on Lenin, in one of his earlier works defined the social democratic movement as "the unification of socialism with the workers' movement." He thus made a clear distinction between two strands that unite in Marxist parties, the activity of the proletariat and the intellectual current of Marxist socialism. Lenin clearly accepted this distinction and defined the task of the movement as the "injection of socialist ideas into the spontaneous workers' movement, so as to ally it with socialist convictions which must stand on a level with modern science." [7] This stress on ideas is in keeping with the Marxist theory of revolution. According to Marx, only the awareness of his own nature and of the social system within which he lived would lead the worker to act, and to act in his true class interest. The proletariat would emerge as a revolutionary force only as it acquired class consciousness. Lenin echoes these ideas in emphasizing knowledge as an all-important agent of revolution. Freedom is inevitable only when necessity (the existing conditions) is recognized. For knowledge is power, and power makes free. "Consciousness," he writes, "is half of salvation." [8] "The slave who is conscious of his slavery and has taken up the fight for his liberation has already half ceased to be a slave." [9]

Knowledge, for a Marxist, is knowledge about oneself. The self, however, is always part of, and formed by, the environment. Hence self-knowledge is virtually equivalent to an understanding of the environment, especially the social environment. The social environment, which forms the individual, is the class structure; self-knowledge therefore amounts to a thorough grasp of Marxist theory, because that theory presents insights into the class structure. Marxist ideas thus constitute the class consciousness that Lenin recognized as an important, if not the most important, driving force in history. The great stress placed on knowledge and ideas, on consciousness, is one of the most characteristic features of Leninism.

In a way this is not remarkable. As we have observed, Marx, too, laid great stress on proletarian class consciousness as the agent of revolution; hence Lenin's emphasis is noteworthy only because the concept had been neglected more and more by

European and Russian Marxists in the late nineteenth century. To the extent that revolutionary schemes and aspirations lost importance to the leaders of the labor movement, they could safely forget about this ideological driving force. If they did continue to speak about proletarian class consciousness, they meant by it not that rational understanding of modern society and its workings which the term denoted to Marx, but rather the workingmen's pride in their class and their devotion to the daily struggle for civil rights and social benefits.

Lenin, however, who crusaded for the proletarian revolution, had to re-emphasize consciousness. Yet there is a difference, at least of degree, between his ideas and those of Marx. The latter had clearly attributed consciousness to the proletariat, and his followers came to use the term "class consciousness." This term can also be found throughout the English translations of Lenin's works. But it is a mistranslation. For Lenin consistently and inevitably used the word "consciousness" (*soznanie* or *soznatel'-nost'*) without any modifier. He had very good reason for doing so, because, unlike Marx, he did not generally attribute the attainment of consciousness to the working class at all.

We shall see that Lenin's opinion of the proletariat — as of many other things — was characterized by ambivalence; and at various times he did concede consciousness, or growing consciousness, to the working class.[10] His generally prevailing opinion, however, was that the proletariat was not and could not be conscious. "The history of all countries," he wrote, "bears out the fact that, through their own powers alone, the working class can develop only trade-union consciousness."[11] True enough, Lenin attributed to the workingmen an awareness of their misery under capitalist conditions; but he was careful to describe the impulse prompting them to revolt against society as instinct, mood, opinion, or, more frequently, as spontaneous feelings, or "spontaneity." * These words describe a nonrational revolt of the mind against society. If the acceptance of the social structure were

* *Stikhiinost'*, from *stikhiia* (element). Hence the adjective *stikhiinyi* has the original meaning of "elemental"; "spontaneous" is a later, more abstract use. In many places the original literal meaning conveys much more strikingly Lenin's conception of the role of the masses in social revolution.

labeled "habit," then spontaneity would be the antithesis of habit, and consciousness would be the rational conception of an order which sought to overcome both habit and spontaneity. Fighting against the forces of habit, consciousness might ally itself with the destructive yet fertile forces of spontaneity, and might even yield to them temporarily. But, in Lenin's opinion, it must seek to remain victorious in the end and eliminate spontaneity altogether, as part of the old order.

Lenin held that the masses were, indeed, dimly aware of a new rational order, of new norms, of some better goal. But only the scientific socialist, he thought, was truly conscious of them. Spontaneity was therefore nothing more than a stimulant to revolutionary action. Instinctive feelings, he held, might indeed coincide with the true interests of those who had them.° But, in the long run, feelings not put to rational tests would run counter to the "true" interests of a class.

Lenin explained the fact that the working class has spontaneity but not consciousness by the conditions under which it has to live in capitalist society: "Workers have to work in the factory as if on a chain gang, and neither time nor possibility remains for them to become socialists." [12] During World War I, shaken by the collapse of international working-class colidarity, he added the explanation that in each country the working class is bound up in narrow sectional and national interests and loyalties, and hence is unable to grasp the problems shared with proletarians everywhere. This notion, too, was one with which Marx and Engels had dealt. On the eve of the Revolution of 1848, they had described communists as "the most advanced and resolute sections of the working-class parties of every country, that section which pushes forward all others; . . . they have over the

° Thus Lenin, in the article "About a Strong Revolutionary Regime," wrote: "According to their instincts, their feeling, their inclination, the majority of the population in Russia are sympathetic to a revolution against the capitalists. . . . But there is as yet no clear consciousness, nor, in connection with it, determination" (Lenin, *Sochineniia*, ed. 2, Moscow-Leningrad, 1926–1932, vol. 20, pp. 342–343; English translation in Lenin, *Collected Works*, London, 1929, vol. 20, book 2, p. 47).

Hereafter, all references to the second edition of *Sochineniia* (Works) will be written as follows: Lenin, vol. — , p. — .

great mass of the proletariat the advantage of clearly understanding the line of march, the conditions, and the ultimate general results of the proletarian movement." [13] Again, "the communists are distinguished from the other working class parties by
this only: (1) In the national struggles of the proletarians of the
different countries, they point out and bring to the front the
common interests of the entire proletariat, independent of all
nationality. (2) In the various stages of development the struggle of the working class against the bourgeois has to pass
through, the communists always and everywhere represent the
interests of the movement as a whole." [14] Lenin's ideas echo these
statements. But, whereas Marx had believed in the spontaneous
growth of working-class consciousness under the impact of capitalist realities, Lenin tended to assume that the workingman was
forever doomed to insufficient consciousness, no matter how
miserable his conditions.*

Yet he spoke of consciousness. Someone was gifted with it. If
it was not produced in workingmen under the pressure of alienation, who possessed it, and whence was it derived?

According to Leninism, the carriers of proletarian class consciousness were bourgeois intellectuals, whose consciousness is
the product of the dialectics of ideas. They become conscious by
carrying the heritage of liberal thought to its logical conclusion.[15]
Intellectuals, thought Lenin, were members of the *bourgeoisie*
or gentry who had been declassed and uprooted by acquiring an
education. Ideas were at work in their heads and were turning
their thoughts toward social criticism. They mirrored the ills of
their society, and the socialist ideas held by bourgeois intellec-

* As Herbert Marcuse has correctly shown, the idea of the workers' loss
of revolutionary class consciousness did not originate with Lenin but with
Eduard Bernstein and other German social democrats, who in the last
decade of the nineteenth century observed this trend in the European labor
movement. We shall see that, as an "orthodox" Marxist, Lenin denied the
revisionist thesis that the workers had lost their class consciousness (or had
never possessed it in the first place). But as a Leninist he accepted it, at
least as a short-run proposition. The difference between him and Bernstein
is that the latter expressed his satisfaction over the waning of revolutionary
aspirations among the ranks of labor, whereas Lenin deplored and strove to
counteract it.

tuals could only be understood by knowing the capitalist society they criticized and wanted to abolish. *

Lenin was careful to add that, initially, there need be no connection between socialist ideas of this sort and the workers' movement.[16] As a matter of fact, he points out that the ideas came first, "and then" Marx and Engels understood that it was the proletariat which would carry them into practice by making the revolution, and undertook to educate the proletariat for this purpose. "All the socialists have to do is to realize which of the social forces, due to its position in contemporary society, is interested in bringing about socialism, and to instill in this force the consciousness of its interests and of its historical tasks. This force is the proletariat." [17]

Not only in regard to Marx and Engels, but also in viewing the subsequent history of Marxist socialist parties, Lenin thought that theory had preceded practice.[18] And this in his eyes was quite as it should be; for the workers, possessing only spontaneous feelings, could not be expected to think about the interests of their class as a whole; instead, they must be supposed to pursue only far less important narrow sectional interests. "From the point of view of the fundamental ideas of Marxism, the interests of the development of society are above the interests of the proletariat — and the interests of the whole workers' movement in its entirety are above the interests of special groups of workers or of any specific aspect of the movement." [19] Hence the organization of the conscious leadership and the elaboration of a party platform must needs precede the extension of the party to the level of the workers.[20]

The Leninist conception of the party is derived from this acknowledged superiority of socialist theory (consciousness) over the spontaneous movement of the working class. The party is

---

* "Tasks for Young Revolutionaries," Lenin, vol. 5, p. 354. Marx and Engels conceded that "of course" communist consciousness could *also* develop among nonproletarians, from contemplation of the conditions of the working class; but, in contrast to Lenin, they held that the origins of communist consciousness were to be found in the proletariat ("Die deutsche Ideologie," in Karl Marx and Friedrich Engels, *Historisch-kritische Gesamtausgabe,* hereafter cited as *MEGA,* Frankfurt, 1927ff, part 1, vol. 5, p. 59).

conceived as the organization, incarnation, or institutionalization
of class consciousness. In it, historical will and purposiveness are
to acquire domination over unguided and irrational instinct and
drift. The party is therefore to be composed of those intellectuals, whatever their background, who have acquired consciousness and, prompted by ideas and convictions, have turned into
revolutionaries by profession,[21] men whose vocation it is to con-
spire against the existing order and to prepare a proletarian dictatorship. The task of the party is "to make the proletariat capable of fulfilling its great historical mission." [22] It should not
"adapt itself to . . . the backward sections of the working class,
but raise the entire working class to the level of its communist
vanguard. . . . The party exists for the very purpose of going
ahead of the masses and showing the masses the way."* Or, to
use the military terminology of which Lenin was so fond, the
party was to be the general staff of the proletarian revolution,
conceiving the strategy of class war, revolutionary attacks, and
strategic retreats, training the cadres, organizing shock troops,
collecting and digesting intelligence, and building up the fighting
spirit of the rank and file. It was to be a military hierarchy, functioning with strictest discipline and according to the command
principle.

The term "revolutionary by profession" has a double meaning
in Leninism. First, it expresses the idea that revolution-making
should be the vocation of party members, the exclusive task to
which they would devote their entire lives. Lenin himself exem-

* From a resolution about the role of communist parties in the proletarian
revolution, adopted at the Second Comintern Congress (*II kongress Kommunisticheskogo Internatsionala, stenograficheskii otchet,* Petrograd, 1921,
pp. 569–570). See also Georg Lukács, *Geschichte und Klassenbewusstsein*
(Berlin, 1923), pp. 53–54.

The resolution quoted gives the following example: "Thus, for instance,
at the beginning of the imperialist war in 1914, the social treason parties of
all countries, in supporting the bourgeoisie of 'their' countries, invariably
referred to the fact that such was the will of the working class. They had
forgotten that, even if this were so, the task of the proletarian party in
such a situation should have been to come out against the opinion of the
majority of workers and to defend the [real] historical interests of the
proletariat, in spite of everything."

plified the devoted professional revolutionary by sacrificing everything — his legal career, his family life, his friendships, and his very emotions — to the self-imposed task of making a revolution. Second, the party members should be professionally competent, and the party itself should be a professional body organized so as to ensure maximal administrative efficiency in its operations. It should therefore develop all those rationalized techniques of administration we associate with bureaucracy, such as centralized controls and decentralized execution, a rational division of functions, hierarchical co-ordination, competency, and managerial responsibility.[23]

This conception of the party was so controversial that it led to the first major break between the Leninist faction and the more moderate sections of the Russian Marxist movement, which had organized itself as the Russian Social Democratic Labor Party. The dispute did not flare up suddenly, but was prepared in a long-drawn-out discussion within the movement, especially involving different conceptions of the role to be played by the central party organ, *Iskra*. It was brought to the attention of the entire party in a dramatic fashion at the party congress held in Brussels and London in 1903, where Lenin clashed with other leaders over the principles that were to govern party organization and membership. Since his followers managed to obtain a majority of votes at this congress (though not on this issue), after the Jewish *Bund* had walked out, they were thenceforth known as the majority faction (Bolsheviks), and his opponents, as the minority faction (Mensheviks).

The Mensheviks clearly and emphatically identified socialism with the working-class movement. They had therefore no use for elitist distinctions between conscious and spontaneous people. Hence they conceived of the party as a loose and democratic organization of the proletariat itself, a broad mass movement in which anyone was welcome as a member if he wished to call himself a social democrat, and as long as he kept paying his dues. Decisions were to be made in this mass party according to democratic rules of procedure; one man's vote was to be as good as another's.

Lenin, however, stressing the leading role of consciousness, firmly refused to be guided by grass roots opinion among the working class and denounced the Mensheviks for making a fetish out of democratic rules. Disdainful of majority decisions,* he wrote that "the important thing is not the number, but the correct expression of the ideas and policies of the really revolutionary proletariat.[24] The Mensheviks, he argued, were perverting the idea of the party as the conscious vanguard; their party was turning into the tail of the proletariat masses,† unthinkingly and opportunistically echoing their unenlightened and fickle political thoughts. A party of this sort, Lenin argued, would become hopelessly enmeshed in the everyday problems of the workers and thereby lose the larger perspective of revolutionary strategy. Fighting none but local and isolated skirmishes, instead of the decisive battles, it would be converted into an integral part of the existing system; "tailisms" would turn the Marxist movement into an appendage of the bourgeoisie. In short, once the movement was submitted to the grass roots opinions of the working class, it would lose sight of its socialist objectives. It would have forsaken Marxism.[25]

With arguments such as these, Lenin and his followers never ceased attacking rival Marxist groups of a more moderate cast as traitors to the cause of revolutionary Marxist socialism, as petty bourgeois muddleheads or paid lackeys of the ruling classes, who would hide the shame of their treason behind the fig leaf of democratic slogans. In Lenin's eyes, they were perverting the doctrine of Marx into a harmless myth; his movement, into a Babbittish pressure group for social reforms. With all this, they were distracting the workingmen's attention from fundamental issues and killing his revolutionary enthusiasm. Hence they were in fact the most vicious and dangerous enemies of the proletariat.

* Lenin referred to democratic majorities, contemptuously, only in quotation marks: "Of what value is a 'majority' when that majority is by itself only a formal thing, whereas materially, in reality, that majority is a majority of parties who carry into effect the deception of the majority by the bourgeoisie?" ("On Constitutional Illusions," Lenin, vol. 21, p. 53; translation in *Collected Works,* vol. 21, book 1, p. 68).

† Hence the expression "tailism" (*khvostizm,* from *khvost* — "tail").

Through all the gyrations of communist policy, Lenin's followers have never revised their opinion about the leaders of democratic socialism.

Chapter 2

The Party and the Masses

The trouble is that revolutions require a passive *element, a* material basis. *Theory is going to be realized in a people only to the extent that it is the realization of its needs. . . . Will the theoretical needs be immediately practical needs? It is not sufficient that the idea strive for realization; reality itself must strive toward the idea.*

MARX

The relationship between "spirit and the masses" . . . is nothing but the perfection, in *"critical" caricature, of* Hegel's interpretation of history, *which in turn is nothing else than the* speculative *expression of the* Christian-Germanic *dogma about the dualism of* spirit *and* matter, God *and the* world. *For this dualism expresses itself within history, within the world of man itself, so that a few chosen* individuals *as* active *spirit confront the remainder of mankind as the* spiritless mass, *as* matter.

MARX AND ENGELS

We have seen the great emphasis which Lenin placed on consciousness, that is, on ideas and leadership. Yet he clearly did not believe that ideas or leaders alone could make history. Ideas alone are considered by Marxists to be mere reflections of reality, and, like Marx and Engels, Lenin would have ridiculed those "reflecting individuals who imagine to have transcended everything in and through their reflection." [1] In short, consciousness by itself is powerless, and Lenin was most acutely aware of it. Indeed, an almost obsessive preoccupation with problems of power characterizes Leninism.

Lenin liked to compare his strategy of revolution favorably with that of Blanqui, with which, by the way, it has nonetheless been identified frequently. Louis-Auguste Blanqui, barricade fighter and underground conspirator, who figured prominently in all revolutionary upheavals in nineteenth-century France, is admired by the Leninists for his revolutionary idealism, but at the same time condemned as a utopian dreamer for failing to appreciate the problem of power. Blanqui and his conspiratorial friends believed in the seizure of power by a small conscious minority, an elite of "legislators" who, after seizing the state, would introduce democracy and hand power over to the common man. "Blanquism is a theory that denies class warfare. Blanquism expects man's delivery from wage slavery, not through the class war of the proletariat, but through a conspiracy of a small intelligent minority." [2]

Lenin, in contrast, believed that consciousness turns into power only with the help of the masses of the population. He never ceased emphasizing that it is the masses who will have to carry out the policy of the party, and that the party therefore remains an insignificant sect if it does not obtain (Lenin said "conquer") a working majority. Paraphrasing Marx, he wrote that "theory becomes material force only when it takes hold of the masses." * Power, he said, must be based "with knowing

---

* "Will the Bolsheviks Be Able to Maintain Themselves in Power?" Lenin, vol. 21, p. 279. The Marxian statement is interesting enough to be cited more fully: "To be sure, the weapon of criticism is no substitute for the criticism of weapons; material force must be overthrown by material force. However, theory too turns into a material force as soon as it takes hold of the masses. Theory is able to take hold of the masses as soon as it demonstrates *ad hominem*, and it demonstrates *ad hominem* as soon as it becomes radical. To be radical means to grab the matter by its root. The root for man, however, is man himself. Evident proof of the radicalism of German theory, hence of its practical energy, is the fact that it begins with a decisive *positive* elimination of religion. The criticism of religion leads to the doctrine that *the highest being for man is man himself,* hence to the *categorical imperative to overthrow all those conditions* in which man is a humbled, oppressed, abandoned, despised being, conditions which cannot be described more aptly than by the exclamation of a certain Frenchman over a projected tax on dogs: 'Poor dogs! They want to treat you like human beings!' " ("Zur Kritik der Hegelschen Rechtsphilosophie," in *MEGA*, part 1, vol. 1, pp. 614–615).

certainty and unconditionally on the majority of the population." [3] Blanquism, he explained, "is the seizure of power by a minority, whereas the Soviets . . . are the direct and immediate organization of the people's majority." *

This emphasis on winning a majority should not be confused with Hitler-like attempts to come to power "legally." Lenin, in dissociating himself from what he thought was Blanqui's naïveté, followed rather in the footsteps of all those philosophers like Plato and Machiavelli, who sought to ally themselves with small elites, aristocracies, kings, tyrants, or other centers of power, in order to transform their ideas into reality. The difference was that Lenin thought of the working class as the decisive center of power in modern industrial society. Hence even though he disdained the opinions and the leadership of majorities, he had a very healthy respect for public opinion when he faced the problem of ensuring the success of revolutionary or other political action. For, "to have an overwhelming preponderance of forces at the decisive moment in the decisive place — that 'law' of military success is also a law of political success, particularly in that fierce, intense war of classes which is called revolution." [4] The proletariat, he wrote, "knows full well that for the success

* "Letters on Tactics," Lenin, vol. 20, p. 104 (translation in *Collected Works*, vol. 20, book 1, p. 124). It is noteworthy that Lenin contrasted his own views with those of a western European socialist, Blanqui, rather than those of some of the Russian Blanquists, such as Nechaev and Tkachëv. Undoubtedly Lenin was familiar with their views as well, but the history of Western revolutionary movements and socialist doctrine was more meaningful and therefore more real to him than the development of the Russian revolutionary movement, in which, strangely, only Chernyshevsky seems to have inspired him to genuine and undivided admiration. Despite his keen appreciation of peculiarly Russian conditions, and his readiness to adjust party strategy to them, Lenin considered himself primarily a member of the international Marxist movement; and, in referring to the past history of revolutionary movements, he preferred speaking about Germany, or England, or especially France.

An additional factor that contributed to Lenin's habit of avoiding mention of Russian revolutionary history was the necessity to use "Aesopian" language. In order to evade censorship, the critic of existing social institutions had to talk about the animal kingdom or other foreign realms, even though the Russian reader trained in deciphering "Aesopian" was perfectly aware of the implicit admonition, *de te fabula narratur*.

of its revolution, for the successful overthrow of the bourgeoisie, the sympathy of the majority of the working masses (and hence of the majority of the population) is *absolutely necessary*." [5]

We thus get a different sort of majoritarianism in Leninist thought. It is not a problem of constitutional legality. "The proletariat wages its class war and overthrows the bourgeoisie without . . . waiting for an advance vote (which is carried out by the bourgeoisie anyway and goes on under its oppressive rule)." [6] Nor is it what one might call a revolution by consent. Instead, Lenin intended to obtain a firm hold of political power through mass support. Only then could the party translate consciousness into reality. "Yes, indeed, the relation between the function of the intellectuals and the proletariat (workers) in the . . . movement can perhaps be expressed pretty accurately by this general formula: The intellectuals nicely decide problems 'in principle,' they nicely draw the blueprint, nicely debate on the necessity of action . . . but the workers do act, and do transform gray theory into living life." [7]

But this involves the party leadership in a dilemma: clearly, the opinions and instincts of the working masses must to a certain extent guide the conscious leader, if he wants to retain his followers. In particular, the communist should not desert the masses when they do act spontaneously, even if their action is mistaken and harmful. [8] Yet to what extent, precisely, should the masses be followed? How much influence should the conscious leader give to the unenlightened thoughts and actions of the common man? How much, and in what way, does the fickle support given by the masses determine the leader's action?

Leninism answers this question by the concept of the revolutionary situation. There are certain moments when a society is ripe for revolutionary action. These moments are determined by the social conditions and by the mood of the masses. The presumption in Leninism is that whenever objective conditions are ripe for revolution, the spontaneous will to action of the masses will also be at the highest point of its development. Yet it is admitted that the mood of the masses may at times be out of tune with actual developments. In any event, it is up to the conscious leaders to assess the strength of both, weigh them against each other, and on the basis of this diagnosis choose the most propitious moment for action. The moment should not be too late, for then the enthusiasm of the masses may have spent itself. Nor must it be too early: "If we speak about civil war before people have grasped its necessity, then doubtless we fall into the error of Blanquism." [9] And the ability to make such an appraisal is one of the necessary qualifications of a truly conscious revolutionary leader. "The art of the politician, and the correct understanding by the communist of his own tasks, consists in the correct appraisal of the conditions and the moment when the vanguard of the proletariat can successfully seize power; when it will be able, during and after this, to obtain sufficient support from sufficiently broad sections of the working class and the non-proletarian working masses; when he will, after that, be able to support, strengthen, and broaden his rule, educating, teaching, and attracting wider and wider masses of the laboring population." [10]

Marxism in its original form maintained that the spontaneous unfolding of historical events produces progress and, finally, a rationally acceptable form of human relations. Leninism is more pessimistic and therefore became a manipulative theory of history. Its aim is to subject the most irrational, spontaneous forces to reason (consciousness) by means of organization; even revolution is made the object of science and rational organization. Yet the irrational forces are recognized as given, and they receive their place in the rationalized scheme of revolution. Their specific function is to help determine the moment of action. They dictate the "irrational *hic et nunc*," as Mannheim calls it.[11] Hence Lenin, with all his stress on consciousness, and his demand that it must gain and maintain the initiative over spontaneity, could during World War I write with confidence that the next Russian revolution would, like that of 1905, start spontaneously, unexpectedly, and locally. He did not consider this an ideal situation; he would have preferred a nation-wide revolution carefully planned in advance by the party. But he warned that the party must be prepared to take advantage of any unique opportunities provided by spontaneous outbursts, because only such outbursts would ensure the mass basis necessary for the establishment of a proletarian dictatorship.[12]

In short, revolution, according to Lenin, can not be the work of conspirators alone; it must be made by an entire people or by an overwhelming majority. Moreover, during a revolution initiative almost inevitably goes to the masses, at least for a while. This is precisely the meaning of the revolutionary situation: the masses have taken the initiative, or are about to take it. It is the test of an able revolutionary leader to make use of these "elemental forces" and ride to power on the waves of spontaneity.

To be sure, Lenin emphasized that these elemental forces which make the wheels of history turn must never be allowed to engulf and overwhelm conscious leadership. Spontaneity must never be permitted to change the direction of the party's action, the party line.[13] And yet, when it becomes necessary in the interests of the power struggle, the party must follow mass opinion even if it means breaking with its own platform. This was Lenin's argument at least in 1917, at the time of the October Revolution, when he rode his party to power on the waves of mass enthusiasm for slogans to which the Bolsheviks subscribed for purely opportunistic reasons. "The vast majority of peasants, soldiers, and workers are in favor of a policy of peace," explained Lenin. "This is not the policy of the Bolsheviks; it is not a 'party' policy at all; but it is the policy of the workers, soldiers, and peasants, that is, of the majority of the people. We are not carrying out the program of the Bolsheviks, and in agrarian matters our program has been taken entirely from the mandates of the peasants." [14]

In this and subsequent instances Lenin went further in "submitting to spontaneity" than was acceptable to some of his party comrades, and he was therefore accused of becoming an opportunist who was allowing the party to get stuck in the morass of public opinion. By following the masses, they argued, the party was descending to their level, instead of lifting them up. Lenin's reply was that the danger of following spontaneity was, of course, very great. Mass unrest is a tricky ally; yet it must be used by the conscious leadership, and the more courageously the better. For only a courageous leader can ride the waves of mass opinion and tame them. They are the element he needs in order to act. The element is treacherous, but without it the revolutionary is paralyzed. "Do not fear the initiative and independence of the masses! Entrust yourselves to their revolutionary organization — and you will see in *all* areas of political affairs the same force, grandeur, and invincibility that the workers and peasants showed in their unity and passion against the Kornilov affair." [15] Moreover, the conscious vanguard not only makes use of mass spontaneity, but also serves to check it by taking the masses in hand: "otherwise the wave of real anarchy may become stronger than we are." [16] If the party were to be destroyed or silenced, the masses would continue to react to the misery of their status; but they would react spontaneously, that is, in a nonrational and hence purely destructive manner. "Where Bolshevism has the possibility of coming out in the open, there will be no disorganization. But where there are no Bolsheviks, or where they are prevented from speaking up, there will be excesses, there will be decay, there will be pseudo-Bolsheviks." [17]

In short, spontaneity, though it is essential to the revolution, must be used judiciously. The spontaneous instincts and actions of the masses are the natural element available to the conscious social scientist, but spontaneity is of use to him only if it is harnessed, transformed into political energy, and channeled into the most advantageous direction. Then it is welcomed, and the more there is of it the better it is for the professional revolutionary.[18] As the mill needs water, so the Marxist wheel of revolution turns only as the human element of mass unrest and mass revolt begins to flow and swirl. Lenin, like Hegel, was optimistic in that he visualized the ultimate triumph of consciousness through unconscious, irrational, spontaneous passions. "God," wrote Hegel, "lets men direct their peculiar passions and interests as they please; but the result is the accomplishment of — not their plans but His, and these differ decidedly from the ends primarily sought by those whom He employs." [19] Lenin reserved the role of God for those men who can make use of the passions of the dissatisfied and oppressed. Their "consciousness" has definite secular aims, whereas the aims of Hegel's God are not recognizable by man.

Up to this point we have simplified Lenin's position to some extent. While it is true that in the main he denied rationality to the workingman, he did not maintain this attitude unhesitatingly. On the contrary, he more than once allowed himself to be led astray by an unusually optimistic appraisal of proletarian consciousness.* Lenin was thus torn between two judgments about the working class. In tracing the ups and downs of his estimate of proletarian rationality, we find that his opinion becomes optimistic as soon as the masses begin to engage in spontaneous revolutionary action, following the slogans preached by himself and his associates. Conversely, as soon as the masses cease to obey the commands or suggestions of the party, his estimate of their consciousness declines sharply. Lenin thus was caught in the same dilemma in which modern democratic theorists find themselves; and in being one of the first men to voice doubts in working-class consciousness, he is one of the pathbreakers of contemporary political thought. In theories of democracy, the rationality of the "common man" is as indispensable a premise as the workers' class consciousness is in Marxism. Although Lenin's faith in it was shaken, he never completely abandoned it because then he would have had to abandon his entire ideology. Somewhere, at some point, his theories inevitably assume that workers will acquire consciousness. Similarly, all ideas of democracy collapse once the faith in the common man's rationality is abandoned. Yet we are even less sure of it than was Lenin, whose lack of faith was based only on political horse sense, whereas ours is intensified by the incontrovertible findings of psychology and anthropology. Democratic theorists of our day are therefore as schizophrenic with regard to this problem as the Leninists, and only those who have no scruples in abandoning democracy as an ideal wholeheartedly accept all evidence about man's alienation and project it into the indefinite future.

The problem of working-class consciousness has an important

* A typical instance is his referring to the Second International as a general staff without an army. The implication here is clearly that the workingmen of Europe were really behind the communists. See his telegram to Serrati and Lazari in Lenin, vol. 24, p. 430. For an example of Lenin's admitting that he had overestimated the consciousness of the masses, see vol. 24, p. 421.

implication for the party: the leaders must ask themselves how much sense it makes to engage in political action without fully conscious support. In particular, how much sense does it make, in terms of Marxist schemes and theories, to seize power before the working class is fully conscious? In the Marxist movement, it had been considered axiomatic that action should be consonant with the development of consciousness. Hence Marxists believed it senseless, irresponsible, or even criminal to undertake revolutionary action, much less think of socialism, before true consciousness was developed among the working class. Lenin did not take a definite stand in opposition to this. True, he denied consciousness to the proletariat; yet he claimed that his party was to remedy this situation by educating the working class, and, as we have just seen, he more than once convinced himself that the task had been accomplished, that the masses were enlightened.

At least he felt it necessary to pretend that such was his conviction, in order to counter Menshevik criticism that the party had engaged in irresponsible adventurism. In reality, Lenin was prepared to take action before the masses were ready for it. Confident that, with the progressive development of capitalism, the proletariat would inevitably come to identify socialism with its own class interests,[20] the moderate socialists favored postponing revolutionary action until the workers had acquired class consciousness. Lenin, on the other hand, appeared impatient with the development of this consciousness and held that waiting for it would mean betraying the revolution. The essence of Marxism, for him, was not the morphology of events outlined by Marx, according to which capitalism was to be transformed into socialism, but rather the consciousness of the inevitable necessity of this transformation, and the desire to achieve it as quickly as possible, by whatever means might be available in a given society. In other words, Marxism was not so much a scheme of historical development as the recognition of the direction in which history was moving and of the historical tasks facing the twentieth century, combined with a method of solving historical problems by means of the class struggle. He could, therefore, concede that the proletariat by itself would never attain anything but trade-union consciousness, thus justifying the educating role of

the enlightened intellectuals; he could even become impatient
with the educational process and condemn excessive reliance on
it as a betrayal of the revolution; yet impatience did not necessarily lead him to despair of the creation of a socialist society, as
it would have led a Menshevik or other defenders of constitutional democratism.* Lenin, in seeking to bring about the revolution, was satisfied with mass support acquired by nonrational
means. The development of true consciousness among the proletariat could come later, under the well-established dictatorship of
the conscious vanguard.† In the meantime, the problem of power
was paramount, and this problem could be solved by relying on
the spontaneous support of the masses, generated if necessary by
propaganda.

In Leninist writings the issue is seldom posed as clearly as
this. The belief that a conscious vanguard is required to lead
the revolution is expressed simultaneously with confidence in the
proletariat. This confidence leads to the firm conviction, often
voiced by Lenin and his followers, that the workers, though not
conscious, will nonetheless join forces with the vanguard and

* The result is a dilemma facing the moderate socialist, who must choose
between socialism and democracy — a dilemma that is one of the causes for
the split within the Marxist movement. The right wing has decided in
favor of democracy at any price; the left, for socialism even if democracy
be lost; while the center has often tried not to see the dilemma at all. In
a story about Karl Kautsky, Eduard Bernstein illustrates the last of these
attitudes. Bernstein had adduced factual evidence refuting the Marxist
theory of the increasing misery of the workers. Thereupon Kautsky, unable
to disprove facts by better facts, simply refused to accept Bernstein's thesis,
on the grounds that it contradicted his own evolutionary socialist dreams:
"If that were true, . . ." he said, "we should never reach our goal. If the
number of capitalists were to grow instead of the number of the dispossessed, then we should get further and further away from our goal the
more that development persisted. Capitalism, not socialism, would then be
strengthened" (Eduard Bernstein, *Die Voraussetzungen des Sozialismus und
die Aufgaben der Sozialdemokratie,* Stuttgart, 1906, p. 178).

† In contrast to both the moderate socialists and Lenin, Marx and
Engels believed in the unity of theory and practice, as has been pointed
out. The hard realities of proletarian life would drive the working class to
action and would at the same time enlighten them. The consummation of
both these developments would come at the time of the proletarian
revolution, "for the change in human nature which produces communist
consciousness on a mass scale can occur only in the practical activity of
making a revolution" (Marx and Engels, "Die deutsche Ideologie," p. 60).

let themselves be guided by it. Yet, if it is indeed true that the workers are blinded by narrow economic interests, why should they be expected to recognize the identity of their ultimate goals with those of the conscious vanguard? Must they not be conscious already in order to remain faithful to the party at all times? Like the Hobbesian concept of the individuals' submission to leviathan, the proletariat's voluntary subordination of its own narrowly conceived class interests to the higher interests of the movement as a whole can be explained only as a rational decision. The worker, if he is to submit to leviathan, must be wholly conscious already. That he cannot be so, Leninism takes for granted. Hence it requires irrational incentives, such as coercion and propaganda, to make the proletariat submit to the conscious elite.

Because Lenin was loath to see this conclusion clearly, the meaning of the word "consciousness" came to be weakened considerably in his spoken and written pronouncements. At times he and his friends seem to have believed that spontaneous feelings of resentment would gradually transform themselves into true consciousness,[21] and there is a persistent tendency to hail these spontaneous feelings themselves as consciousness. What is even more remarkable is that the word "consciousness" was often used simply to denote the workers' acceptance of the vanguard's leadership and of their own humble role as rank-and-file soldiers of the revolution, regardless of how this acceptance had been generated. Hence even mass support acquired by irrational means of persuasion was often regarded as an indication of the consciousness of the masses. This self-deception was necessary whenever Lenin wished to reassure himself concerning the common man's rationality; it was equally necessary as a justification for radical action by the party. Lenin's impatient radicalism and his conviction that he had the masses squarely behind him mutually supported each other.*

* Thus in 1917 Lenin was convinced that he had the masses behind him because they were in conscious agreement with his aims: "If they tell us the Bolsheviks have thought out some sort of utopian story like the introduction of socialism in Russia, and that this is an impossible thing, then we answer: but in what way could the sympathy of the majority of the workers, peasants, and soldiers have been drawn to the side of

Yet every time Lenin deceived himself in this manner, the subsequent development of mass opinion disappointed him further, and strengthened anew his conviction that the vanguard was needed to lead the common man. Each manifestation of mass support for the party was hailed as a growth of the workers' consciousness; each subsequent manifestation of mass resistance to the party confirmed his secret conviction that the workingman was forever locked in the fetters of capitalist modes of thought and would have to be liberated by force. Pending his liberation from the bonds of false consciousness, however, the workingman's support of the party had to be assured by non-rational means, because he himself would have to act to free himself.* Thus each optimistic appraisal of the workers' consciousness led Lenin to greater contempt of the common man's rationality. Ultrademocratic leanings went hand in hand with elitist practices.†

---

utopians and dreamers?" (Lenin, vol. 22, p. 236). See also the conclusion he drew from the success of the October Revolution: "The first task of any party of the future is to convince the majority of the people of the correctness of its program and tactics. . . . Today that task, which of course is still far from completion and can never be fully exhausted, has in the main been solved; for the majority of workers and peasants in Russia . . . are certainly on the side of the Bolsheviks" (vol. 22, p. 441). In his polemic against Kautsky, one year later, he went even further and asserted that the Russian peasants had been conscious even in 1905 (vol. 23, pp. 401–402; translation in *The Proletarian Revolution and the Renegade Kautsky*, New York, 1934, pp. 90–92).

Lenin frequently obtained overly optimistic conclusions concerning the consciousness of the masses from a corresponding overestimation of the enemy's class consciousness. By ascribing well-developed class consciousness to non-Leninists, he could thus consider every victory over them as a token of the growth of true consciousness in the proletariat.

* In a speech given in May 1919, Lenin frankly criticized those who insisted on the fulfillment of the "campaign" promises of 1917, calling them deceivers of the people and enemies of the Soviet regime. The promises on which his party rode to power, he claimed, had catered only to the opinions of the masses, not to true consciousness; and such promises do not count. The speech was entitled, "On the Deception of the People by Slogans of Liberty and Equality" (Lenin, vol. 24, pp. 279–383). "Just because the revolution has started," he wrote earlier, "the people have not turned into saints" (vol. 23, p. 186; translation in *A Letter to American Workers*, New York, 1934, p. 19). For detailed arguments and conclusions in the same vein, see vol. 21, pp. 458–464.

† It should be remembered that a similar ambivalence characterized the

This ambiguity can be traced also in another set of Leninist ideas, namely, the conception of the party's task in bringing consciousness to the workingman. As long as "consciousness" is considered to be tantamount to rational, scientific judgment, the party's task is an educational one. But when the word is used in the sense of the mere readiness to follow the party's orders, the task is one of manipulating the masses.

It is clear that any choice between education and manipulation is decided by the educator's faith in his pupils' ability to absorb and use the knowledge, doctrine, and method that may be given them. The educator imparts his truths in order to influence the minds and actions of his pupils and to give them certain standards of behavior, of whose utility and expedience he is convinced. He desires to shape men in his own image. If he believes that the pupils have the ability to arrive at these standards of behavior by the same intellectual path he himself trod, he will educate. In such measure as he lacks that faith, he will be tempted to use manipulative means to make his charges behave in the desired manner.*

One form of manipulation is the influencing of minds by non-rational messages of communication, customarily called propaganda. An individual educates as long as he imparts to his students that information and that scientific method which he

---

thought of Marx, who in theory extolled the rationality of the proletariat, but in the privacy of his study expressed doubts about it. The difference between his case and Lenin's was that the latter incorporated these doubts in his theories even though he never entirely abandoned his faith in the workers' consciousness. In Lenin's writings the dilemma is therefore expressed more openly. Incidentally, his doubts of the workers' rationality must be contrasted with his emotional attachment to proletarians as actual human beings, the fact that he was a master at winning over working-class audiences and felt comfortable only in the company of workers and other simple folk. In this he was noticeably unlike Marx.

* Erich Fromm has made a very similar differentiation between education and manipulation: "Education is identical with helping the child realize his potentialities. The opposite of education is manipulation, which is based on the absence of faith in the growth of potentialities" (*Man for Himself*, New York, 1947, p. 207). For further discussions of the concept of manipulation, see Lasswell, Leites, et al., *The Language of Politics: Studies in Quantitative Semantics* (New York, 1949); and Philip Selznick, *The Organizational Weapon; A Study of Bolshevik Strategy and Tactics* (New York, 1952), chapters 6–8.

himself is convinced are most nearly true. He propagandizes when he gives out information or teaches methods that are a distortion, misrepresentation, or contradiction of what he is convinced is most nearly true. In other words, the distinction between education and propaganda is a subjective one, and reflects the educator's confidence in the student's ability to learn.

Leninist terminology tends to confuse us here, for what we have called "education" Lenin called "propaganda," using the word in the same way as missionaries of the church speak of "propagating the faith." What we have called "propaganda," Lenin calls "agitation." Agitation to him denotes the activity of inciting the masses to action by playing on their instincts and passions, whereas propaganda in his vocabulary refers to the educational activity of spreading the communist doctrine and method; its aim is to make its recipients truly conscious. Lenin has made his distinction between the two words quite clear:

> A propagandist, when he discusses unemployment, must explain the capitalist nature of the crisis; he must show the reason for its inevitability in modern society; he must describe the necessity of rebuilding society on a socialist basis, and so on. In a word, he must give many ideas all together, so many that all of them will not be understood by the average person, and in their totality they will be understood by relatively few. The agitator, on the other hand, will pick out one more or less familiar and concrete aspect of the entire problem, let us say, the death of an unemployed worker as a result of starvation. His efforts will be concentrated on this fact, in order to impart to the masses a single idea — the idea of the senseless contradiction between the growth of wealth and the growth of poverty. He will strive to evoke among the masses discontent and revolt against this great injustice and will leave the full explanation of this contradiction to the propagandist.[22]

The characteristic form of agitation, as perfected by Lenin, is the political slogan, a simplified form of communication that can be used not only to impart knowledge but also to arouse the masses to action and familiarize them with the party, again in as direct and concrete a fashion as possible. Lenin's wife tells of the origin of a typical slogan:

> When the party program was being discussed at the Second Congress, Vladimir Ilyich proposed, and strongly defended, the slogan

of returning to the peasants the "pieces" of land that were cut off
from them in the reform of 1861.

It seemed to him that in order to attract the peasantry it would be
necessary to advocate a concrete demand corresponding as closely as
possible with the needs of the peasantry. In exactly the same way as
the social democrats began their agitation among the workers with the
fight for hot water, for reduction of working hours, for punctual pay-
ment of wages, so the peasantry had to be organized around a concrete slogan.[23]

It is interesting to note how the words "to organize" crept into
a paragraph about agitation. The reason is that organization is
but another method of manipulation; and nothing perhaps was of
greater interest to Lenin than this means of influencing the
masses. Lenin conceived of the proletarian revolution as the
product of great minds, who, conscious of inexorable trends,
would create order and progress out of chaotic elements by
organizing the raw material of history in a rational fashion. His
deep sympathies for the working class were rationalized by the
fact that it lent itself most ideally for such organization by the
conscious vanguard. Marx had considered the proletariat the
Chosen People because, thrust into inhuman conditions, it had
been so alienated from its humanity that it could speak for
tortured mankind as such; it had been so completely cast out
of human society that it would be totally opposed to the existing
order and could therefore overthrow it. In Lenin's eyes, on the
other hand, the proletariat is the chief instrument of conscious
history-makers because it can be awakened from its political
stupor into action.[24] Most important, however, the working class
had been already organized in the modern machine shop; it had
been organized by its life in the big city's tenement districts. It
would therefore lend itself to even more deliberate organization
on a national scale, and this would permit the centralization of
the revolutionary effort in the hands of a national general staff.[25]

Lenin throughout his life was intensely preoccupied with
problems of organization. His aim was to perfect the instrument
of revolution-making into a machinery (*apparat*) that could be
used effectively as the generals of the revolution might see fit
to use it. He thought of the party as an institution in which
rationality had taken concrete form as a mighty historical force.

The secret of its strength would lie in the fact that the party was to act as an organization through which consciousness could get hold of the masses. It was to be a sort of transmission belt for imparting the will of the leaders to the rank and file of the followers and fellow travelers. The party apparat would enable the leadership to make the masses act whenever the wires of organization were pulled. For organization always has a purpose, and where the party would do the organizing, or acquire a hold over the organization, the purposes would be determined by its leaders. It is therefore often possible, in discussing Leninism, to use the terms "organization" and "propaganda" (in the customary sense) interchangeably.*

Lenin developed the concept of what we today call the front organization. The party should not only have leaders and rank-and-file followers; it should in addition develop a sort of open superstructure, an appended network of mass organizations, undogmatic, elastic in the way they were organized and in the activities they pursued, sensitive to the shifting requirements of local and temporary conditions, but firmly guided in whatever they were doing by the party's leaders.[26] We perceive here the first conception of totalitarian politics: Lenin seems to have envisaged an ideal situation, in which the whole of society would be converted into a network of front organizations, and the entire organizational and associational life of the country would be guided by the conscious leadership, through its control of the apparat.†

---

* If, for instance, we follow Lenin in his explanation of what he means by his call for the "organization of the rural paupers" (Lenin, vol. 23, p. 59), it becomes clear that he means a propaganda campaign to enlist the rural paupers in a crusade against the kulaks.

† In his attempt to extend party control over all social activities, Lenin drew heavily on the experience of the Continental Marxist movement. While the social democratic parties of Europe can not be accused of totalitarian tendencies, it is true that they expanded their organizational empires far beyond those of other political parties. Together with the trade-unions, their press empire, their consumers' co-operatives, sports clubs, women's groups, schools, youth organizations, social insurance enterprises, and other affiliate undertakings, the social democratic movements virtually constituted a state within the state, or a society within society. The difference between them and the Leninist apparatus was that the latter aimed to be a state *against* the existing state and a society *outside* the existing society.

The party as conceived by Lenin is therefore far more than a conspiratorial group of Marxist intellectuals. It is of necessity a dual organization of leaders and followers, or rather, a system of organizations grouped in concentric rings around the conscious leadership: "The smallest possible number of the most homogeneous possible groups should lead the movement, past masters in the business of professional revolution-making. The greatest possible number of the most diverse and heterogeneous groups from the most various layers of the proletariat (and of the other classes of the people as well) should participate in the movement." [27] There is, of course, no question in Lenin's mind that the conscious leaders are the most valuable part of the movement. Not only is it vital that they remain ideologically sound and retain real leadership in the party,[28] but it is also clear to Lenin that they are less expendable than any other group. Hence in times of trouble, when the class struggle goes against the proletariat or when the consciousness of the masses is at a very low ebb, Lenin's chief concern is to retain the nucleus intact. The proletarian armies may desert, but the general staff must remain.* For even if the mass basis vanishes temporarily, the preservation of the central organization will guarantee the ultimate victory of the proletarian cause.

Nonetheless we cannot characterize Lenin's party adequately by contrasting its small nucleus of professional revolutionaries to the mass party envisioned by the Mensheviks. Leninism, too, required a mass basis; indeed, it was much more skilled and successful than the Mensheviks in organizing the masses for its own purposes. The difference lies in the manner in which the masses were to be recruited and organized, in the relationship between leaders and followers, and in the sociological composition of the highest leadership cadres, not in the fact that one or the other branch of Russian Marxism was more eager for mass support.

* "In the period of the decisive triumph of the counterrevolution which has followed the dissolution of the Second Duma, the force of circumstances has prescribed the following task for all party activity: to preserve the party organization created in the years when the enthusiasm of the proletarian struggle was at its highest, despite the efforts of reaction, and during the deep decline of the proletarian class struggle . . ." (Lenin, vol. 14, p. 99; translation in *Selected Works*, New York, 1943, vol. 4, p. 21).

In short, although Lenin at times denounced manipulative methods,* his general tendency was to be impatient with the working class. He felt that there was no time to make the masses conscious; instead, they had to be organized. "The habits of the capitalist system are too strong; the task of re-educating a people educated in these habits for centuries is a difficult job which demands a lot of time. But we say: Our fighting method is organization. We must organize everything, take everything into our own hands, . . ."[29] Social forces are there to be used by the conscious history-maker. Spontaneity is something that can be manipulated. Hence his insistence on organization, discipline, central direction, and leadership.

At the same time Lenin tended to deceive himself concerning the novelty of this approach by constantly obscuring the difference between education and manipulation, between conviction and constraint. The reason is that, for him, agitation and manipulation were but part of the educational work. The party leader manipulating the masses through the transmission belts of organization was only to goad them into acting rationally. The agitator whose task was to arouse the masses to anger and action was not to tell lies but merely to simplify the truth. This simplified truth, the slogan, was not intended to deceive the proletariat; it functioned as a sort of political shorthand, necessitated by the presumably limited understanding of the workers. The aim of slogans and of agitation in general was to awaken the workers, and this awakening was meant to be but the first step in their education for consciousness. It is therefore not astonishing that Lenin used the terms "education" and "propaganda" interchangeably. Since in his opinion education meant the inculcation of Marxist doctrine, the term "communist propaganda" became synonymous with the term "education." There are pas-

* "To conceal from the masses that [our policy of] attracting bourgeois specialists by extremely high wages is a step away from the principles of the commune would mean to lower ourselves down to the level of bourgeois politicians and to deceive the masses. To explain openly how and why we took a step backwards, then to discuss publicly what measures there are to catch up on what has been lost — that means to educate the masses and, on the basis of that experience, together with them, to study how to build socialism" (Lenin, vol. 22, p. 447; translation in Selected Works, vol. 7, p. 323).

sages in his works where he seems to draw a distinction between them, for instance, when he told the Eighth Congress of Soviets that "the dictatorship of the proletariat was succesful because it knew how to combine coercion and conviction." * Yet, from the context, it seems very likely that both these terms as they are used here refer only to manipulation.

According to Marxist theory, communism denotes a certain state of mind, even a change in human nature, which is according to Leninism, facilitated by education. The primary educational instrument, wrote Lenin, must be the "force of example." This would work, for instance, in a situation where the masses out of habit or force of tradition stubbornly retained outmoded methods of production. If the party were to take the initiative in setting up model organizations or creating more efficient methods, the success of these new ways would force the most stubborn traditionalist to adopt them. Lenin, in speaking of the "force of example," remarked that it was basically a method of *moral* persuasion. Yet if it did not work, he continued, it should be backed up by *coercive* "persuasion." The "force of example" is thus clearly a mixture of coercion and education.[30]

We have seen that Lenin confused the effects of education and manipulation by giving the term "consciousness" a wide and ambiguous meaning; it came to denote any willingness on the part of the workers to follow the commands of the party. Hence he failed to distinguish between genuine public opinion and opinions fabricated by the vanguard, and was sharply disappointed whenever the masses deserted their leaders, and manipulation was resorted to.

* Lenin, vol. 26, p. 32. See the discussion of the roles of consent and constraint in creating political power in Carl J. Friedrich, *Constitutional Government and Democracy* (Boston–New York, 1946), pp. 584–590. Similarly, when Lenin tells communist school teachers that "the task of the new education is to tie the work of teaching in with the tasks of the socialist organization of society" (vol. 23, p. 66), the careful reader will be at a loss to say with certainty whether this education is to teach skills to the masses so that they learn how to work with modern machinery, whether it is to persuade them to accept the dictatorship of the party and have confidence in a better future, or whether Lenin had in mind the creation of a new collectivist man, the education of the masses to genuine consciousness. Most probably Lenin, if asked about this, would have said that education in Soviet society would comprise all of these aspects.

In the actual development of the party's relation to the Russian working class, this reliance on manipulation as a short cut to success in revolution had ominous consequences. So long as manipulation was used, the process of education could not go on. The original mission of the vanguard, that of raising the masses to consciousness, tended to be forgotten because of the more immediate problem of keeping the party in power. Manipulation tended to replace education altogether. The possession of power requires a continual appraisal of public opinion, and yet the manipulative methods which seek to mold that opinion tend to blind the rulers themselves to the actual trends. The stress on manipulation, utilizing means in which coercion played a conspicuous role, resulted in making brutal suppression of criticism seem to be an easier way of staying in power than a sensitive and careful incorporation of mass opinion into public policy-making.

The vanguard's initial lack of confidence in the workers doubtless tended to widen the gulf of mutual misunderstanding by making the workers react to events in an increasingly less rational or enlightened fashion, and this in turn increased the leaders' initial contempt of public opinion. A vicious circle of education and manipulation led to the inevitable defeat of all efforts at educating the common man to consciousness. What made the circle vicious was the problem of power, coupled with the Leninists' impatient refusal to wait for "history to take care of itself."

Chapter 3

Democracy

The only thing that follows from Hegel's way of reasoning is that the state in which the "manner and formation of self-consciousness" and the "constitution" contradict each other is no true state. I dare say it is trivial to observe that a constitution which was the product of a bygone consciousness can turn into an oppressive fetter on a more advanced consciousness, etc., etc. What should instead be pointed out is that what would logically follow is the demand for a constitution having in itself the aim and the principle of progressing in step with consciousness . . .

MARX

The capitalists and their followers are but an insignificant little bunch. How could they, then, under universal suffrage, hold up the transition to socialism?

KAUTSKY

The social order is stronger than the constitution of the state. As long as capital holds the "commanding heights of the economy," it compels the state to obedience against its own interests, by means of its economic power and through the systems of ideas which develop out of economic power relations, the democratic equality of the franchise notwithstanding.

BAUER

In capitalist society, given some sharpening of the class struggle which forms its foundation, there must be either a dictatorship of the

bourgeoisie or a dictatorship of the proletariat. Any dream about some
third alternative is the reactionary lamentation of the petty bourgeois.

LENIN

A similar preoccupation with problems of power characterizes the Leninist attitude toward democratic processes and democratic traditions. Democracy, in its most radical, anarchistic
form, constitutes part of the ideal society toward which Lenin
and most other Marxists were striving. The "withering away" of
the state picturesquely formulates this ideal, which, incidentally,
was professed in the very earliest writings of Marx. In a democratic state, Marx wrote, the general will of the "real" people
becomes incarnate in the actions of the state. "Democracy is the
solution of the *riddle* of all constitutions. Here the constitution
is . . . constantly reduced to the *real* men, the *real people,* and
posited as their *own* work." [1] Freedom, he wrote in the same
article, is the identity of private or special interest with the
interests of the community. When these collide, it is, formally,
the state which decides between them, and it makes these
decisions in the name of the community. In reality, however,
Marx held, the state has always been, itself, the creation of
special interests.[2]

The political ideal of the young Marx is thus posited clearly:
the state, in order to make democracy a reality, must be liberated
from the rule of special interests. It must be transformed into an
instrument of the "real" people — a Marxian variant of Rousseau's General Will. As soon as this is accomplished, however,
the state will itself have become superfluous. Once the interests
of the individuals or groups and the community have come to
coincide, no mediator is necessary between them. The General
Will can express itself directly, without the aid of political
institutions. "The most recent French writers have interpreted
this to mean that in true democracy the political state perishes,"
Marx pointed out, indicating his agreement.[3]

Now, the method of analysis developed later by Marx and
Engels was nothing else than an attempt to single out the
special interests which, through the instrument of the state,
could dominate society and by that token corrupt the institution

of the state itself. Once it was accepted that it is classes which are the antagonistic forces within societies, then it followed that that agreement on fundamentals which in liberal theory is the premise of the democratic state could, in the language of Marxism, be expressed only as the abolition of all class differences. The only kind of society that would be able to attain the political ideal of liberalism was, therefore, according to Engels, "the society that organizes production anew on the basis of a free and equal association of the producers." * Then the state would die away. "The first act in which the state actually steps out as the representative of *all* society . . . is simultaneously its last independent act as a state." †

In this theory of a stateless society, Marxism promises to fulfill the liberal ideal, though this fulfillment is, in a sense, but a by-product of another ideal, the attainment of socialism. We should note further that this promise of direct democracy in a classless society was accepted by most followers of Marx and Engels, and forms part of the Leninist tradition as well. To Lenin it was so commonplace that he seldom troubled to discuss it, with the significant exception of the weeks shortly before the October Revolution, when he devoted an entire work to his ideas about the future society. In this sense, the Marxist tradition embodies liberal ideals of democracy.** It diverges from liberal democracy

---

* Many statements made by Lenin echo this; for instance, the following: "If we are not to mock at common sense and history, then clearly we can not speak of 'pure democracy' so long as different *classes* exist, but can speak only of *class* democracy" (Lenin, vol. 23, p. 345; translation in *The Proletarian Revolution and the Renegade Kautsky*, New York, 1934, p. 25).

Other examples may be found in Lenin, vol. 23, p. 351, and vol. 21, p. 378; translations in *The Proletarian Revolution*, p. 32, and *The State and Revolution*, New York, 1929, p. 122.

† *Herrn Eugen Dührings Umwälzung der Wissenschaft* (ed. 2, Zürich, 1886), p. 271. In a letter to Bebel of 18–28 March 1875, Engels wrote, "As soon as it becomes possible to speak of freedom, then the state, as such, ceases to exist" (printed in Karl Marx, *Critique of the Gotha Program*, New York, n. d., Appendix I, p. 58).

** The Leninist notion of the withering away of the state has a somewhat anarchistic character. Lenin wrote: "We establish as our final aim the liquidation of the state, i.e., of any sort of organized and systematic constraint, of all coercion of human beings in general. . . . Striving for socialism, we are convinced that it will grow into communism and that, in

not in the rejection of democratic ideals, but in the rejection of democratic practices pending the realization of these ideals. There is a latent conflict within the Marxist movement over the question whether or not the classless and stateless society can be attained through democratic processes, and few Marxist leaders have taken an unambiguous stand one way or another. In general, Marx's belief in the rationality of the broad masses led him to believe in democratic processes and to fight for

---

connection with it, all necessity for the coercion of men in general will disappear, all necessity for the *subordination* of one man to another, of one part of the population to another part; for people will *get used* to observing the elementary conditions of sociability *without constraint* and without subordination" (Lenin, vol. 21, p. 426; translation in *The State and Revolution*, p. 187).

Yet Leninists have insisted on a sharp differentiation of their own theories from those of anarchism (and, in talking about anarchists, they tend to think primarily of Bakunin). The very conception of the gradual withering away of the state can be contrasted to the anarchist advocacy of an immediate abolition of the state. Democracy (or the "abolition of the state") can not be "made" or decreed, but must grow organically because it depends on specific sociological conditions.

The difference between Leninism and anarchism is made more glaring by the fact that, with the latter, the democratic ideal is a purely negative one, denoting the absence of all constraint and subordination, whereas the stateless democracy envisioned by Lenin has a positive content. This content is that "administration of things" of which Engels wrote when he defined the withering away of the state as a "change from the political rule over men to an administration of things and a leadership over processes of production" (*Herrn Eugen Dührings Umwälzung der Wissenschaft*, p. 277). Such an administration of things clearly involves authority, planning, control, and co-ordination, as the phrase "leadership over processes of production" indicates, beyond doubt. Lenin indicated his agreement with this in a speech given in May 1918, in which he said: "There is no doubt — the further the gains of the October Revolution advance, . . . the greater and higher the role of the soviets of national economy will become; they alone among all state institutions can look forward to maintaining for themselves a lasting place, which will be all the more lasting the nearer we come to the establishment of a socialist system and the less necessity there is for a purely administrative apparatus, an apparatus in control of government, strictly speaking. *That* apparatus is doomed after the resistance of the exploiters has been definitely smashed, after the working people have learned to organize socialist production — that apparatus of government in the proper, narrow, restricted sense of the word, that apparatus of the old state is doomed to die; but an apparatus of the type of our Supreme Soviet of National Economy is bound to grow, develop, and become strong, fulfilling all the most important active functions of an organized society" (Lenin, vol. 23, p. 36).

democratic reforms, for the widening of the franchise, for constitutional guarantees, for civil liberties and equality before the law. The resulting universal participation in politics would, he thought, inevitably lead to the rule of the proletariat. In this context it is irrelevant whether or not he thought that the attainment of constitutional democracy would have to be won in a revolutionary struggle. What matters is his belief that, given democratic and constitutional processes, the victory of socialism was assured. Wrote Engels, "If anything is certain, it is that our party and the working class can come to power only under the form of the democratic republic. This is indeed the *specific form for the dictatorship of the proletariat.*" [4]

Subsequent Marxist politicians, including Lenin, accepted this and similar statements. But Lenin, after quoting it with obvious approval, thought it necessary to add a comment: "Engels," he wrote, "here repeats in a particularly emphatic form the fundamental idea which runs like a red thread throughout all of Marx's work, namely, that the democratic republic is the *nearest approach to the dictatorship of the proletariat.*" [5] In writing this, he seems to have thought that he was but paraphrasing the words of Engels and elucidating their meaning. In actual fact, however, his passage marks a significant difference in the attitudes assumed by the two men toward political democracy, as we shall see presently.

On one thing Engels and Lenin agreed: while democracy would be fully realized in the coming socialist order and was thus a feature of the ideal society, the short-run appraisal of democratic institutions depended on their value in the revolutionary struggle of the proletariat. The question concerning this value has always plagued Marxist theorists. It was often put by asking whether or not the democratic constitutional process set up by bourgeois regimes might ever become a "neutral agent" and, as such, correctly express the will of the proletarian masses.

Marx himself did not live to witness the full flowering of democratic government in Europe through the extension of the franchise to the entire adult population. Engels outlived him long enough to be aware of it. Still, Marx perceived the trend sufficiently to state that the conquest of power by the proletariat through legal, constitutional means might be possible in those countries of western Europe where popular sovereignty had in fact been realized. Engels, in his critique of the Erfurt Platform of the German Social Democratic Party (1891), mentioned England, France, and the United States as democratic countries that might fit this description; he made this assertion, however, in an attempt to curb similar optimistic opinions about the efficacy of democratic institutions in Germany. He thought that the constitution there was nothing but the "fig leaf hiding the shame of absolutism," and that any reliance on constitutional and parliamentary means in the German class struggle would betray the cause of the proletarian revolution.[6]

In his last years, however, Engels viewed the rapid growth of the social democratic electorate in Germany with great satisfaction, and he voiced the conviction that, given time and the continued opportunity to carry on party propaganda within the limits of a truly liberal constitution, the proletariat could not fail to gain the reins of political power. After all, he wrote, "the time of surprise attacks, of revolutions carried through by small conscious minorities at the head of unconscious masses, is past."[7]

The proletariat, he continued, had now become the advocate and the defender of constitutional democracy; it had acquired a vested interest in the democratic method, as the surest way toward the proletarian revolution. "The irony of world history turns everything upside down: we, the 'revolutionaries,' the 'rebels' — we are thriving far better on legal methods than on illegal methods and revolt."[8] He added, however, that in the same measure as the proletariat benefited by constitutional methods, the old ruling classes were trying to take political concessions away from it. The bourgeoisie saw itself obliged to abandon the pretense of democratic government and to resort to "illegal" laws for the oppression of the people's will. And, as the bourgeoisie was thus turning away from liberal practices, Engels invoked — irony of all ironies! — the political contract by which the princes had bound themselves to abide by the will of the majority. Should they break that contract by their unilateral decision, the proletariat, in turn, would no longer be obliged to abide by it. The right to revolution, which is, "after all, the only real 'historical right,' the only right on which all modern states without exception rest," would then revert to the people, as represented by the proletariat.[9] And so Engels, indeed, affirmed the desirability and theoretical possibility of winning the revolution by constitutional, democratic means; yet, just because such means were being used, he visualized the decline of liberal democracy, as the capitalist class would react by revoking political liberties and thus force the proletariat into taking violent revolutionary steps.

Lenin's inital position was that of the first program of the Russian Social Democratic Workers' Party, which was modeled closely on the Erfurt Platform. Like the latter, the Russian platform posited as the initial goal of the party the creation of a democratic republic of a radical liberal character. Hence Lenin, in the first two decades of his political life, argued with vehemence that the creation of a liberal, democratic, constitutional Russia was an indispensable precondition of all further successes of the proletarian movement. Yet at the same time he began to emphasize more and more the possibility, or even the inevitability, of the ruling classes' revoking all constitutional rights and processes as soon as they became a threat to continued bourgeois rule. Finally, after the initial and indeed modest constitutional reforms granted by the tsar during the Revolution of 1905, Lenin never ceased to stress the fundamental inadequacies not only of these reforms but also of the most far-reaching democratic institutions. By the second decade of this century, Lenin's attitude had thus become thoroughly ambivalent. On the one hand, he continued to stress that democratic institutions were a favorable environment for revolutionary struggle, although we shall see that he came to use the very word "democracy" in a rather unusual sense. On the other hand, he more and more emphasized the inadequacies of democratic institutions, claiming that capitalism could never be abolished within the framework of constitutional democracy. No political reforms, no extension of political liberties could, in themselves, lead to the victory of socialism: the most liberal type of constitutional democracy was precisely the typical political form of mature capitalism.

According to the Marxist view, democracy in its historical development is a curious paradox, because its two outstanding features are in sharp contradiction. Constitutional democracy, as the Marxists see it, has always been in effect the dictatorship of the capitalist class; yet it entails the formal recognition of the equality of all citizens, a recognition of which universal suffrage is the most basic institutional expression.[10] Eduard Bernstein, defining democracy as the "absence of class rule," immediately modifies this definition by arguing that the absence of class rule is only a principle, a postulate. Democracy is that organization of society "in which no class *can claim* a political privilege as against the collectivity." Hence it means the "abolition of class rule in principle, though it is not yet the actual abolition of classes."[11] In other words, under political democracy there is formal equality for all. No one is privileged, theoretically. Yet actual privilege is still maintained; there is actual inequality of classes and therefore of power. Bernstein expressed this ambiguous nature of democracy by recalling that the German word *Bürger* means both "citizen" and "bourgeois"; hence the concept of the *bürgerliche* state expresses both the dictatorship of the bourgeoisie, which is to be abolished, and the presumably neutral agent of the general will of all citizens, through which the aims of democratic socialism can be achieved.*

Marxism looks to the history of constitutional democracy for an explanation of the paradox. According to this view, the bourgeoisie came to power on the slogan of political liberty. In its revolutionary struggle against the *ancien régime* it needed the support of broad masses of the population, and it attracted this support by its persistent demands for liberal political reforms. As Laski wrote: "Historically, in fact, political democracy, throughout Western civilization, is the price the middle class had to pay for the support of the masses in the struggle with the

---

* Bernstein, p. 128. Incidentally, Marx and Engels berated Max Stirner for obscuring the difference between *bourgeois* and *citoyen* by his use of *Bürger*. See their "Die deutsche Ideologie," p. 182.

feudal aristocracy for power. It welcomed the support until victory was certain; it has been doubtful of its consequences ever since." [12] For the growth of . the proletariat in number, strength, and class consciousness went hand in hand with the subsequent development of capitalism, and the bourgeoisie continued to be forced into a growing dependency on the working class. Because of this dependency, it was forced to put the democratic slogans on which it has come to power into practice. Although the most radical constitutions of the decades immediately following the French Revolution still restricted the rights of citizenship to property owners, the franchise had to be extended further and further, and every extension, every forward step in the recognition of the formal political equality of all, increased the demands for more liberties. Even so, many Marxists insisted that the paradox of democracy remained unresolved, that the formal "equality of all" guaranteed by the franchise did not mitigate the actual inequality of power.

Otto Bauer explained this paradox by a very clever definition of democracy as a system of distributing power, without coercive means, in accordance with the social status of individuals, groups, or classes: "Democracy is that form of state within which the distribution of power in the state is determined *exclusively* by the social factors of power, but is not shifted in favor of any one class through the application of material means of coercion." [13] What are these decisive social factors of power? Bauer furnished the following list of factors: (a) the numerical strength of the classes; (b) the manner, strength, and efficacy of their organization; (c) their functional position in the process of production and distribution; (d) the level of their political consciousness; and (e) their cultural and educational level.

Although this definition of democracy appeared in an anti-Leninist pamphlet, at first glance there seems to be little in it to which Lenin or his followers would have objected. Lenin, like Bauer, would have stressed the fact that political forms are of interest mainly because they constitute specific manners of distributing power. He would have further agreed with Bauer that democracy indicates the free play of power factors, yet he would have added that the game is rigged in advance. It is not necessarily the vote which decides, or other formal methods of democratic decision-making; the decisive power factors are of an informal nature and are distributed unequally within society. Simply because power plays freely, the formal equality of every citizen is a sham. Bourgeois democracy, Lenin wrote in 1919, means that decisions are ostensibly made by votes, but those votes are influenced by financial interests.[14] In all this he was in agreement with Bauer.

Lenin would probably have criticized Bauer's definition on at least two counts. In the first place, he would have considered Bauer's definition of democracy too abstract. His point would have been that Bauer should have indicated which of the power factors mentioned was the most decisive one. Which is stronger in the free play of power factors, the level of education possessed by a class, its political consciousness, its numerical strength, its organization, or the hold it has over the essential means of production and distribution? To put it more bluntly: who wins in a democracy, the ruling minority or the exploited masses of the population?

The question in this form is loaded; nonetheless, Lenin himself has given conflicting answers to it at different times, and his appraisal of the usefulness and desirability of democratic institutions has varied accordingly. Indeed, as is so often the case, he subscribed to opposite views at the same time, without being aware of the contradictions in which he had involved himself. On the one hand, he fought for democracy, partly for propagandistic reasons, but also because he thought that democracy was only one step short of the victory of the proletariat. On the other hand, he did not cease insisting that the deciding factor of social power was always and inevitably control over the means of production. Capital, he held, exerted the greatest influence over the consciousness, aims, and actions of all citizens; hence it was the deciding factor. According to Lenin, all the "social factors of power" listed by Bauer could have been epitomized by private property, which in democracies determines political action. As he put it: "The democratic republic is the very best possible political framework of capitalism, and therefore, once capital has got hold . . . of this best of all possible frameworks,

it establishes its power so firmly, so truly, that *no* change, be it
of personalities, institutions, or parties of the bourgeois democratic republic, will cause this power to waver." [15] Variations
on this statement can be found abundantly throughout Lenin's
writings.

Democracy, then, according to this view, may look like a
free play of forces, but in reality the will of the people is
perverted by the all-pervading influence of capital. All the
alleged benefits of constitutional democracy are debunked as
"constitutional illusions," a term used to describe not only the
half-hearted concessions granted in Russia after 1905, but even
the most liberal constitutional regimes. For there, too, the working masses would inevitably be frustrated in their attempt to
influence the course of politics. "To decide once every few
years which member of the ruling class is to oppress and suppress
the people in parliament — there you have the real essence of
bourgeois parliamentarism." [16] Similar comments are made on all
institutions characteristic of liberal democracy: freedom of
speech, press and assembly; the right to vote; equality before
the law, and so forth.

The second reason Lenin would have quarreled with Otto
Bauer's definition of democracy is this: he would have objected
to the sharp dividing line drawn between "social factors of
power" and "material means of coercion," because he tended
to regard all methods of rule as coercive and dictatorial, whether
the rule was enforced by the most unmitigated police state or
by the subtlest means of influencing public opinion. In reading
Lenin's works we get the feeling that he hardly appreciated
in all its fullness the role which influence ("social factors of
power") plays in liberal democracies. Instead of pointing out, in
the manner of, say, Thurman Arnold or Harold Laski, the many
subtle ways in which big money takes hold of society and
determines political decision-making, he tended to generalize
from his observation of democracy in Prussia and Russia and of
the wartime emergency governments in Europe during World
War I. Hence, instead of the economic power of capital, it was
the political organs of the police, the standing army, and the civil

service, that seemed to him to be the main power factors favorable to capitalism, presumably because they were the hired servants of the business class. He therefore viewed democracy not so much as a subtle way of ruling through influence, but more as a method of ruling by plain coercion. Where he did mention the influence of capital, he tended to brand this influence as corruption and systematic bribery.*

His view of democracy as an openly coercive system of government becomes particularly apparent in passages where he tries to refute the claim that democracy means the protection of minorities. Lenin's assertion was that such protection is given only as long as the business class deems it convenient. "Minority protection is given by the ruling party in a bourgeois democracy only to another *bourgeois* party, while the proletariat in every *serious, deep, fundamental* question gets martial law and pogroms instead of 'minority protection.' " [17]

Adducing the bloody history of the 1871 Paris Commune, Marx had similarly stated that "the slightest improvement in [the proletariat's] position remains a utopia within the bourgeois republic, a utopia that turns into a crime as soon as [the proletariat] wants to realize it." [18] Lenin eagerly seized upon the slaying of Karl Liebknecht and Rosa Luxemburg as further proof:

If people under arrest, that is, people who have been taken into the custody of the state authority, could be slain without punishment by officers and capitalists, under a government of social patriots, then the democratic republic under which such a thing was possible is the dictatorship of the bourgeoisie.

"Liberty" in one of the freest and most advanced republics of the world, in the German republic, is liberty to kill, without punishment, the arrested leaders of the proletariat.†

* This failure to distinguish between different intensities of coercion allowed him, in turn, to shed all restraint when his own party came to power and to exercise his dictatorship by all the means at his disposal. We often attribute our own motives to our adversary in order to justify our own hostility.

† Lenin, vol. 24, p. 11. For further comments on the hypocrisies of liberal democracy, see Trotsky's bitter comments on the ficticious character of the right to asylum, made in the last chapter of his autobiography (*Mein Leben*, Berlin, 1930, pp. 552ff).

According to Lenin, therefore, constitutional legality was nothing but the capitalists' shield against revolutionary change, and it would remain capitalist dictatorship. "Bourgeois democracy, the value of which is undisputed for the education of the proletariat and as a school for battle, is always narrow, hypocritical, mendacious, and false; it always remains democracy for the rich, a bluff for the poor." [19] Hence it is basically inadequate as a means of bringing about a proletarian regime. In the long run, it would mean betrayal of the revolution were the proletariat to wage its class struggle exclusively within the range of democratic institutions. Politics, in the eyes of Leninism, is amoral. Conversely, all and any political means, as long as they are conducive to further the proper ends (as defined by the Leninist), are acceptable. As Trotsky wrote in the fiery Manifesto of the First Comintern Congress:

In the last struggle for life or death against capital, to demand of the proletariat that it piously observe the demands of political democracy would be the same as demanding of a man who is defending his life and existence against highway robbers that he observe the artificial and conditional rules of French wrestling, which have been established by his enemy and are not being observed by that enemy.[20]

At the time of the October Revolution, Lenin went even further than that. Not only was democracy a luxury which the revolutionary proletariat could not afford; he now asserted that it was also a false ideal. Abandoning himself, for a brief period of some months, to anarcho-syndicalist ideas which he was later to drop abruptly, he expressed himself against democracy because it was "a form of *state;* yet we Marxists are enemies of *any sort* of state." [21] At the same time, he repeated that the democratic state was, historically, the "normal" superstructure of capitalism, and he was emphatic in his assertion that this political shell of an obsolete, exploitative mode of production must be done away with completely. Or, as he put it, the democratic state, as the most powerful weapon in the hands of capitalism, must be smashed to pieces. Of his moderate socialist opponents, he said:

They have not understood that a vote within the framework, the institutions, within the habits of bourgeois parliamentarism, is *part* of the bourgeois state apparatus, which must be smashed and broken up from top to bottom *in order* to realize the dictatorship of the proletariat, for the transition from bourgeois democracy to proletarian democracy.

They have not understood that *all* serious questions of politics are decided, not at all by votes, but by civil war, when history places the dictatorship of the proletariat on the order of the day.[22]

As we have indicated earlier, he held these views simultaneously with an opinion of democracy that was much more favorable. The hypocrisy and illusions of bourgeois democracy notwithstanding, Lenin constantly fought for the extension of constitutional rights and the elimination of predemocratic political institutions, and so have his followers ever since. These efforts can be viewed as a propagandistic attempt to put the ruling classes on the defensive by using their own slogans against them, a strategy that has been part of the socialist tradition even since the French Revolution. The implication is that democracy may be a sham as long as capital rules, but it is still part of the platform of all socialist parties, who argue that the rule of the proletariat will better guarantee the reality of democratic practices.

Lenin and his followers, however, have never shown much interest in appealing to the ruling classes, even by such indirect means as putting them on the defensive. Their concern is with the working class or, more broadly, with all those who work with their hands, be they factory workers, coolies, or peasants. It is they who are to recognize the inadequacies of bourgeois democracy, and they are to learn this lesson not only through instruction from the conscious leaders, but through practical experience. They are to demand their constitutional rights, they are to ask for the extension of democracy, not because of the benefits they might thus obtain, but because the leaders expect that these benefits will not be granted. Every time the proletariat demands its constitutional rights, Leninist doctrine expects that it will be cheated of them. The fight for democracy is therefore designed as an eyeopener, or, as Lenin put it, as an "education and school for battle."

Yet any concessions made by the ruling classes, all extensions of civil and political liberties, do come as a help to the workers in the class struggle, by training the masses to participate in politics. In turn, this training will help the leaders to manipulate the workers, particularly in that mass participation allows them to gauge the mood of the common man, whose sympathy is essential for revolutionary action. "The universal franchise is an indicator of the maturity with which various classes understand their problems. It indicates how various classes are *inclined* to solve their problems. The *solution* itself of these problems is given not by the vote, but by all forms of the class struggle, including civil war." [23] Most important, however, democracy is desirable as a tool for the acquisition of power. Since the civil and political liberties of democracy facilitate waging class warfare in the most intensive manner, a democratic, constitutional republic is "the most convenient arena for the struggle between the proletariat and the bourgeoisie." [24] Its advantage for Lenin and his followers lies in its acknowledged tendency to assure "that a free, enlightened people learn to manage all its affairs — but chiefly in order that the working class be able to fight freely for socialism, that is, for a state of affairs in which there will be no rich and poor, in which all the land, all the factories and mills will belong to all those who work." [25]

Democracy is the "most convenient arena" for the class struggle because it provides freedoms that no other form of government provides. Leninism has never been reluctant to make use of these freedoms. On the contrary, perhaps the most important motive that prompted Lenin and his followers to fight for democratic reforms was the realization that these freedoms will benefit not only the owners of the means of production, but also those strong in numbers, consciousness, and organization. And Lenin repeatedly exhorted the party to utilize democratic freedoms to the utmost. "The tactics of the proletariat must consist in the utilization of the rights that have been given under the pressure of its blows, in the organization of workers' conventions for deciding the question whether or not to continue the strike, in the organization of a militia for the protection of revolutionary rights, in the presentation of demands for a full amnesty . . ." [26]

We see thus that Lenin regards democracy in a society divided by the class struggle as conducive to a sharpening of the class struggle, and therefore conducive to revolution and civil war. Or rather, in Lenin's eyes, democracy really is tantamount to civil war; for the closer a society approaches full and unfettered democracy, the more openly does the cleavage between the classes show up, and the more freely rages the class struggle.[27] Pure democracy is therefore not only seen as the "last form of class rule," [28] but also considered the purest form of the bourgeois order, in that it stimulates the underlying class conflict and lets it break into the open.[29]

These differing views of democracy are part of the Leninist tradition. To both of them the well-trained Leninist subscribes simultaneously, even though emphasis may be shifted from one to the other as the situation warrants. The seeming contradiction in which the Leninist involves himself by maintaining both views at the same time is resolved by the overriding view that consciousness is higher than democratic procedures. In its broader meaning of "rule of the people," democracy is, indeed, part of that socialist system of values which is always treated as self-evident and hardly ever discussed systematically. Hence Leninism "is for" democracy. Moreover, the optimistic aspect of Leninism contributes to a favorable attitude toward constitutional democracy, for the Leninist has faith in the class struggle — he believes that its outcome will be favorable, and that democracy furthers it. In addition, the fight for democracy has propaganda value. By continuously stressing the inadequacies and injustices of bourgeois democracy, the Leninist seeks to undermine democratic loyalties and community spirit; and the fight for the extension of democratic rights serves as an education and as battle training for his own loyal rank and file.

This appraisal is made by Leninism of all reforms and advantages granted by the ruling classes. Leninist tradition has found a number of derogatory labels for communists who disdain reforms altogether or refuse to make use of institutions that are part of the bourgeois political system, and this tradition is based on the political battles Lenin himself waged against, say, the "Boycottists" (who wanted the party to boycott the Duma elections), the "Otzovists" (who wanted to recall the Bolshevik delegates from the Duma), and the "Left Communists" (who opposed the conclusion of the Brest-Litovsk Treaty and many other measures taken by the regime during the Civil War). Lenin argued that the parliamentary fight, the fight for economic benefits, and the fight for reforms of any kind must be considered an intrinsic part of the over-all class struggle.

For, once more, the benefits granted would either be useful as weapons, or they would be taken away again, and hasten the disappointment of the working class and their disillusionment with democracy. One way or another, the party could not lose. Each partial victory would lead either to the revocation of liberties granted under the duress of mass unrest or to further and further concessions. In either case the result would be a sharpening of the class struggle. As Lenin wrote with such confidence, "semivictories in revolutions, those forced, hasty concessions on the part of the old regime, are the surest token of new, far more decisive, sharper civil disturbances, which will involve broader and broader masses of the people." [30]

This highly optimistic appraisal, however, is accompanied by repeated warning of caution: democracy may be a pleasant dream and a convenient weapon to boot, but so long as it is *bourgeois* democracy it cannot be trusted by the party. Nor can any reforms whatsoever be trusted that are the gift of the ruling classes. Lenin never ceased denouncing all benefits granted by the rulers of the prevailing system as bluff, deception, or unimportant palliatives. How, he asked, could it be otherwise when reforms are implemented by capitalists? "Where except in the imagination of sentimental reformists are there any trusts capable of worrying about the condition of the masses rather than about the conquest of colonies?" [31] This skepticism applies particularly to far-reaching reforms. Lenin did not hesitate to consider them scientifically impossible. He thought that, so long as the old ruling classes were in power, they could not be expected to make any concessions endangering their rule over society. It is an old axiom of Marxism that no ruling class ever destroys itself: in Lenin's words, "The history of mankind has not yet seen examples of a ruling and suppressing class voluntarily giving up its right to rule, its right to oppress, its

right to tremendous profit from enslaved peasants and workers." [32]
In any event, whatever reforms might be won would be secure
only when they were protected by the dictatorship of the
proletariat.

In addition, a pessimistic note pervades Leninist doctrine in
regard to this matter. Not only is democracy untrustworthy;
the working class cannot be trusted with democracy and reforms,
either. An improvement in the workers' standard of living or an
extension of their political rights is regarded with the greatest
suspicion, because it might tend to corrupt the fighting spirit
and class consciousness of the rank-and-file followers of the
party. As heatedly as he fought against the romantic left-wingers
who scorned parliamentary activities and the fight for gradual
reforms, Lenin battled against what he called "reformism," the
tendency to be satisfied with the reforms gained from the
hands of the ruling classes.

The Marxists, as distinct from the anarchists, recognize the fight for
reforms, that is, for improvements in the situation of the working
people that leave the power in the hands of the ruling class. But at
the same time the Marxists wage a most decisive struggle against
reformists who directly or indirectly limit the endeavors and activities
of the working class to reforms. Reformism is a bourgeois delusion of
the workers, who will always remain wage slaves in spite of individual
improvements — as long as the rule of capital is a reality. [33]

The socialists do not renounce the struggle for reforms. They must,
for instance, even today, vote in the parliaments for all, even the
smallest, improvements in the position of the masses. . . . But it is
simple bourgeois bluff to preach reforms for the solution of questions
that history and the actual political facts of life have posited as
revolutionary ones. [34]

Reformism, then, is a dangerous perversion, or deviation, from
the proper path to be followed by the party. Obtaining reforms
from the ruling classes must never become an end in itself, or
even a very important subsidiary end; it is merely one of the
many tactical advantages for which the party keeps fighting. [35]
And even here caution is required, for reforms are not always
unmixed blessings. The tactical advantages they bring with
them may be outweighed by psychological setbacks.

To put it bluntly, even while Lenin urged his followers to fight for reforms, he nonetheless believed that reforms corrupt. His gloomy views concerning working-class rationality, together with the practical experience he had had, led him to think that reforms and concessions, once they have been won, work to alleviate the situation of the proletariat and thus make the workers relax in their class struggle. Hence he could write that "Reformism, even when it is completely sincere, actually turns into a means for the bourgeois perversion and weakening of the workers." [36] Or, more sharply, "A reform is a concession which the ruling classes make *in order* to slow down, weaken, or obscure the revolutionary struggle, in order to break the strength and energy of the revolutionary classes, to darken their consciousness, and so on." [37] And with this same suspicion Leninism regards all improvements, political or economic, of the workers' lot except those wrought by the party itself. A real reform of the existing system, short of its complete overthrow in a revolution, is considered impossible.

This notion of the impossibility of real reform is, significantly, axiomatic not only with Leninism; it recurred again and again among political and social thinkers of nineteenth-century Russia. Whether they were on the side of the ruling classes or on the side of the underprivileged, the sharpest and keenest intellects of Russia seem to have despaired of reforms and of evolution. If they favored the ruling classes, that is, if they stood for "order," they tended to think that even the slightest concession to demands from below would lead to further and greater demands and to a destruction of the entire existing system. If they were opponents of the regime, they were prone to denounce all compromise solutions as worse than outright slavery. If this "all or nothing" attitude reflected the actual possibilities, then anyone starting with a belief or hope in evolutionary development would sooner or later be forced to choose sides.

A case in point is that of M. M. Speransky.° A man in his

° M. M. Speransky (1772–1839) rose from humble origins to ministerial rank in the administrations of Alexander I and Nicholas I. While he distinguished himself as a capable and imaginative administrator both in St. Petersburg and in Siberia, he is best known, perhaps, for his repeated efforts to devise a constitutional order for tsarist Russia.

high position could not have helped swinging from a surprisingly
radical *theoretical* desire for the evolution of democratic liberalism to a *practical* advocacy of the most abject divine-grace
absolutism, in a society of privileged nobles and enslaved
peasants. His idealism resembled Engels' characterization of
Kant's categorical imperative — "powerless, because it asks for
the impossible, and consequently will never achieve any real
results." [38] Speransky's ratiocinations were based on a clear
recognition of the interrelation of the rise of the bourgeoisie and
the development of liberal constitutionalism; they were supported
by his belief that reaction could lead only to revolution. Yet
these very premises resulted in practical projects and "reforms"
designed to put tsarist absolutism on an even firmer social and
legal basis. He based his decisions on the argument that a social
basis for liberal institutions was completely lacking in the Russia
of his day. But although he believed that such a basis might
be created by institutional reforms, that is, by erecting the
political superstructure of liberalism in which a nascent bourgeoisie might gradually grow and be educated, he nevertheless
saw fit to stress the dangers to the existing order that lay in the
"premature" creation of liberal institutions. Hence he was even
against general education: enlightenment would, after all, be a
most cruel and inhuman gift to slaves, and it also would lead to
revolution. Speransky discussed these problems in a mood of
gloomy disappointment and resignation; he spoke of a vicious
circle of reform and reaction, out of which he saw no immediate
escape. He consoled himself by positing the inevitability of the
gradual development of another, more liberal social basis; time
would do away with the vicious circle. Yet, as we see from his
fear of education, he was in the final analysis afraid even of such
a long-range evolution, and so he tried to devise means of arrest-
ing the course of history.*

° For these discussions see M. M. Speransky, "Vvedenie k ulozheniiu
gosudarstvennykh zakonov," in *Istoricheskoe Obozrenie*, 1898, no. 10 (St.
Peterburgs, 1899); also Nikolai I. Turgenev, *La Russie et les Russes* (Paris,
1847), vol. 3, pp. 423ff. For a secondary account see Sergius Swatikow,
Die Entwürfe der Änderung der russischen Staatsverfassung (Heidelberg,
1904). That such intellectual developments were not confined to Russia
is shown by but cursory glances at such cautious liberals as Walter Bagehot

At the other extreme we find a man like Nikolai G. Cherny-shevski, who denounced the peasant reforms of 1861 as a piece of dastardly deception and, in the interest of eventual revolutionary change, voiced his preference for outright reaction over such half measures — much to the pleasure of Lenin, who hastened to place himself in the Chernyshevski tradition.[39] "All or nothing!" That is the attitude which Leninists take toward any mitigation of existing hardships or exploitative relationships, even while they eagerly seize upon all advantages given them by the spread of democracy.

---

in England, Benjamin Constant in France, or Baron Louis de Geer in Sweden.

Chapter 4

The "Operational Code"

Chernyshevsky has already said: a man who is afraid of getting his hands dirty should not be active politically.

LENIN

The whole art of conspiratorial organization must consist in utilizing everybody and everything . . . and at the same time maintaining leadership *over the entire movement.*

LENIN

Again and again we are led back to the realization of the importance that "consciousness" plays in the image which the party's leaders formed of their organization and its tasks. The impatience with history that characterizes communism can be derived only from an absolute consciousness of man's destiny. It is possible that a firm conviction of the inevitability of socialism could lead to a happy quietism, born of the unshakable belief that all roads lead to the Good Society and that man's historical destiny will be fulfilled in due course, as soon as the conditions have ripened. The typical Leninist impatience stems, instead, from a hidden pessimism, creeping doubts that history has not been going in the right direction, or perhaps, that the danger of its deviating into utter chaos is ever present. This second possibility was implied as early as the *Communist Manifesto*.

To put this differently, we might say that consciousness, in the Leninist sense, consists not only of the abstract knowledge of where history is going, but also of a very concrete knowledge of the existing world, its social structure, its economic functioning, and its political constellations. The world must be viewed on various levels of abstractness or concreteness, from the vast schemes of Marxist historiography down to the analysis of what Lenin called the "current moment," that temporary constellation which is with us now and will be changed presently. And consciousness includes the full knowledge of the world on all these levels.

Still, in order to understand Lenin's feverish impatience, his activism, a third element must be recognized as constituting part of consciousness. This element is moral. The Leninist takes action, or is eager to have an opportunity for action, because he is evaluating the world around him. He is casting value judgments, usually negative ones; hence his desire to wreak changes. Leninist consciousness is not contemplative, but activist. Theory, Lenin used to say, is of no value except as a guide to action. He knew, without having to discuss it at any length, that the world had to be changed. As an orthodox Marxist, moreover, he was aware of the general scheme of development, the algebra of revolution. What was still required was the arithmetic of the specific situations and the specific actions to be taken in them. The formulas that in the abstract were familiar to any Marxist and, in modified form, to any Leninist, had to be concretized. The over-all values and the broad consciousness of historical developments had to be supplemented by a precise estimate of the momentary constellation of forces, and only then could the most appropriate action be taken to change the balance of forces in the party's favor, so that history could be pushed on and on toward the final goal. It is this preoccupation with the proper action to be taken during any fleeting time-span which is, according to Lenin's view, the mark of the conscious revolutionary leader, and the ability to make correct assessments and to devise correct programs of action is the only valid criterion of consciousness that Lenin recognized. Hence his mania for precision and realism both in analysis and in action, his hatred of carelessness, vagueness, inefficiency, shilly-shallying, phrase-making, and of those endless discussions without results that were so typical

of Russian intellectuals. Leninist dialectics, in stressing concreteness, often fights against these habits.

But the emphasis on concreteness is also related to the manipulative attitude that Lenin and his followers took toward all features of the world around them. For the Leninist, all things, all
institutions, and particularly all people are forces that are always
in a certain balance. In relation to the party, these forces play a
double role. On the one hand, they are obstacles in the party's
road toward the final goal, or even toward the more intermediary
goals, such as the attainment of absolute power. They are therefore objects of the party's hatred; and they are hated not only
because they do constitute obstacles, but also, more generally,
because they are features of a social system that in its entirety is
hated and despised. Indeed, everything that exists, every institution, every social group, every class, every habit or culture pat-
tern.is part of the capitalist system or of a precapitalist system
and is therefore regarded with suspicion and contempt by the
Leninist. Yet every one of these contemptible features of the past
(or present) is at the same time something that can be used by
the party in its fight for power, its fight against the existing system, its fight for communism. Rather, these features of the existing society not only *can* be used, they *must* be used, if the party
is to succeed. They are the material, the only material, with
which the party can work; they are the element (*stikhiia*) that
makes the wheels of history go around, and the party must act as
the general staff of social engineering in this interplay of forces.
For the party, society constitutes not a laboratory but a universe
of forces, basically unfavorable and hostile, but in which judi-
cious manipulation can create a new balance more favorable to
the party's aims.

This universe of hostile forces is the instrument on which the
party's leaders play their revolutionary tune, in accordance with
that "operational code" which is but part, albeit an important
part, of Leninism. The Machiavellian principles of this code are,
basically, determined far more by personality than by doctrine,
even though Nathan Leites has shown how heavy a doctrinal
cloak has been woven around the various courses of action that
can be taken, or around the various attitudes, actions, and so

forth, that are condemned by this "operational code." [1] For this reason Professor Leites is justified in using psychoanalytical symbols in his discussion of the operational code. It should, however, be useful to see this code in its relation to broader Marxist traditions, problems, and doctrines. Leninism can be treated as a state of mind, but it can be treated with equal legitimacy as a systematic political theory. The reader should keep in mind the fact that these two views must complement each other, because the theoretical and psychological aspects are interdependent.

The attitude on which the entire operational code is based is the deep-seated hostility toward everything that exists, and the desire to manipulate the features of a hated environment. The desire to manipulate leads to a strong striving for domination, since things, people, institutions, can be manipulated only by those who have acquired power over them. This power can take an infinite variety of forms. Hence the operational code is a set of precepts revolving around the problem of control: How can the party acquire control over people and institutions? How can it avoid being controlled by them? How can it acquire complete mastery of any situation, without in its turn being mastered by the hostile forces that make up the world? * What is important to us here is not the answers given to these questions, but the questions themselves, that is, the preoccupation of the Leninist strategist with the wish to control and the fear of being controlled.

* The preoccupation of Leninists with problems of controlling the forces of the outside world has been brought out not only by studies of Leninist thought, but also by works on Soviet government and politics, such as Merle Fainsod's outstanding study *How Russia is Ruled* (Cambridge, Mass., 1952). The reason is the very simple one that this preoccupation with methods of control has led to the growth of a police state type of government. To many students, Soviet politics revolves around problems of control and hence around police state methods. Yet control, though an important objective of Soviet governmental policy, is but a negative one. In addition to holding their population in check, the leaders of the USSR have always had additional, positive objectives, which lead to the formulation of economic, social, educational, cultural, and other policies. Their own preoccupation with control often makes us forget about these policies, which are in a way more fundamental. Moreover, it has often been forgotten that the emphasis on control is itself a policy, derived not only from the leaders' feeling of insecurity, but also from ideological considerations such as those developed in the present work.

Another important part of the operational code concerns attitudes toward any allies that the party may make. Eager to utilize all forces that might assist the party, Lenin impressed on his followers the need to accept the help of outsiders whenever it was offered, and to ally themselves with forces that might be pursuing some of the same goals. Alliances are very desirable to the revolutionary party, as we shall see in Part Two, where we shall discuss a number of different alliances made by Lenin. Making alliances, however, does not mean that the party approves of its allies, or trusts them, or thinks of them in any favorable light. On the contrary, allies are distrusted. They are considered undependable, treacherous, ill-willed, if not agents of the bourgeoisie. Allies must be controlled by the party as much as possible lest they obtain mastery over it. They must be abandoned and betrayed at the proper moment, lest they anticipate the party by abandoning and betraying it.

These considerations are not based on abstract Machiavellian cunning, but on reflections concerning the nature of all political alliances made by outsiders with the party. If we investigate such alliances, we shall always find that they are made because the party and the hostile outsider share a common goal. Inevitably this goal will be a negative one: what is shared is a common enemy, who must be weakened or destroyed. The two allies may not pursue even this joint goal with equal vigor; one might be more inclined than the other to come to terms with the common enemy. This would, of course, be cause for mutual distrust. But even the very best of alliances will end and give way to hostility when the common enemy has been defeated. At that moment the Leninist remembers the causes which divide him from his ally and resumes his hostility without shedding any sentimental tears over the joint action they took before. All alliances are *ad hoc*, and therefore ephemeral.

The Leninist does not, however, usually wait until the end of a joint undertaking to remember that his ally is basically another enemy. He remains aware of the latent divergence of purposes all the time. Hence his attitude toward all allies is one of continual distrust and vigilance. There is an ever present fear of everyone and everything, a fear of being betrayed, of being provoked, of being trapped into action that will benefit the enemy. As Leites has pointed out, the Leninist is beset by fear even of himself, his emotions, his inaction, his poor judgment, anything in himself that might do the cause of the party harm and that of the enemy good. Consciousness imposes terrible responsibilities on those who possess it, and the life of a professional revolutionary is expected to consist of continual sacrifice. Lenin himself tried to live up to this ideal. He worked hard on himself, trying to kill emotions, interests, predilections, that might interfere with his work.° He imposed a rigorous schedule of physical exercise on himself, in order to keep fit for his profession. He consciously and deliberately sacrificed friendship, warmth, and beauty for the sake of the party, and he demanded the same rigor of his close associates. This, too, is part of the operational code.

The entire code may be said to be derived from the overriding principle of *expediency,* a principle which deserves some explanation in the light of the development of Marxist doctrine. The original Marxist theory of revolutionary development had no need to be preoccupied with strategy, because it was a theory of a more chiliastic character. The revolution, which according to Marxism would develop spontaneously out of the inevitable breakdown of capitalism, would at once usher in a society in which expediency was no longer required; instead, men would act, again spontaneously, in accordance with their liberated in-

---

° For instance, Lenin's widow reports that he gave up playing chess because "chess gets hold of you too much and hinders work"; he quit skating because it "tires you out and makes you sleep too much"; and he dropped Latin, because it is so absorbing that it hinders work (N. K. Krupskaia, *Memories of Lenin,* London, 1930, p. 35). About his brother Alexander, who had a keen interest in biological studies, he is reported to have said that he would never make a revolutionary because he spent too much time studying worms (Krupskaia, p. 5). Note also the well-known statement Lenin made while listening to a friend playing a Beethoven sonata: "I can't listen to music too often. It affects your nerves, makes you want to say stupid nice things and stroke the heads of people who could create such beauty while living in this vile hell. And now you mustn't stroke anyone's head — you might get your hand bitten off. You have to hit them on the head without any mercy . . ."

nate rational and moral judgment. Marxism thus breathed a fighting spirit, but the fight was to be waged in a spirit of almost boundless optimism.

The socialist reform movement which developed in Europe during the last quarter of the nineteenth century took over this optimistic scheme, but more and more lost the original fighting spirit. The hopes propounded by Marxism increasingly turned into a justification for renouncing revolutionary action. Yet the orthodox theoreticians refused to revise Marxism to fit the new practices of the labor movement, hence a growing discrepancy between the theories and the actions of the Marxist parties. The revisionist revolt around the turn of the century was an attempt to realign theory with practice by a thorough-going attack on most of the principal theoretical shibboleths of the orthodox. Under fire, the latter were forced gradually to accept most of the revisions. Some radical leaders nonetheless attempted to unite a new and vigorous revolutionary movement with an optimism that was based on a firm belief in the maturity and revolutionary class consciousness of the proletariat.

Lenin's position was somewhat ambiguous, in that his long-range views were the opposite of his short-range analysis of the situation. In the long range of historical perspective, he looked at the world through the eyes of Marx and subscribed to everything the latter had said about the inevitable breakdown of capitalism and the dawn of socialism. In that sense Lenin was an orthodox Marxist, and he joined other orthodox believers within the Second International in their fight against revisionism. At the same time Lenin's short-range analysis of the situation tended to yield different results. In place of the fighting optimism typical of Marx, he substituted a fighting pessimism, based on the realization that things were not developing in as smooth and rapid a fashion as the Marxist algebra of revolution had foretold. Hence Lenin's attempt to inculcate revolutionary spirit into the labor movement by education and by propaganda, in order to make it the fighting tool of a class-conscious elite. Hence his stress on organization as the means by which this elite could manage to dominate other men and make them act according to the party's will. Hence also his preoccupation with correct strategy, which, based on a scientific analysis of the current moment, was to incorporate the most expedient means to further the party's ends — a strategy in which radicalism and activism were to be made effective by good political horse sense. This combination yielded a few very simple rules that form the basis of the operational code: fight as long as the remotest chance of victory is still given; never give up until the movement has been repelled decisively.* This rule is complemented by another: do not engage in battle if you know you are licked from the start.† Further: use all means available to carry on the struggle.** At the same time, do not rely on any of the means employed, for they are all but means, and can be scrapped, thrown away, replaced. Do not become a slave of the tool you employ.††

This double view of the world, long-run and short-run, is an important key to the understanding of Leninism. Lenin's party fights, not the revolution, but *toward* the revolution. The revolutionary situation, in which the party can fight for the purpose of establishing itself (and the proletariat) in power, is the moment for which the party yearns, and for which it always keeps itself prepared. Lenin acted on the assumption that this revolutionary situation was itself an objective for which the party must fight,

* From the numerous examples Lenin's own political life offers, we might cite his decision to boycott the elections to the First Duma, his stubborn support of the Moscow uprising and barricade fighting of December 1905, and the Red Army drive on Warsaw in the summer of 1920. The first two examples are consequences of his firm belief throughout 1906 that the revolution of the preceding year had not been decisively beaten, but had suffered only a temporary setback.

† As examples, we might cite Lenin's decision to turn toward the New Economic Policy or his advocacy of concluding the Treaty of Brest-Litovsk. Both issues will be discussed in greater detail in subsequent chapters.

** For example: legal as well as illegal organizations; the party as well as "front organizations" of followers and fellow travelers; or terroristic methods (such as assassinations of individuals and bank robberies), customarily condemned as anarchist foolishness, but resorted to in particular cases.

†† For example: the ease with which the Constituent Assembly was dismissed even though the Bolsheviks had been loudest in calling for its convocation; Lenin's decision to resign from the editorial board of *Iskra* after his antagonists had won a majority on it, despite (or perhaps because of) his belief that this party organ was the primary cell around which the entire party would have to grow; or his readiness to forget, for the time being, the slogan "All power to the soviets," when the soviets had turned decidedly anti-Bolshevik.

and fight a long and bitter battle — by weakening the enemy, by strengthening itself numerically, ideologically, organization- ally, financially, and by gaining advantageous positions in any other way. This everyday struggle may be a war of movement, a stalemate, or a siege; whatever its form and its outcome, it is but a preparation for the final and decisive revolutionary battle. For that very reason, however, its temporary importance may be greater.

Leninist strategy thus fights for a number of objectives simul- taneously. In Part Two of this work, for instance, we shall see that Lenin himself was fighting for both a bourgeois and a prole- tarian revolution. More generally, the party always outlines two objectives, a long-range one and a short-range one, and its pro- gram of action is therefore divided customarily into two parts, a maximum program and a minimum program, the latter being conceived as an intermediary objective, from which the final goal can be reached more easily. We might say that the minimum program constitutes a means to an end. Yet, in Leninist practice, it easily turns into an end in itself. For if the minimum program is to succeed, it must be carried out totally, unhesitatingly, and ruthlessly. The fight for it must occupy the minds and plans of the party without interference from extraneous matters, and the very thought of longer-range goals might constitute a distraction that would interfere with the pursuance of the more pressing immediate tasks. The means thus turn into absolutes, and the end, at least for the time being, becomes a mere myth.

In using terms such as "goal," "ends," "means," and "program of action," we have slipped into moral terminology. The positing of any goal is an ethical proposition, and it should once again be emphasized that such a proposition lies at the basis of Leninist theory. But, once this moral proposition is accepted and becomes the star by which the party is guided through the choppy waters of the present, Leninism becomes dissociated from conventional morality. The party is indeed preoccupied with finding the proper means toward the end. It sees this, however, not as an ethical, but as a pragmatic, problem. For the Leninist, the diffi- culty lies not in devising morally acceptable means, but only in finding ways by which the end can be attained in the fastest and surest manner. If Lenin had talked in moral terms at all, he would have said that no means are more or less reprehensible than any other means, because, after all, this is an altogether reprehensible world. He who fights for a moral goal would betray that goal, would submit to this unmoral world, if he restricted his choice of means by moral considerations. He would thus himself be unmoral. As Engels put it, a truly human ethic will be possible only after the very memory of classes has vanished from society. Until then, the only acceptable moral considerations are rules of expediency designed to further the success of particular classes in their class struggle. Every class has its own moral code, and Lenin could therefore speak of proletarian morality; proletarian morality, however, is nothing else than expediency. Bolshevism, wrote Lenin, "stands on the point of view of expediency: We shall support [any other group] depending exclusively on whether or not we should then be able better to strike a blow against our enemy." [2]

Lenin was thus emphatic in his view that the end justifies any means, and that the means can find no other justification than that it serves the end. And the end, for him, was never constituted by good intentions; it could only be good results. It is not the motive behind the use of means, but success in reaching the objective that justifies the application of any means. Only the likelihood of success, he wrote, would justify taking revolutionary action.[3] But, if success depends on ruthlessness and unscrupulousness, the Leninist must not be squeamish. "We know," wrote Trotsky in 1918, "that if there are obstacles on the way they have to be swept away. If this sweeping away of obstacles increases the ruin [of Russia] for a while, then all this must be rewarded a hundredfold by the policy of economic creativity which the working class must develop after its seizure of power." [4]

The principle of expediency, of course, is but an ideal, which may or may not be attained by the party in the practical execution of its tasks. The Russian word for "expediency" is *tselesoobraznost'*, which means, in literal translation, "conformity to the goal." The party's pragmatism, in other words, is supposed to be purposive, while at the same time its idealism should never

transcend the bounds of what is pragmatic. Action should conform to theory, but theory must not go beyond the limits posed
by the existing situation. Here we have a resurrection of the
Marxist notion of the unity of theory and practice, though with
significant changes: Marx believed that, in the process of revolution, the old, baneful dichotomy between theory and practice
would spontaneously disappear. But, when in Leninism the notion of this synthesis of thought and action is transferred to the
everyday class struggle that is a preparation for real revolutionary action, it turns into a mere postulate. The unity of theory
and practice is seen not as a given fact, but as an ideal toward
which the party must strive.

And the ideal is not easily attained, as can be shown very
quickly. For the two elements of the synthesis, lofty ideals and
hard-headed realism, are hard to define. What *is* a realistic appraisal of a situation, or a realistic act? What are the realistic
limits of possible action? These questions can be answered only
by acting first and seeing the results afterwards, by probing the
limits of possible success, in short, by a continual process of trial
and error, a thoroughly pragmatic procedure that could be entirely divorced from theoretical considerations. Again, who can
say which practical steps do, and which do not, conform to the
ideals proclaimed by the party? On the one hand, there is the
optimistic assumption that all roads eventually lead to communism, and the practical doctrine that all forces must be manipulated, and all means must be used in the fight for intermediary
objectives. On the other hand, the leaders know that no force,
no method employed, is entirely reliable; everything that is used
by the party is part of the evil present; from the point of view
of doctrinal purity, therefore, the party is in danger of sullying
its hands whatever course of action it takes. In practice, the
leaders have accepted this situation and seem to have lost most
of their scruples. But this acceptance means that the ideals which
form the foundation of Leninist theory have turned into "long-
range" truths not necessarily related to the party's practices.

Aware of these dangers, Lenin forever fought a dual war
against two deviations from what he considered the most expedient course to be followed. One of these deviations is the path of

opportunism; the other, that of ultraleftism, or ultraradicalism (no universally applicable term has been coined to label this second deviation). Opportunism may be defined as the readiness to adapt the party's course of action too much to ephemeral conditions of the moment. The opportunist is a man who forgets or neglects the goals toward which action should be oriented. He has become a mere tactician, whose actions are adjusted to momentary situations to such a degree that he becomes the slave of events. His actions therefore bog down in the mire of spontaneity. The ultraradical is a leader so preoccupied with the final goal that he tends to disregard the material obstacles separating him from it and therefore becomes unrealistic in his actions. Obsessed with the ideas of socialism, he cannot bear to have his hands soiled by compromises or alliances of any sort. Preserving his radicalism at all cost, he will engage in a blind and futile struggle against the existing order, ending in defeat and frustration. Very typically, Lenin tended to believe that ultraradicals were more dangerous to the party than opportunists. The latter, he thought, at least did not pretend to be radical, and therefore would, in the end, be defeated by the loss of their working-class following. But the ultraradicals would attract and lead astray the class-conscious proletariat, particularly after it had been disillusioned by the opportunists.

Communist historiography maintains that the party has never strayed from the correct path, but that the Leninist "center" has always steered a firm course between the Scylla of opportunism and the Charybdis of ultraradicalism.* Apart from the possible hypocrisy inherent in this proclamation of the party's infallibility, this statement could be verified only if it were established just what constitutes a "correct" appraisal of conditions and possibilities, and just how any action might be reconciled with the long-

* In actual fact, Lenin's alleged "center" position is a gross distortion. His policies zigzagged from "right" to "left" depending on his analysis of the situation, and each time he made a sharp turn he would leave some followers behind who were not ready to turn with him at that particular moment. We can, perhaps, generalize on the pattern by saying that Lenin would usually swing toward a more radical course when crises were affecting the surrounding world, while turning toward more opportunistic policies when the party itself was in danger of defeat, decay, or annihilation.

range aims and theories of the party. But that is not possible. The dilemma of the faithful Leninist who wants to avoid deviations is almost as great and troubling as the dilemma of the neurotic person toward the object of his ambivalence, and in both cases the ambivalence leads to erratic and irrational behavior. The ambivalence with which Lenin looked at everything that existed is, of course, a very "dialectical" view, a view of things from every possible angle and every historical perspective. At the same time it is that dualistic view of things which crept into Marxism when the unity of theory and practice was revealed to be a myth or, at best, a mere postulate. Now, far from being abnormal, ambivalence is an all-pervasive, universal human trait. Its existence in social theory and politics has not yet been studied sufficiently. It would be surprising if the relationships among classes, groups, and parties were not marked by as many conflicts in aims and emotions as are relationships among individuals, and we cannot expect that the social philosopher will be able to erect his social and political ideas on the basis of values that are altogether compatible. Ambivalence can therefore be taken for granted as an inherent trait of all value systems and political programs, and to bring it into the open is to perform a service. Life poses dilemmas, and to recognize them not only is an act of wisdom, it should also lead to more intelligent action. We can cope with our problems better if we see them in all their complexity.

Yet to see dilemmas is one thing; to live with them is another. The politician with a simple, unsophisticated, black-and-white view of the world may in the long run go down in a defeat whose approach he was too blind to see, but in the short run he has fewer problems. A simple view of the world leads to a simple code of behavior. A dialectic view can lead to paralysis. If the conflicting elements of an ambivalent attitude were carried to their logical conclusion, no action would be possible at all; all slogans, programs, alliances, would be "undialectical." Still, the Leninist compels himself to live with dilemmas and to act, though he is constantly torn by his ambivalence toward the means he employs. Or, rather, the party is torn internally, and the struggles that rage within it are struggles over nuances in ambivalence. Leninists always fight each other over which means are less unreliable than all others, which are most useful, which part of the program demands immediate attention, and how the advantages of usefulness compare with the dangers of unreliability — short-range losses to long-range gains.

Chapter 5

Democratic Centralism

However small a number of new thoughts and ideas may constitute real progress, the fact remains that all further development is possible only through new ideas, which first come up only as minority ideas. Any suppression of all ideas coming from minorities within the party therefore means damaging the proletarian class struggle and holding up the maturing process of the working class.

KAUTSKY

. . . the measure of the method's accuracy lies in the strength of those who rule in its name.

MILOSZ

As we have seen, the "operational code" is nothing but a set of attitudes that underlie the making of decisions. But decision-making also presents organizational problems. Decisions have to be made by a collective body, namely, the party or some group or committee speaking for it; and, from fairly early times in his political career, Lenin was interested in establishing the party as a decision-making machinery that would fulfill several demands:

First, its decisions should be correct.

Second, they should be made in an acceptable manner, to wit, a democratic manner. The problem of finding the right solutions was from the beginning involved in the democratic tradition from which all left-wing radical movements, including Leninism, had started. In party affairs, Lenin always carried the word "democracy" in his mouth, and was eager to show that he had not forsaken these democratic traditions.

Finally, decisions should be arrived at efficiently, speedily, and without undue friction — a practical problem in which Lenin was keenly interested.

The formula Lenin found for the resolution of the problems has become famous. It is the "principle of democratic centralism." [1] This principle implies that the process of making and executing party decisions is to be a synthesis of democracy and organization, of freedom and order, of dissent and unanimity. Although the synthesis of such opposites might seem almost impossible, it is nevertheless possible to single out certain elements of, say, dissent as well as unanimity, existing side by side within the party organization. For instance, there is a natural unanimity, or agreement, concerning the ultimate goals of the movement, a basic unanimity of will which Lenin believed to be of the utmost importance because it would, he thought, prevent conformity from leading to blind conformism within the party. For it would not be enforced discipline that would hold the party together, but a spontaneous self-discipline that would even give centralism and tight controls a basically democratic character. Lenin liked to speak of the party as a genuinely collectivist organization, freely, consciously, and joyfully submitting to the leadership imposed upon it by the senior members.[2]

This unanimity of purpose, Lenin hoped, would lead to a good deal of unanimity in decision-making. But even if it did not, he expected that it would lead to the self-discipline of submitting to decisions reached in the party councils. One of the basic rules of democratic centralism is that decisions reached by the party must be accepted unanimously by the membership. There may be full discussion of what is to be done; perhaps there *ought* to be such full discussion. There may even be sharp disagreements that are reconciled only with great difficulty. But, once a final decision has been made, it must be accepted by all, and not only on the surface. The agreement is expected to be wholehearted and sincere.

This principle is based partly on the realization that it would not be advisable, even if it were feasible, to make *large* minori-

ties conform to the will of the majority. Unanimity is not necessarily the imposition of a decision on grumbling dissenters; it
can also be the result of compromise. And, when the party is
split wide open over a policy problem, the very principle of
unanimity demands that a compromise solution be found.*

Nevertheless, the chief aim of the demand for unanimous approval of party decisions is to make the party into a disciplined
fighting organization capable of going into concerted action. As
Lenin wrote very early in his political life, unanimity is required
for the task of executing decisions.[3] Hence his demand for absolute discipline in carrying out any decision once it has become
official. To the members, the party's resolutions should have the
force of law.[4]

In short, party decisions should be made by a process of free
deliberation, in which every opinion is heard. Once a decision
is reached, however, it should be accepted by each member in-
dividually, and any further criticism of the decision is considered
a breach of party discipline. Dissent is possible only before a
decision becomes party law. After that, criticism may still be
expressed, but it should concern only the manner in which the
program is being carried out.†

* Such a wide-open split developed, for instance, over the question of
how to make use of former tsarist officers in the newly formed Red Army.
According to a note in the printed minutes of the Eighth Party Congress
(*Protokoly VIII S"ezda RKP(b)*, Moscow, 1933, n. 48, p. 497), the
following took place: "After the concluding words of V. Smirnov and G.
Sokol'nikov, the congress accepted L. Trotsky's theses as a basis by a
majority of votes. A roll call vote taken thereafter gave the opposition a
sizable minority: The vote for G. Sokol'nikov's resolution was 174 delegates,
for V. Smirnov's resolution, 95. Such a voting outcome on a most timely and
important question naturally could not satisfy the party." In consequence,
a compromise resolution was drafted by an *ad hoc* subcommittee consisting
of representatives from both factions, and this compromise resolution was
accepted unanimously by the congress (*ibid.*, p. 498).

† We must be careful to keep in mind that Lenin applied the principle
of "freedom of criticism and unity of action" only to his own Bolshevik
Party, but not to the larger Social Democratic Party of which the Bolsheviks
were a faction. Within the Russian Marxist movement as a whole, Lenin
was careful always to retain the fullest freedom to criticize decisions made
and to pursue his own course of action. And every time his efforts came
up against the centralist and unitarian tendencies of his opponents, he
pleaded the principle of intraparty democracy, at least inasmuch as he
troubled to justify his own breaches of party discipline at all.

Apart from certain details concerning party discipline and centralization, this formula of "free criticism plus unity of action" is almost the whole meaning of "democratic centralism." We shall presently see that this is no more than a verbal solution of the problem of combining free discussion with discipline. One reason is that the function of carrying out decisions cannot be separated entirely from that of making decisions, particularly in the communist movement. Given the demand that every member must loyally adhere to formally accepted decisions, given further the conception of the party as a perfectly co-ordinated machine for action, given, finally, the party's custom of carrying out every decision by a total effort in which all available resources are marshaled — given these characteristic traits of communist thought and behavior, any criticism of the manner of execution is likely to be condemned, because it might jeopardize the total pursuit of the goal that has been established and thus endanger the party's policy. For this reason, it was unrealistic of Lenin to allow criticism of the manner of execution while simultaneously demanding absolute loyalty to all decisions.

Another fallacy of Lenin's was his idea that the party is unanimous concerning its goals. What is true instead is that the goals themselves change continually. Not only the method of execution, but the entire program of the party must be redefined again and again. If, however, the principles of democratic centralism forbid the criticism of agreed-upon policies, who has the right to suggest that any such policy has, perhaps, outlived its usefulness, or should be re-examined in the light of changed circumstances? Any such suggestion from a rank-and-file member or even from a highly placed leader may be branded as a breach of party discipline, so that, in practice, the free discussion provided for by the formula of democratic centralism can be restricted at will by the party command. A policy problem, or even an analysis of prevailing circumstances, must be considered a settled question as long as the leadership continues so to consider it. Any theoretical or practical problem can therefore be debated openly only after the leadership has decided that it is to be debated. The command then doubtless prepares its own solution and submits this to the membership for discussion. Such discussion became more and more an empty formality, in practice, since questioning the leaders' wisdom was considered a violation of the principle of unanimity. The "democratic" part of democratic centralism has thus withered away in practice. The formulas still live on, and might, of course, be made more meaningful at any time in the future.

Lenin's principal argument for centralized direction and control by the party command was that only firm leadership would be able to steer the movement through difficult periods, the implication being, of course, that only the leaders can know what is best for the movement. "Only central, all-party institutions can, during the present period of the regrouping of party forces, be authoritative and strong representatives of the party line, on the basis of which all genuinely party forces and all genuinely social-democratic elements might rally." [5] At the same time, Lenin consoled the rank-and-file members by the affirmation that only the exigencies of the fight against tsarist absolutism forced him to advocate such strict centralization: "Under free political conditions our party can and will be built entirely on the principle of elective leadership." [*]

These arguments of Lenin's are probably rationalization. We come closer to the real issue when we realize that all discussion was suspect to him, because it was a waste of time and because it might threaten the unity of the party in action. It was this unity which he sought to preserve under all circumstances, even at the price of gagging dissenting groups that might become a

[*] Draft resolutions for the Third Party Congress, Lenin, vol. 7, p. 132. At the time this sentence was written, Lenin probably meant that in a future constitutional democracy the party might turn into a broad mass party. For in the next sentence he wrote, "*Under autocracy* this cannot be realized for the entire mass of the thousands of workers who are in the party" (italics added). Yet we know that he did not consider a democratic constitution to come under the heading of "free political conditions." Only the stateless communist society of the future deserved such a description. Yet, by the time that society had been reached, not only would there be no more leadership, but there would no longer be a Communist Party. Consequently, so long as the party has not reached its ultimate objective, it will be dictatorially organized.

nuisance to the men in command.* He tried unsuccessfully to define the limits of legitimate disputes: "Without debates, conflicts, without a war between opinions, no movement, including the workers' movement, is possible at all. But without a merciless fight against the degeneration of conflicts into quarrels and squabbles, *any* organization is *impossible*." 6 The trouble is that no one can define the moment at which a legitimate conflict turns into an illegitimate squabble. As Grigori Zinov'ev stated the issue at the Eighth Party Congress: "Opposition is a lawful thing. Nobody has a thing against it. And the congress has been called just in order that each group of our party may speak its opinion. But when an opposition does not come down to brass tacks, when it advances prescriptions which will be harmful to the party — that must be rejected." 7 Again, who determines what proposals made by an oppositionist are going to harm the party?

Lenin held that centrally directed, co-ordinated action was the secret of success for a revolutionary party. He had the utmost respect for organization, so much so that we might say he made a fetish of it. Organization, to him, not only meant strength — this was but one of the axioms on which the Marxian theory of revolution was based — it also meant rationality. Somehow, Lenin seems to have believed that the party, as organized consciousness, consciousness as a decision-making machinery, had superior reasoning power. Indeed, in time this collective body took on an aura of infallibility, which was later elevated to a dogma, and a member's loyalty was tested, in part, by his acceptance of it. It became part of the communist confession of faith to proclaim that the party was never wrong. Nor could it be inefficient, for there is no inefficiency in rational organization. Mistakes of judgment or bungling in executing orders can only be made by individuals, and the presumption is always strong that these individuals by making mistakes have shown themselves lacking in consciousness. This is tantamount to disloyalty.

* As early as 1899 Lenin expressed indignation over a breach of discipline, consisting in the publication by a comrade of views divergent from party orthodoxy. See Lenin's letter about Bulgakov, quoted by L. B. Kamenev, "Lenin 1897–1899," in Lenin, vol. 2, p. xxvii.

Hence inefficiency is seen as the result of ill intent. Bureaucratic mistakes are seen as rebellions against the party by criminals, wreckers, saboteurs, or counterrevolutionaries.* The party itself never makes mistakes.

We see that Lenin was a revolutionary of a rare type: a revolutionary with a bureaucratic mind, for whom a high degree of organization in human affairs represented progress, order, and rationality. His mistake was to believe that this had anything to do with either democratic ways of making decisions or with efficiency and correct policy. Seen in historical perspective, bureaucracy has indeed been an important means of rationalizing administrative processes. Where goals are agreed upon, standard procedure can·take the place of more informal decision-making. Hence the bureaucratization of decision-making usually works well on a fairly low level, because low-level decisions are made by the bureaucrat within the framework of carefully outlined policies. But it is fallacious to assume that bureaucratic procedure can solve policy problems. Administrative apparatus are designed to carry out decisions and directives, but they must obtain them from outside. Lenin erred in drawing an insufficient distinction between making and executing policies. The reason is that he really thought of Marxist theory as an operational code, or a "guide to action." The conscious party bureaucrat need only apply this code to a given situation, and the correct procedure would become evident.

In actual fact, every significant change in the situation led to sharp disputes concerning the correct steps to be taken. And the only remedy that Lenin could devise against these corrosive tendencies was the establishment of the principle of command, to guide the party in legislative procedure. According to this

* Sorel observes that this attitude was also common during the French Revolution. He traces this back to the *ancien régime,* arguing that the kings would confuse the disciplinary surveillance of their bureaucratic underlings with the task of suppressing crimes. The French Revolution, he says, took over this habit and therefore guillotined defeated generals and muddling administrators as being traitors or enemy agents. "Un tel crime," he continues, "suppose que l'État peut être mis en péril tout entier par le fait d'une personne; cela ne nous paraît guère croyable" (*Réflexions sur la violence,* Paris, 1905, pp. 148–149). Of course, it seems even less believable in the context of historical materialism.

principle, the elected leaders had the right to issue commands that were binding on all lower organizations.

The party is in a position in which the strictest centralism and the most stringent discipline are absolute necessities. All decisions of higher headquarters are absolutely binding for the lower. Every decision must first of all be executed, and only after that an appeal to the corresponding party organ is permissible. In this sense, outright military discipline is indispensable in the party at the present time.[8]

The only thing that remained of democracy in democratic centralism was the rule that higher organs should be elected by the rank-and-file membership.

The main principle of democratic centralism is that of the higher cell being elected by the lower cell, the absolute binding force of all directives of a higher cell for a cell subordinate to it, and the existence of a commanding [*vlastnogo*] party center [whose authority is] undisputable for all leaders in party life, from one congress to the next.[9]

But even this was vitiated in practice, for in actual fact the party soon became a rigid hierarchy in which the top ranks were filled entirely by co-optation.

Lenin had originally thought the problem of selecting a corps of really enlightened leaders easy to solve. Enlighten the proletariat, he had written; use your organization, your apparatus, to imbue the entire working class with the spirit and method of Marxism, and then there will no longer be any need for a leadership cadre.[10] But this solution merely reaffirms Lenin's insistent demand for the education of the working class, and both his ideas on party organization and his appraisal of the limited consciousness of the proletariat, developed later, are in contradiction to the optimism displayed here. It was not long before he frankly demanded that leaders be co-opted by those in command of the party. In a revolutionary organization, he argued, there is no room for decentralization of command, or even for elections. When he was warned that unfit persons might rise to the top through such methods of selection, he expressed confidence that they would certainly be eliminated promptly.[11] His stubborn protection of the *agent-provocateur* Roman Malinovsky, against the well-founded attacks of his most trusted comrades, illustrates how consistently he lived up to the policies he advocated. At the same time, the clumsy and costly habit of purging the party occasionally had to be developed as a means by which the unfit and unworthy might be eliminated from leading positions.

And yet the whole setup functioned pretty well, while the party was commanded by a strong leader who ruled it with an iron grip. What was wrong was that Lenin was foolishly satisfied that he had given the party a well worked out standard procedure of decision-making, whereas he had really given it centralized control with some trappings of democracy. Although this did work as long as a central personality was there who commanded everyone's respect and obedience, upon his death rival cliques, informal organization, and wire-pulling behind the scenes took the place of orderly decision-making, precisely because regular procedures had not been worked out by Lenin and "democratic centralism" had remained an empty formula. Obedience to the leader, which had been mostly voluntary in Lenin's days, became a matter of constraint under his successors. And as we shall see, orthodoxy, or the ability to make correct decisions, became identified with the power to make decisions. In his earliest book, Lenin had written that "the highest and only criterion of doctrine remains its correspondence to the actual process of socio-economic development." [12] This statement amounts to "the doctrine that is most nearly true is most nearly true." In actual practice, the only thing which could prove a Leninist right in the eyes of his party comrades was success in action, for it is by acting on the world that the Leninist proves he has understood the "actual process of socio-economic development." In order to buttress his claim to infallible correct judgment, the party leader must be ever ready to prove the correctness of his program by committing the party to it.

In some ways this coupling of power with responsibility is a very sound principle, which works to make theorists more conscious of practical implications, and practitioners, of theoretical considerations. No theory can be propounded that will not be tested in action at once. This principle places a particularly heavy responsibility on the shoulders of the theorist, a responsibility intended to ensure that he refrain from criticism unless it is realistic and constructive. Only such criticism is permitted as advances alternative policies that can be tested at once. At the Eighth Party Congress, Zinov'ev formulated this as follows:

> There is, it seems to me, nothing wrong with opposition as such. Every comrade, if he reckons that the party and the Soviet ship should be taken in another direction, may speak up about it; that is right. But an opposition which does not know whither to direct the ship is bad. Only in that case can we accuse an opposition.
> We are used to self-criticism, no one is afraid of it. But when our opponents take up the attention of a mighty party assembly for several hours without having a serious plan, then we cannot recognize them as serious.[13]

It was, however, inevitable that this pragmatic impatience with high-flown theoretical chatter and with purely negative criticism would make any oppositionist hesitate considerably before coming out with any new proposition, unless he was ready to see it tested, perhaps found unsuccessful — or condemned in advance as heretical. For, as we shall see, the men in command could not possibly admit that their own policy was incorrect. The ability to commit the party to action is coupled with the leader's claim to orthodoxy, and, conversely, the fountain of the exclusively correct solutions is always the individual or group in control over the apparatus. Hence the marked tendency of both Lenin and his successors to stifle leading intellects in the party who did not happen to be in that favored situation. Moreover, the pragmatic test of theory is not always applicable. Where the theoretical program of action is so long-range that success or failure can not be apparent for a long time, there can be no proof or disproof of claims to have found the correct solution, so that, again, any claim rests either on the faith of the rank and file or on power.

But let us return once more to the pragmatic test. How does a Leninist act? He acts by making the proletariat or the masses act for him, and in order to accomplish this he must first obtain influence over them. The medium of influence is the party. Hence a communist who wishes to verify his theories must have authority in a party through which his theory can take hold of the masses and be carried out, successfully or unsuccessfully. If there happens to be no party available, he will attempt to found one, as G. V. Plekhanov and his associates did in Russia. If a party is already in existence, he will attempt to gain influence in it, and such struggles for influence go on in every party. An alternative is to leave the old party and to build his own rival apparatus, if he believes himself strong enough to do this. That is what Lenin, Trotsky, and other leaders did when they felt that they, and not the leaders in power, had the "correct" program of action. Once the party has established a monopoly of power, however, the masses are no longer free to choose between parties, and then the dissenters can only attempt to wrest control of the party, and thus of the masses, away from the current leaders. In so doing, however, they place themselves in opposition to the party (as represented by those in command), and, where the party has identified itself as the vanguard of the entire nation, unsuccessful dissenters become enemies of the people by definition. Even before the Bolsheviks came to power, unsuccessful dissenters were inevitably branded as enemies of their class, whether this enmity was conscious or unconscious, willful or unwilling, and this ostracism was accepted so readily by all Leninists that dissenters who turned out to be too weak sometimes expected to be purged or otherwise disciplined.

The leader who is convinced that he alone has preserved orthodox interpretations and programs of action can not but seek by all means to keep "his" apparatus firmly in his own hands, least deviationists obtain a hold over it and abuse it in an attempt to verify their own theories, an attempt which he must consider to be doomed to failure. For another leader's taking over would imply that the displaced leader's interpretation of Marxism and Leninism was wrong, that his own theory was not the perfect expression of proletarian class consciousness.

It might be argued that an open-minded leader would give his opponent at least the opportunity of trying out his theories. After all, the opponent, too, claims to be a Leninist, and they would therefore presumably agree on all important goals. It might be argued that the leader would be all the more inclined to make such a concession because he felt that his rival's attempt to experiment with "incorrect" policies is bound to fail; events would prove his own course right. Yet, the leader of a party can not in fact be expected to allow a dissenter such freedom. For the society in which the party will be used is not a laboratory in which experiments can be made at will. Each experiment changes the society itself and has its effect on the party apparatus, and the party is considered too precious and fragile an instrument to be used for anything but decisive action. An operation, once initiated, can not be reversed or eradicated, either in its effects on the environment or in its effects on the party itself. The party is expected to equip and organize itself for a definite strategy, and any change of course would require a radical reorganization and reorientation, which would be likely to weaken the party at least temporarily. This makes for a spectacular lack of flexibility, in a party that prides itself on its readiness to adjust its tactics to the needs of the current moment. In part, lack of flexibility is a consequence of Lenin's predilection for bureaucratic procedures. But it is also related to the totalitarian character of Leninist thought and action. For the Leninist there are no halfway measures; there is no cautious reconnaissance into new methods. An action is taken in hand, or it is not. A decision one way or another commits the party not only organizationally, but also ideologically and psychologically. Hence the habit of going whole hog, when changes in policy are finally made — the famous zigzag pattern of Leninist policy, of which Lenin was quite aware, but which he explained in terms of the "changing situation." "A very frequent change in the line of our policy will be demanded from us, which may seem strange and incomprehensible to the superficial observer. 'How about it,' he will say, 'yesterday you made promises to the petty bourgeoisie, and today Dzerzhinsky announces that [they] . . . will be stood against the wall. What contradiction!' " [14] In the final analysis, this zigzag pattern, too, is a consequence of the fact that "democratic centralism" was but a crude and weak formula that did not enable Lenin to establish workable decision-making procedures.

PART TWO

The Russian Revolution

Chapter 6

The Task of the Proletariat
and Its Auxiliary Forces

If I say, "It is necessary *to build a new Russia* in this certain way, *say, on the basis of truth, justice, or the equalization of labor, etc.," that would be subjectivism which is going to lead me into the realm of chimeras. Actually, the class war, and not my very best intentions, will define the structure of the new Russia. My ideals concerning the structure of the new Russia will be nonchimeric only when they express the interests of an actually existing class whom the conditions of life compel to act in a definite direction. By adopting this point of view of class-war objectivism, I am by no means justifying what actually exists; on the contrary, I am pointing out in this very actuality the deepest (though at first sight unseen) sources and forces of its transformation.*

LENIN

LENIN'S PROGRAM UNTIL THE REVOLUTION OF 1905

Lenin's ideas concerning leadership, organization, and the decision-making process were of crucial importance, not only because they shaped the Communist Party of Russia and its sister organizations all over the world, but also because they provided a working model for totalitarian parties of all types. To many democratic critics of Leninist thought, these ideas have seemed to be the essence or even the whole of Leninism. In reality, however, they are only part of a larger whole and derive their meaning, if not their justification, only within the broader framework

of the theories Leninism had adopted or developed concerning
the dynamics of contemporary society. Leninist leadership and
organization has purpose and direction, and these must be sought
in Lenin's theory of revolution. To be sure, within the context of
the Russian Marxist movement as a whole, where many non-
Leninists shared significant portions of his ideas, Lenin was
notable mainly for his amoral approach to tactical problems (the
"operational code") and his ideas on party organization. To a
Russian Menshevik, Leninism is characterized exclusively by
those traits, because in many other questions he may be in agreement with Lenin. We, however, have to investigate all of his
political thought, not only those parts in which his disagreement
with other Marxists was most decisive.

When Lenin called himself a Marxist it meant, to him, that he
had accepted the axiom of the moral and actual inevitability of
the proletarian revolution. In his eyes, the acid test of a Marxist
was his unceasing striving toward this revolution. This revolution
was seen as a political act, the seizure of power by the leaders
of the proletariat, so that the establishment of a proletarian dictatorship was Lenin's guiding aim. Once again we see at once
why he had to be preoccupied with problems of political
strategy.

In war and in politics, strategy depends "on the situation and
the terrain." Therefore, Leninist strategy cannot be understood
without a knowledge of the environment in which he found
himself, namely, tsarist Russia toward the end of the nineteenth
century. If we take a very broad view of Russian society, perhaps the outstanding trait distinguishing it from the West is its
backwardness, a much-abused concept that has two connotations,
an economic and an ideological one. Economic backwardness
requires little explanation. In nontechnical language, it might be
defined as the inability of a country's economy, due to under-
development of means and methods of production, to match the
productivity of other countries' economies. It can be measured
readily. Under certain circumstances (by no means inevitably),
socially conscious persons in the society will realize that they are
living in a backward society. They will regard this backwardness
as a problem to be solved, so that it becomes an ideological issue.

Not only was modern Russia measurably backward, but the social thought of rulers and dissenters alike tended to revolve around their consciousness of the fact.

To trace the many historical circumstances accounting for the underdeveloped state of Russia's economy would lead us too far astray. We can but note some of its characteristics, such as the predominance of agriculture over all other economic pursuits, and the relative absence of cities and towns and of the city and town culture characteristic of western Europe, with its deeply rooted crafts, trades, and tradition of civic autonomy. Intimately connected with Russia's backwardness, through an involved historic evolution, was not only the main division of Russian society into a land-owning privileged gentry and a serf population comprising the vast majority of Russians, but also the firm rule of an autocratic emperor standing above all law, aided by an all-pervading bureaucracy. In so characterizing Russian society we have to be aware, first, that all these features are found also in the West, though not in the same preponderant measure, and, second, that ever since the dawn of the modern age Russian society has shown tendencies toward westernization, though this should not be imagined as a unilinear development. These tendencies were given a strong boost by the Crimean War, which made it obvious that the old social order based on serfdom was about to collapse.

The society into which Lenin was born in 1870 was in the throes of rapid change. Less than a decade before, an epochal step had been taken in liberating the serfs from legal bondage by a tsarist decree which in the subsequent two decades was followed by far-reaching administrative and judicial reforms designed to streamline Russian government following Western models. This series of reforms gave a boost to the development of a money economy, to capitalism, and to modern industrialism. Railroads were built, coal mines were dug, modern factories sprang up, cities grew, and new social groups and classes developed to fulfill the various functions required by industrial societies. Meanwhile, the tsarist state, under the urging of certain military and business groups, began to expand into the less civilized areas of Central Asia and the Siberian Far East. The khanates of Khiva and Bukhara were made into dependencies, and Russia vigorously participated in the efforts of other Western powers to carve up China into spheres of influence. As in the early decades of capitalism in the West (though not necessarily for the same reasons), this development was accompanied by serious dislocations bringing emotional and economic misery to broad sections of the rural and urban population. Moreover, the growth of industrialism in Russia, in contrast to that in western Europe, was accomplished to a large extent through the initiative of foreign investors and governmental interference. At the same time, it was not accompanied by the development of liberal democracy: the government remained autocratic, and dissent tended to take socialistic rather than liberal directions.

In a society marked by tremendous inequalities of burdens, opportunities, and rewards, and by rapid social change with accompanying dislocations in the social structure, the development of movements of dissent can be taken almost for granted. But in a state ruled autocratically, all social thought is the privilege of the ruler and his chosen advisers; in everyone else it is subversive and is regarded as a crime. In spite of such discouragement, burning issues created by rapid social change and aggravated by more and more intensive contact with the West compelled generation after generation of Russian intellectuals to engage in the subversive activity of discussing their country's problems. The covert quality of the discussions could not but influence the organization, activities, and ideological content of Russia's intellectual movements. Russian social thought tended to be radical and dogmatic. According to the measure in which it was the product of isolated intellectuals, in touch more with European radical thinkers than with the "people" as a whole, it also tended to be irresponsible. At the same time, intellectuals thirsting for change could not help becoming aware of their alienation from the mass of the population and of their resulting powerlessness. Russian revolutionary thinkers were therefore forced to discuss the relationship of intellectuals to the masses, of leaders to followers, of the thinkers' "consciousness" to the people's "spontaneity." Most of all, they had to see how the revolutionary strivings of broad sections of the population might be fitted into their own intellectual schemes.

For centuries Russia had been shaken periodically by violent peasant unrest, in which non-Russian nationalities often participated. Since the age of the French Revolution, liberal and socialist ideas had infiltrated into an educated minority, the "intelligentsia"; and after the Great Reforms a professional class grew which in various ways was committed to liberal ideas. Finally, as capitalism developed, and as the serious famine of 1891 severed broad sections of the poorer population from the land, a proletariat grew up that from the very beginning was strongly under the influence of radical thought. Lenin began his political activity just at the time of the first serious outbursts of working-class violence, the Yaroslav strike of 1894, which was but the most important one of a whole wave of strikes in 1893–1895.

It is clear from these developments that the thought of Marx and Engels about political strategy, unsystematic and fragmentary as it was, could not serve as an adequate guide to anyone devoted to their cause who wanted to fight for it in a country like Russia. Marx and Engels had relied on a large and mature working class to seize power when the number of capitalists had been reduced to a minimum. In Russia, however, the number of proletarians was small in comparison to the total population. Moreover, capitalism, far from being on the decline, was still growing. The number of people engaged in business was small, not because competition had ruined most of them, but, rather, because Russian capitalism was still in its beginnings. Russia remained overwhelmingly a country of peasants. Who was to serve as the historical force in such a country? Who was to play the revolutionary role most Marxists wanted to be played?

And what kind of revolution was it to be? It could not very well be expected that a proletarian revolution in Russia, or any revolution whatsoever, would usher in the socialist society predicted by Marx and Engels. Russia's grain-producing peasant society could not be expected to produce that abundance of industrial products which is, according to Marxist theory, one of the essential preconditions of socialism. Hence even a proletarian revolution in Russia would have to have different results from those expected in western Europe. It might, perhaps, be viewed as a contributory development in the broader perspectives of a world-wide revolution. In any event, a Marxist in Russia was forced to think about the role that a peasant country like his own might play in the Marxist scheme.

To the question, "Who is to make revolution in Russia?" Lenin's first answer would have been, "proletarians and bourgeois intellectuals." But Lenin very early recognized that there were other classes or groups in Russian society who might become interested in making a revolution. Such groups might not share the ultimate aims of the Marxist movement, but they would be interested in change, they would be forces of unrest, negation, destruction. And, since the destruction of the old order would have to precede or accompany the construction of the new, Lenin was keenly interested in all such forces of destruction, and tried to ally his party with them. His appraisal of these forces, however, underwent periodic changes, and we shall therefore consider his analysis of the role various classes in Russia would play and of their usefulness to the cause of revolution. We shall furthermore trace the changes in Lenin's ideas on the nature of the revolution that could or would or should be made with these available forces.

As Lenin surveyed the Russian social scene in the last decade of the nineteenth century, he came to the conclusion that Marx had been right in his analysis of historic trends, and that his findings were applicable not only to western Europe but also to Russia. In the light of Russia's peculiarities, this conclusion is surprising. We should note, however, that Lenin was not alone in this opinion: the entire Marxist movement, which had struck its first feeble roots in such alien soil in the 1880's, was based on this idea.

In this respect it was in sharp contrast to the thought of the Narodniks (populists, from *narod* — people) a radical group that arose in the 1860's and 1870's after the Great Reforms. Its intellectual traditions can be traced back to Herzen and even to the "slavophile" philosophy of the 1840's. Asserting the uniqueness and superiority of Russia and her social, political, and moral traditions, the Narodniks fought not only against the old order, but also against the spread of modern industrial capitalism. They called for the overthrow of the old regime, the expropriation of the landlords, and the establishment of some sort of peasant socialism based on the traditional Russian peasant commune. Starting as an abortive attempt by radical intellectuals to go *v narod* (to the people) and arouse the peasants to rebellion, the Narodniks turned into an underground group of conspirators pledged to individual terror against the tsar and highly placed members of the bureaucracy. In the 1890's, when all Russian radical movements consolidated into nuclei of political parties, the Narodniks founded their own party, the party of Socialist Revolutionaries, whose left wing was devoted to the fight for a socialism based on the age-old village community, while its right wing simply fought for a radical solution of the peasants' hunger for land.

In a process which we cannot treat in this book, the Russian Marxist movement originated within, and in opposition to, the Narodniks and won its first spurs in fighting against them. The outstanding theoretician leading this fight was Georgi V. Plekhanov, whose vigorous preaching of orthodox Marxism, "scientific socialism," was directly sharply, even mercilessly, against Narodnik ideas. Inspired by Plekhanov, Lenin, too, began to develop his ideas in writing anti-Narodnik tracts.[1] In these pamphlets he insisted that Russia was not different from the West and that the development of industrial capitalism as outlined by Marx was the path which Russia, too, was about to take. The Great Reforms, he asserted, had irreversibly transformed Russia into a bourgeois society with all its familiar contradictions and its irresistible drift toward the proletarian revolution. In his very first publication he asserted that there had already been two distinct stages in Russia's capitalist development: the Great Reforms, which, he claimed, opened the way for capitalist social relationships and for the entire superstructural array that accompanies them; and capitalism, which, ever since the early nineties, had been the dominant mode of production in Russia.[2] The political form of Russian society, he wrote, was the "class state." [3] His principal economic work, completed in

1899, was devoted to a thorough examination of the rapid development of capitalism in Russia, both in the cities and in agriculture.[4]

In this very work, however, Lenin showed his awareness of the relative importance that agriculture held in the Russian economy. Consequently, even though he claimed that the Marxist sociology of capitalism applied to Russia, he could not fail to observe that his country showed certain peculiar traits of its own. Indeed, Lenin did take into account the fact that the predominance of the peasantry in Russia's economy would necessitate changes in the Marxist sociology there. In a purely capitalist economy, he wrote in 1899, there are, indeed, only two classes, the bourgeoisie and the proletariat. The former possess capital and use it for the exploitation of the labor of others; the latter, constituting the great majority of people, possess nothing but their labor power and are therefore obliged to sell it to the capitalists in order to make a living. Before capitalism develops fully, however, a precapitalist bastard class continues to exist, the petty bourgeoisie, and a country's relative backwardness expresses itself in the prevalence of petty bourgeois elements.*

* "Our Program," Lenin, vol. 2, p. 491. As conceived by Marxism, the petty bourgeoisie is composed of small shopkeepers, craftsmen, traders — in short, of small independent producers and middlemen. Hence it can also include the farmer, though not the peasant still bound to the soil. Still, many Marxists include in the petty bougeoisie those who *aspire* to become small producers; and in this sense the Russian peasant, independent only in legal fiction, could be included. The petty bourgeoisie is thus that class which formed the backbone of preindustrial town society. In Marxist eyes they are people unable to adjust to the industrial age because industrialism has made them obsolete as a class. The typical petty bourgeois therefore desires the return of the Good Old Days before the machine age, the big city, modern technology, and mass communications. His politics consists of wrecking machines, abolishing department stores, breaking up monopolies. At the same time he is assumed to aspire to become bourgeois, an independent and fully competitive producer. This, in Marxist eyes, is a hopeless aspiration, for the small producer, fighting a losing battle against large-scale industrial capitalism, faces a slide down the social scale that threatens to make him a proletarian. Yet he hates and fears the working class while envying the bourgeoisie. In the eyes of Lenin, its struggle against industrialism makes the petty bourgeoisie the most reactionary of all classes, more reactionary at any rate than the "big" bourgeoisie (see, for instance, his article "The Tasks of the Russian Social Democrats," Lenin, vol. 2, p. 176; translation in *Selected Works*, vol. 1, pp. 501–502). In practical politics the petty bourgeoisie would, he thought, waver forever between the bourgeoisie and the proletariat. It would there-

In his early years Lenin attempted to reconcile the prevalence of the petty bourgeoisie with his characterization of Russia as a capitalist society by regarding (and virtually dismissing) the peasantry as a phenomenon belonging to the past, hence doomed to disappear before long. In viewing the peasantry and assessing its role, Lenin thus projected "inevitable" future developments into the present and based his strategy on this futuristic analysis of Russian society. In his eyes the peasantry was a dying class, which was rapidly being split into two sections, a small minority of capitalist farmers and a vast majority of rural paupers. True enough, he saw revolutionary dynamism in these paupers, but only because their pauperization was transforming them into proletarians, in the classical Marxist sense of the word. Only the peasant who had become conscious of his transformation into a proletarian interested Lenin.

In fact, Lenin's bitterness against the Narodniks stemmed from his opinion that they prevented the peasantry from becoming aware of its proletarian destiny, by maintaining that it was a class in its own right, and not a doomed one, either. Lenin thought that the Narodniks were delaying the growth of consciousness in the peasantry. In addition to fighting against their preachings, he proposed practical measures to attract "those elements of the petty bourgeoisie which gravitate toward the proletariat." [5] This does not mean that he proposed to make concessions to them, by, for example, incorporating some of their typical demands and aspirations in his party platform. On the contrary, Lenin before 1905 believed that he could, instead, instill proletarian consciousness into the peasantry by a process of education. This was not to be accomplished by lectures or pamphlets alone; in his opinion, only hard facts that are seen and

fore be a very dubious ally, unreliable, even treacherous, liable to desert the battle and go over to the ruling classes at any moment.

Since many if not all the failures of Marxist prognoses about trends in capitalist society can be ascribed to the fact that "pure" capitalism is being distorted by the survival of the petty *bourgeoisie*, this class is the chief scapegoat in all Marxist apologetic literature. An ideological study surveying the uses of the term would therefore constitute a virtual history of Marxist social theory. Such a study would reveal the flexibility of this concept, which has been used as a label for any group not fitting into the simple bipolar schemes Marxism seeks to apply.

felt and resented will stimulate men's minds. The educational
method he proposed was therefore the active promotion of class
war in the village. He wanted to sharpen the antagonism between
rich peasants and rural paupers; he wanted to show the poor that
their old methods of resistance were useless, to demonstrate
to them that their plight was a consequence of the growth of
capitalism in Russia. Thus he hoped to convince them that the
proletarian revolution alone promised them a better deal.[6] He
wrote in 1902,

> We recognize the class struggle as the central fact in Russia's
> agrarian order. We build our entire agrarian policy (and, conse-
> quently, also our agrarian program) on the straightforward recognition
> of that fact with all the consequences evolving from it. Our principal
> and next aim is to clear the road for the free development of class
> war in the village, the class war of the proletariat that is directed
> toward the realization of the final goal of the world's social democracy,
> toward the conquest of political power by the proletariat and to-
> ward the creation of the basis for a socialist society . . .[7]

The political program corresponding to this was a fight for
radical democracy. It might astonish the reader to hear this, after
our discussion of Lenin's views on democracy. The explanation
is that in Chapter Three we were discussing these views without
reference to their development in time; we merely juxtaposed
different and at times conflicting aspects of the appraisal which
Lenin and his followers have made of democracy. We saw that to
Lenin, democracy was the typical superstructure of capitalism,
and the workingmen had a stake in it because under a democratic
constitution they might come to power more easily. Lenin's
early demand for constitutional democracy was based on the
first of these considerations and is connected with the futuristic
character of his analysis of Russian society. We saw that he
believed Russia would follow in Europe's footsteps, but, impatient, he asserted that Russia was substantially already like
and part of the West. Lenin saw the function of liberal democratic institutions in Russia to be, not helping the proletariat
come to power, but facilitating and accelerating Russia's westernization. His cry for democracy was a measure of warfare against
the old order, the tsarist dynasty, its bureaucratic state apparatus,

the privileged, land-owning gentry, the army, and the police. All these classes, persons, and institutions were considered by Lenin to be the last obstacles in Russia's road to a capitalist society. Or rather, he asserted that this transformation had already taken place; it was merely obscured by the tsarist political structure. Hence he could write: "In order to clear the road for the free development of class warfare in the village, it is necessary to remove all remnants of the feudal order which are at present *covering up* the beginnings of capitalist antagonism within the rural population and are preventing them from developing." [8] Political action was thus seen as the midwife who could tear the new society from the womb of old institutions. Superstructural means, to use Marxian parlance, would help to reveal sub-structural change. "The fight of the Russian working class for its liberation is a political fight," Lenin wrote as early as 1895, "and its first objective is the achievement of political liberty." [9]

In consequence, Lenin called on the proletariat to support all liberal parties in the fight for political liberty. His minimum program, in these years, was to bring about what he called the bourgeois revolution in Russia. It therefore consisted of demands for universal, direct, equal, and secret elections, for political and civil liberties, for the liberation of the peasantry from the inequalities imposed by the Great Reforms, and also for a certain amount of social legislation.[10] Lenin's minimum program up to 1905 was thoroughly liberal: he expressly warned against any open emphasis being placed on socialist long-range aims, and against a flippant attitude toward the minimum objectives. He argued that any admission by his followers that liberal democracy was only the minimum aim would lead them to half-heartedness in supporting these demands. Speaking about a draft for a party platform that was being discussed, he wrote, "It is fully sufficient if we say that the autocracy is retarding or repressing 'the *entire* social development': that means that it is incompatible also with the development of capitalism." [11] This caution on Lenin's part reveals the value he placed on the alliance of his party with other enemies of tsarist autocracy, be they peasants, bourgeois, or even members of the gentry.[12] In his eyes, his principal allies in these years were the representatives of the bourgeoisie; this class, he thought (as did all other Russian Marxists at the time) shared with the proletariat a deep and irreconcilable hostility to the tsarist order. Yet because the bourgeoisie was in addition the natural enemy of the working class, it could not be fully trusted. True enough, according to the Marxist scheme of development it was the natural desire of the business world to bring about the so-called bourgeois revolution. But at the same time the existence of an even more revolutionary class tended to make the middle class afraid of revolutionary action, and thus prone to betray "its own" revolution.

All these arguments were familiar to Russian Marxists, and were quite generally accepted by them. There was no agreement, however, concerning the consequences to be drawn from these considerations. One school of thought might be characterized roughly as follows: The next revolution which has to be fought in Russia is the bourgeois revolution; the principal force that will fight it is the bourgeoisie. The bourgeoisie will fight it more enthusiastically if it is not at the same time troubled by forces further to the left. For this reason, the proletariat should refrain from disturbing the bourgeoisie in its fight against autocracy; it should not by its radical slogans frighten the middle class into becoming counterrevolutionary. Instead, it should lie low until the bourgeoisie has played its revolutionary role to the very end. One group, the so-called Legal Marxists, went so far as to imply that the proletariat should refrain from playing any active, or at least any leading, role in the coming bourgeois revolution.*
These Legal Marxists emphasized the constructive goals capi-

---

* In general, this trend was later represented by the Menshevik wing of the Russian Marxist movement. Since the temptation has often been great to view Menshevism through the eyes of that party which came out victorious in the Russian revolution, many students have tended to make the Mensheviks appear much more moderate and cautious than they were. It is worth remembering that in the Second International and in the interwar socialist internationals, the Russian Mensheviks were usually on the left wing.

The "Legal Marxists," one of the Russian strains of revisionism, were the intellectual precursors of Menshevism and thus the founders of moderate Marxism in Russia. There was no direct connection between Legal Marxism and Menshevism because the Legal Marxists drifted to the right very soon and left the camp of socialism altogether.

talism still had to fulfill in Russia. They warned against premature revolutionary struggles and premature political action of
any sort, lest capitalism be prevented from coming to its full
flowering. This fear of political action led directly to "econo-
mism," the ideology of a moderate Marxist group that succeeded
the Legal Marxists. They proposed outright to let the bourgeoisie
fight its own political revolution; the proletariat, meanwhile,
should restrict its activities to trade-unionism and other attempts
to improve its economic conditions.

Lenin's conclusions were different. True, he too maintained that
the proletariat should for the time being forget its maximum
objectives, but it should do so only in order to pursue its
minimum aim, the bourgeois revolution, with the greatest vigor.
This vigor was essential precisely because the bourgeoisie was
likely to betray "its own" revolution. As a matter of fact, Lenin
almost from the beginning argued that the bourgeoisie would
turn counterrevolutionary no matter what the proletariat did,
while attempts on the part of the workers to appease the middle
class would only promote reactionary measures. Conversely, the
radical spirit of the proletariat would act as the prime mover
of revolutionary developments. When the most revolutionary
class began to march toward its goal, it would set all other
classes into motion. The action of the proletariat would thus be
the spark that would touch off the bourgeois revolution.

This "theory of the spark" is a typically Leninist way of
arguing, which we shall see applied in other fields later. It can be
regarded as a substitute for the rigid determinism of "orthodox"
Marxism. In Lenin's eyes, such determinism leads to political
inaction, because it implies that the revolution will develop by its
own inner dynamics without having to be promoted, and that
vigorous action by the proletarian movement might only spoil its
chances. Lenin's attitude of distrust is in sharp contrast to this.
He was always swimming against the current, but, as a Marxist,
he still needed a determinist rationale for doing so. The theory
of the spark, probably little more than an optimistic myth with
hardly any basis in reality, provided this for him. That the theory
of the spark ("the activity of the working class will set the
bourgeoisie in motion to make the bourgeois revolution") is in

direct contradiction to Lenin's fears that the bourgeoisie, fearing socialism more than reaction, would be ready to betray "their own" revolution should be obvious. Both arguments were adduced to support his demand that the proletariat should undertake the role of leading the bourgeois revolution. In subsequent pages we shall see further instances of Lenin's tendency to use mutually contradicting arguments to support his policies.

To sum up: Lenin in the years around the turn of the century showed an intense hatred of tsarist autocracy and an equally intense impatience with the Russian peasant. With a very guarded faith in the revolutionary potential of the bourgeoisie, he proposed that the working class lead it and even the liberal gentry in the bourgeois revolution, which would "bring out" the capitalist nature of Russian society in its clear and naked reality. His main hatred was directed, first, against those Marxists who warned the proletariat against premature revolutionary activity, and second, against the Narodniks, who were, he thought, confusing the peasants about their inevitable destiny and thus retarding their evolution toward consciousness. We shall see that, in the period following the Revolution of 1905, Lenin changed both his analysis of the political constellation and his program of action.

THE REVOLUTIONARY DEMOCRATIC DICTATORSHIP OF THE PROLETARIAT AND THE PEASANTRY

Lenin's reaction to the Revolution of 1905 provides a good case study of his operating procedure in applying and reformulating his revolutionary strategy. The revolution had come as the climax of a growing wave of strikes, beginning shortly after the turn of the century, to which peasant disorders, student demonstrations, political assassinations, and increasing demands for liberal reforms were added. A more immediate cause was the disastrous war against Japan, which turned into a series of severe defeats and converted the various opposition movements into a revolution. In spite of early attempts by the tsar to make concessions to the liberal opposition, fuel was added to the flames of revolution by the events of "Bloody Sunday" (January 9, 1905), when troops fired on a peaceful mass demonstration of workers who had gathered in front of the St. Petersburg Winter Palace, killing many. The revolution failed, in part because of the lack of co-ordinated leadership. Such leadership was lacking because of the great difference in the aims and aspirations of the various social strata participating in the revolution.* Another deciding factor was the continued loyalty of the guards regiments, which happened to return from the Far East just in time to put down the Moscow uprising of December 1905. Finally, the uprising failed because the masses and their leaders were insufficiently prepared for an all-out revolution. There had been very little time for the revolutionary parties to organize mass support. All of the parties were weak and scattered. Working-class solidarity certainly did not come up to Lenin's hopes. To be sure, the workers of Moscow went to the barricades, but the workers of St. Petersburg and of the railroad did not prevent the transport of the guards who put the uprising down — a lesson that the revolutionary parties put to good use in 1917. In addition to psychological unpreparedness, there was also material unpreparedness. The armaments, for instance, were thoroughly anachronistic and inadequate (which, incidentally, explains Lenin's preoccupation with the technical problems of an armed uprising after 1906). The leaders of the revolutionary parties, moreover, had hardly any chance to take over direction of the workers and peasants, and where they did so they did not always calculate correctly. Lenin himself made serious errors, in overestimating the enthusiasm of the workers and the possibilities for renewed revolutionary conflicts.[13]

In the early months of 1905, as the revolution began to develop and gather momentum, Lenin, then living in exile in western Europe, attempted to explain the events he learned about through the press by previously developed theorems, and to formulate programmatic slogans. His first impression was that the events in Russia were fully confirming his past analysis and prognosis. He therefore concluded that the situation called for

* Trotsky pointed out the lack of co-operation between the workers and the peasants of Russia and blamed "the political stupidity of the *muzhik*, who in his village sets the squire's manor house on fire and grabs his land, but who in his soldier's uniform shoots at the workers" (*Russland in der Revolution*, Dresden, 1909, p. 37).

pursuing his long-advocated strategy with new vigor — the time for the bourgeois revolution had finally ripened. The bourgeoisie was on the march, and the proletariat was showing them the way.

But in the summer of 1905 Lenin thought he saw signs that the revolutionary enthusiasm of the liberal bourgeoisie was lagging, after the tsar had made a number of empty promises of reform. He was not, however, easily discouraged. He maintained that the interests of the middle class could not but come in conflict with the old regime, and that this conflict would be sharper the longer it was retarded. Hence he concluded confidently that the revolution would end in the downfall of tsarism and the establishment of bourgeois democracy, if only the proletariat kept on leading all other elements of discontent in revolutionary radicalism. The proletariat, he wrote, must be the class that chooses the movement for action after gathering around it as many forces as it can. When these forces of revolution are at the peak of their organization and consciousness, and when the enemy is at his weakest, then the population must rise in revolt, and tsarism will collapse. "At that moment the proletariat will rise at the head of the revolt in order to win liberty for the entire people, and to guarantee to the working class the possibility of an open and broad struggle for socialism, a struggle which will be enriched with all of Europe's experience." [14]

With that phrase we are reminded by Lenin that behind the minimum program of the bourgeois revolution there stands the maximum program of the proletarian class struggle and the proletarian revolution. The relationship between these programs, in Lenin's mind, was this: the closer the party comes to accomplishing the minimum program, the more actively its leaders have to think about the maximum aims. The closer democracy comes, the more it must be used for the purpose of revealing its bourgeois character. The faster the bourgeois revolution progresses, and broader masses participate in it, the more should a Marxist remember the special aims of his movement, the more aloof he should keep himself. Lenin therefore called for tighter organization, firmer class consciousness, and the jealous maintenance of the party's independence within the whole movement for bourgeois democracy.[15] In other words, the development of the revolution caused him to move away from the idea of an alliance with liberalism, and later led him to a complete break with the liberals that could never be healed.

Meanwhile, his attitude toward the peasantry underwent an even more decided change. In February of 1905 Lenin received his first news about widespread peasant disturbances, but he did not feel compelled thereby to make alterations in his analysis of the situation. In his pamphlets and letters he welcomed the revolutionary peasants as a friendly force, as long as they were joining the fight against tsarism, but he categorically refused to support the peasants' aspirations toward the division of the gentry's land among themselves. The proletariat, he wrote, has not the slightest interest in supporting the formation of a new class of capitalist farmers in Russia; this would only mean the replacement of one type of capitalism by another.[16] "We must," he wrote, "stand firm on our own proletarian class point of view: we must organize the rural proletariat as we do the urban, and combine them in an independent class party. We must explain to the peasants the hostile clash of their interests with those of the bourgeois peasantry and must call them to battle for the socialist revolution. We must show them that salvation from oppression and misery lies, not in the transformation of some parts of the peasantry into petty bourgeois, but in the replacement of the entire bourgeois order by a socialist one." [17]

Two developments caused Lenin to rethink his policies. One was the proclamation of the October Manifesto, and the reaction of the liberal bourgeoisie to it. The other was the intensification of the peasants' revolutionary activity, and the highly imaginative way the tsarist government dealt with it (see pp. 129–130). The first of these developments led Lenin to reappraise the role and reliability of the bourgeoisie in the bourgeois revolution, and to make corresponding changes in his political and organizational program. The second was responsible for his changed attitude toward the Russian peasantry.

In the Manifesto of 30 October 1905, Nicholas II promised his people to establish a representative assembly, called the Duma, which was to have a positive function in the legislative

process. An extended franchise was to make the Duma a truly
representative body, and granting the customary civil liberties
was to make Russia a more democratic state. The publication of
this manifesto marks the turning point of the Revolution of
1905. That Lenin sensed this very well is apparent from his
comments at the time.[18] But despite this awareness he was not yet
ready to admit that the revolution had been defeated. Instead,
he urged new and more vigorous revolutionary action, and
heartily supported the last-ditch effort of the revolution in
December of 1905, when the working class went on strike on a
mass scale and fought on barricades in the streets of Moscow.
This uprising was suppressed by the guards regiments recently
returned from the front, and Lenin had to admit that, at least
for the time being, the revolution had passed its peak. It was
obvious to him that the proletariat had gone to the barricades
too late. The moment of the enemy's greatest weakness and of the
masses' greatest enthusiasm had been missed. Immediately the
Moscow uprising became the focus of heated debates between
the two wings of the Russian Marxist movement. The moderates
denounced it as a desperate and foolish adventure, while Lenin
heatedly defended it, accusing the moderates of timidity and
opportunism.

At the same time, Lenin considered the reasons for the failure
of the uprising. What, he asked, had changed the mood of the
country before the workers of Moscow delivered their blows?
His answer was that the October Manifesto, by appeasing some
and neutralizing other factions within the Russian bourgeoisie,
had transformed it into a defender of the new *status quo*. Two
liberal parties formed as a result of the October Manifesto, a
conservative group, the Octobrists, who united on the basis of
complete satisfaction with the concessions made, and a left-wing
opposition, the Constitutional Democrats ("Cadets"), who accepted the reforms as a working compromise that might serve as
a basis from which to fight for further gradual reforms. Viewing
these developments, Lenin declared that the bourgeoisie had
forsaken its own revolution and had turned into His Majesty's
Loyal Opposition.[19] It had lost all significance in the revolutionary struggle that constituted Lenin's minimum program. He

had never denied the possibility of such a development, but his strategy had up to that time been based, nonetheless, on the more optimistic belief that the bourgeoisie was compelled by historical necessity to fight for radical democracy. This belief he now abandoned, arguing that the bourgeoisie had sold its services to the counterrevolution for the mere semblance of a constitution. Soon he was to maintain that it could not have been otherwise; in 1908 he stated, "The fact is that the group which in Europe constituted the core of revolutionary democracy — urban guild handicraft, the urban bourgeoisie and petty bourgeoisie — *had to* turn toward counterrevolutionary liberalism in Russia." [20] Nor was he at a loss to explain the reasons: the pressure of international capital and the Russian middle class's fear of the masses. In 1915, he wrote:

We Bolsheviks have always said, especially since the spring of 1906, that the Cadets and Octobrists represent the liberal bourgeoisie as a *united* force. The decade from 1905 to 1915 has confirmed our view. In the decisive moments of the struggle, Cadets and Octobrists together have betrayed democracy and have gone to help the tsar and the landlords. . . . The international setting of the Russian revolution as well as the strength of the proletariat have made that behavior of the liberals inevitable.[21]

After 1905, Lenin was quick to draw the political consequences of this situation as he saw it. The tenuous and uneasy alliance which "the proletariat" (meaning, his party) had made, however unilaterally, with the liberals was now canceled, and open class war with the bourgeoisie was the slogan he advanced.[22] Further, a new aspect was added to his views concerning the usefulness of democracy in the proletariat's class struggle. Until 1905 he had, however vaguely, subscribed to the view that the working class might very well come to power by legal means, given political democracy, though he did not trouble to point out precisely what circumstances might favor a revolution by consent. In any event, democracy had, somehow, been considered to be the normal transitional stage between tsarism and the proletarian revolution; it would take the form of a constitutional republic that might function smoothly for an undefined historical period. Should it function well, it might give the proletariat a chance to seize power by legal means. The acceptance of the October compromise by the liberal bourgeoisie, followed by twelve years of tsarist constitutionalism, gave this vague optimism a severe blow. As we have seen, Lenin continued to fight for the extension of democratic rights and institutions. But we also saw that the word "democracy" gradually acquired a different meaning. It no longer connoted a relatively stable regime in which the classes might muster their forces for new revolutionary battles, using both constitutional and unconstitutional means. Democracy meant now the acute dissolution not only of the old regime but also of capitalist society. It would be achieved only at the moment when civil war between the two main classes had broken out.

The new strategy concerning the peasantry which Lenin developed after 1905 was based on the assumption that an agrarian revolution in Russia might create the best possibilities for erecting the dictatorship of the proletariat. In western Europe, the peasantry by the middle of the nineteenth century had become a thoroughly conservative, not to say reactionary, force in politics. No political movement had been more keenly aware of this than Marxism, so that Lenin's original appraisal of the peasantry as the most reactionary of all classes was but the repetition of a Marxist cliché. In Russia, however, the situation was different. There the great reforms of the second half of the nineteenth century had indeed liberated the peasants from what might be called feudal bondage. But they had not thereby become free and independent farmers. Instead, they had been thrown into a new bondage to their former lords, a financial bondage fortified by the perpetuation of the village community as the primary political entity. They remained second-class citizens, politically under the tutelage of their old masters, discriminated against because they were subject to different legal codes and procedures. Politically, socially, and economically, therefore, the Russian peasant had reasons to be thoroughly dissatisfied with the reforms, which had been introduced with sufficient fanfare to add a sense of betrayal to his bitterness. An inchoate but burning awareness of having been wronged spread among the peasants, and the spirit of revolt was alive not only among the self-appointed spokesmen, but also among the vast rank and file of Russia's rural population. A specter was haunting the Russian ruling classes, one that had haunted them for decades or even centuries. It was not the specter of communism, but that of the *Pugavhëvshchina*, a nation-sweeping *jacquerie* like that led by Emelian Pugachëv in the eighteenth century.

The Revolution of 1905 had been remarkable because for the first time in Russia's history a peasant uprising had been combined with revolutionary activity on the part of the proletariat and the liberal bourgeoisie, a combination which threatened the *status quo* with unprecedented force. Both Lenin and the ruling classes of Russia (not to mention other political groups) drew important lessons from this new experience, and, in some ways, they all drew the same lesson: they discovered that the peasantry was a potential ally of the utmost importance.* The decisive nature of the resulting shift in Leninist strategy is somewhat obscured by the fact that Lenin continued to apply his customary terms to the peasantry. He never ceased to divide them into different classes and layers, sometimes distinguishing between six or seven different strata. Nor did he cease to differentiate between them and the industrial workers. And still, after 1905, the very word "proletariat" gradually acquired a broader meaning, to include all those who sell their labor power to capitalists, including not only rural labor but even the intellectual proletariat. At the same time, the term "proletariat" was more and more neglected; in its stead Lenin began to speak of the masses, the poor, the have-nots, or the toilers.† For instance, "The Soviet of Workers' and Soldiers'

---

* Lenin was joined in this discovery not only by Prime Minister Stolypin and the Mensheviks, but by the self-styled spokesmen of the Russian peasantry, the socialist revolutionaries, who were only now discerning the revolutionary potential of the peasants. See Oliver H. Radkey, "Chernov and Agrarian Socialism," in Ernest J. Simmons (ed.), *Continuity and Change in Russian and Soviet Thought* (Cambridge, Mass., 1955), pp. 65–66.

† Later Leninist writings usually make an effort to express the difference between these two sources of mass support by distinguishing between *rabochie* (workers) and *trudiashchiesia* (toilers). The latter translation is rather unhappy, although sanctioned by official use in English-language communist publications; in Russian, the term roughly denotes "all those who work with their hands." In present Soviet usage it has been extended to include all those who work for a living, so that cabinet ministers and

Deputies is the embryo of a workers' government, representative
of the interests of all the *poorest* masses of the population, that is,
of nine tenths of the population . . ." [23] Both in Russia and elsewhere, Leninism after 1905 became a movement which based its
strategy on the broad masses of the population, deserving the
name "proletariat" only in a wide sense, because they were
composed more of peasants than of workers. "The very concept
of masses has changed in the last years. What was considered
'the masses' in the era of parliamentarism and trade-unionism
has now turned into upper layers. Millions and tens of millions
who have been living outside of political life are now transformed into the revolutionary mass." [24] Lenin here seems to be
slipping into typically Narodnik attitudes, and the accent on
toilers rather than workers (the very term, toilers, being taken
from the Narodnik dictionary) is indeed in agreement with the
political ideas of the leader of the Socialist Revolutionaries,
Victor Chernov. There is one important difference, however:
Lenin's attachment to the toilers was motivated not by emotions,
but by strictly tactical considerations. The masses of toilers
comprised the army which would fight the revolution for him.

The revolution for which these broad masses were supposed to
fight was still, in Lenin's mind, the bourgeois revolution. Lenin's
minimum program was still to bring about "bourgeois democracy" in its most radical form. This could be achieved, he
thought, even against the wishes of the bourgeoisie itself. It was
to be a bourgeois revolution brought about by the proletariat
and the peasantry; for the peasant was regarded as a bourgeois
— or petty bourgeois — who still nursed grievances sufficient
to make him revolutionary. "The petty bourgeoisie will in the
decisive moments swing left," he wrote with confidence. "It is
being pushed to the left not only by our propaganda, but also
by a number of objective factors . . ." [25]

Thus the peasantry took a place in Lenin's strategy corresponding almost exactly to the place heretofore given to the liberal

---

best-selling novelists are "toilers." It has thus assumed the meaning of
Hitler's *Arbeiter der Stirn und der Faust*. Again, the difference between
"workers" and "toilers" is similar to the difference between the French
ouvrier and *laboureur*, or the German *Arbeiter* and *schaffendes Volk*
(another national socialist term).

bourgeoisie. At the same time, this change entailed the formulation of more differentiated and specific aims than those of the
previous program. For one thing, Lenin argued that the Revolution of 1905, however unsatisfactory its outcome, had nonetheless
done away with Russia's *ancien régime*. Or, rather, the *ancien
régime* was doing away with itself. Even the most reactionary
elements, Lenin observed, "are placing themselves entirely on
the ground of capitalist development; they are decidedly drawing
up a European program that is progressive in the economic sense;
it is necessary to emphasize this especially . . ." Simultaneously,
he paid tribute to the political acumen of the tsarist bureaucracy
by adding that "our reactionaries are distinguished by the
extreme clarity of their class consciousness. They know very
well what they want, where they are going, and on what forces
they can count." [26] For this reason, the choice for Russia was no
longer a choice between "feudalism" and bourgeois democracy;
nor had the time yet come for the choice between capitalism and
socialism. For Russia, the choice was now among different kinds
and degrees of capitalism: reactionary tsarist capitalism or democratic peasant capitalism; an abortive revolution like that of 1848
or a thorough-going one like that of 1789.[27] The time was past
when Lenin found one kind of capitalism to be as bad as every
other.

When Lenin said that the ruling classes were accepting
capitalism, he had in mind particularly the reforms instituted in
the years after the 1905 revolution by Prime Minister Peter
Stolypin, in an attempt to ward off another peasant revolution.
The liberal middle class had been appeased by the October
constitution. The peasant, however, was not so easily satisfied by
constitutional reforms. He wanted improvements in his social and
economic position; he wanted to see the inequities and inadequacies of the Great Reforms removed. Any tsarist minister
who was to undertake to satisfy these demands would face the
difficult task of giving the peasantry sufficient benefits without
violating the property rights of the landed gentry. The Stolypin
reforms had the marks of a brilliant solution. Among students of
Russian history it is almost unanimously accepted that, had
these reforms had time to be fully worked out, Stolypin's aim of

transforming the peasantry into a conservative force would have succeeded.

The reforms, first of all, liberated the Russian peasant from the financial burdens imposed on him by the Great Reforms of the 'sixties. In addition they encouraged the breaking up of the village commune, and gave individual peasants an opportunity to enlarge their holdings and to transform themselves into self-sufficient, independent farmers. What Stolypin wished to achieve was the creation of a broad stratum of relatively prosperous individual farmers side by side with the remaining gentry latifundia. The fate of the not-so-successful peasants was not discussed very much, but it is pretty clear that Stolypin expected the majority of the peasantry to be pushed off the land in a process of natural selection of the fittest, so that they would be freed for wage labor.[28] It is not known whether or not he realized what a powerful boost this would have given to the development of industrial capitalism in Russia. A Marxist like Lenin, however, could not help being aware of this at once.

The prospect might have pleased a Marxist, who could have derived satisfaction from the assurance that the proletariat would soon grow into a numerous and powerful class in Russia. But Lenin thought differently. He saw in the Stolypin reforms a diabolically clever scheme by which tsarism tried to appease that class which (as Lenin now admitted) held the balance of power in Russian society and, as the "independent factor" of Russian politics, could decide the issue of all future revolutions. Lenin foresaw that, if these reforms were carried out, influential parts of the peasantry would be cured of revolutionary radicalism, and he doubted whether the remainder would be transformed into class-conscious proletarians quickly. Instead, he visualized their transformation into a poor peasantry, seasonal wage laborers, yet bound to the land, demoralized and politically unreliable, a rural *Lumpenproletariat.* The proletarian revolution, which

---

* Like the petty bourgeoisie, the *Lumpenproletariat* (literally either "proletariat in rags" or "scoundrel proletariat") functions as a scapegoat in Marxist attempts to explain the failure of proletarian revolutionary activities. The nature of this stratum is not easily defined. Marx himself seems to have had in mind those of the utterly poor proletarians who have not been made conscious but have been demoralized by their misery. They

Lenin never forgot despite his preoccupation with the minimum program, would be robbed of its mass basis.

Lenin's criticism of the Stolypin reforms was not that they would usher in capitalism, but that their capitalism would be of a reactionary, stagnant type, a Prussian capitalism instead of the "American" variety to which he contrasted it.[29] Prussian capitalism, he wrote, would perpetuate the tsarist regime, which he thought to be a replica of the Prussian political system, while American capitalism — would bring the democratic republic. The former would perpetuate the Russian gentry; the latter would expropriate it. Stolypin's reforms, he argued, did not go far enough, and would therefore have to be imposed on the masses by force. "We shall explain to the people," he wrote, that these measures "can be realized only through the unlimited coercion of the majority by a minority, for decades, by means of a wholesale extermination of the progressive peasantry." [30] For that reason alone the new political liberties, even if they were granted in good faith, could not help turning into their opposite. "Without suppression of the masses by force, a 'Cadet' 'peaceful' constitutional development *can not* be realized," he asserted bluntly.[31] Prussian capitalism would mean, at best, a slow, gradual, development toward a more progressive capitalism; American capitalism would stimulate immediately that sharp class war between capital and labor which would end in the proletarian revolution. One would mean painful and tortuous progress; the other, rapid modernization. Why, asked Lenin, should the party be satisfied with one step if it could see the entire road clearly ahead? Why ask for a little bit of reform if the fullest result could be obtained by a decisive battle? [32]

Lenin's ideas about American capitalism seem to have been fashioned after Jeffersonian democracy. Lenin obviously thought of it as a community of free farmers organized in a democratic republic. The expropriation of the gentry and the transformation

---

therefore drift into crime, prostitution, strikebreaking, and political irresponsibility. Neither Marx nor his followers have, to my knowledge, given sufficient explanation of the fact that some workers acquire consciousness while others are demoralized. A systematic analysis of the use of the term in the writings of Marx might add to our understanding of his conception of the proletariat itself.

of the Russian peasant into a free "capitalist" farmer of the
French or American type would encourage the most efficient
exploitation of the soil and thus constitute economic progress.
In reading Lenin's pamphlets of the period around 1906–1908
we can watch the curious spectacle of the father of Bolshevism
turning into an apologist of pure competition and bourgeois
individualism.[33]

The most important distinction between the two types of
capitalism in Russia, however, lay in who would wield the
most political influence. Lenin's preference for "American" over
"Prussian" capitalism stemmed from his deep conviction that in
the latter society political and social leadership would be exercised by the gentry and the bureaucracy, whereas in the former
it would be in the hands of the proletariat. "Economic inevitability unquestionably causes and is effecting the most far-reaching upheaval in Russia's agricultural order. *The question is
only whether this is to be brought about by the landlords led by
the tsar and Stolypin, or by the peasant masses led by the
proletariat.*"[34] This question was of the utmost importance,
because the nature of Russia's ruling class in the near future
would directly determine the immediate and long-range course of
her history.

In the era of bourgeois transformations (or more correctly, of
bourgeois revolutions), bourgeois democracy in each country is
shaped one way or another, takes on one or another form, is infused
with these or the other traditions, recognizes one or another minimum
of democratism — according to how far the *hegemony* during the
decisive moments of national history goes, *not* to the bourgeoisie, *but*
to the "lower elements," to the "plebeians" of the eighteenth century,
the proletariat of the nineteenth and twentieth centuries . . .[35]

If there is one theme which Lenin stressed most frequently
and urgently in the years between the two revolutions, it was
that all of Russia's further history should be enacted under
vigorous proletarian leadership. Contrasting the quietism of the
Mensheviks with the impatient activism of his own faction, he
mocked the faith of the moderates in the dialectics of history.
The Mensheviks, he wrote, believe in the "liquidation of the old
order through a process of mutual struggle between the elements

of society," whereas he insisted "that we, the party of the proletariat, must carry out this liquidation." [36] Again, he denounced
the Mensheviks for their "tailism," that is, their tendency to
regard the working class as the left wing, or "tail," of the radical
bourgeoisie, or as a mere pressure group, or "prime mover," of
radicalism. He argued instead that the proletariat should assume
active revolutionary leadership, give Russia's developments their
dynamism, direction, and aim, and carry these developments to
their "logical" conclusion even over the dead body of liberalism.[37]
With an almost obsessive devotion to detail he worried even
about the precise phrasing by which to describe the relationship
between the working class and the peasantry. He rejected such
expressions as, "the proletariat should lean on the peasantry,"
and "the proletariat should fight with the help of the peasantry,"
in favor of "the proletariat should lead the peasantry." [38]

This, then, was Lenin's view of the tasks facing the working
class: in Western Europe, it should prepare itself for the seizure
of power; in Russia, it should lead the peasantry in the fight
for radical democracy.

In Europe, the real political content of social democratic work is
the preparation of the proletariat for the struggle for power with the
bourgeoisie, which now has full rein in the state. In Russia, the
problem *so far* is *only the creation* of the modern bourgeois state,
which will either be similar to a *Junker* monarchy (in case of the
victory of tsarism over democracy) or to a bourgeois democratic
peasant republic (in case of the victory of democracy over tsarism).
And the victory of democracy in modern Russia will be possible only
if the peasant masses follow the revolutionary proletariat and not
treacherous liberalism.[39]

The next question was how the Russian peasant could be made
to follow the leadership of the proletariat. This problem was
discussed at great length during the congress of the Russian
Social Democratic Labor Party held in Stockholm shortly after
the revolution, in 1906. The transactions of the congress
amounted to a stock-taking of the revolution, and when the
peasant problem was discussed, all Russian Marxists agreed in
recognizing that the peasantry had come to play an important
role. But differences appeared in evaluating it. Lenin's Bolshe-

viks, with their theory of the treason of the bourgeoisie, were eager to ally themselves with the peasantry, and, in order to cement this alliance, Lenin advocated the expropriation of all gentry estates and the distribution of all land to the peasants. The Mensheviks, on the other hand, continued to insist that the bourgeoisie was a progressive, not a conservative, class, and would still have to be supported. Plekhanov developed an interesting theory of Russia as an "Asiatic society," * and became one of the chief spokesmen for those who cautioned that the peasantry was an unenlightened force of the past, a source of Russia's despotism and backwardness.

In discussing the implementation of his plan to lead the peasantry, Lenin at this congress startled his comrades by advocating that all land be nationalized and then put at the disposal of individual peasants. Menshevik spokesmen argued with him that nationalization could be effected only in societies where capitalism had already been carried to the peak of its development. Moreover, they held that nationalization would increase the influence of the centralized state and its bureaucracy; hence it would strengthen antidemocratic, reactionary political institutions. Instead of nationalization, they proposed a scheme of local and regional autonomy in the administration and ownership of land. During the Revolution of 1905 such an arrangement had been initiated spontaneously by the peasants of Livonia and Kurland (contemporary Latvia), after seizing the estates of fugitive German barons, though the swift defeat of the revolution had not permitted such a new order to establish itself. Arguing against this scheme, Lenin advanced several

* Conceptions of a specifically Asiatic or Oriental type of society were current in the middle of the nineteenth century and found their way into the works of Marx, particularly the long-neglected first draft of *Das Kapital*. Karl August Wittfogel, an outstanding student of Asiatic societies, and himself a former Leninist, has made attempts to bring the concept back into currency as useful for the understanding of many societies past and present, including tsarist and Soviet Russia. At the same time he has made interesting ideological studies of the fate which this term has had, particularly among Marxists and Leninists. See his "The Ruling Bureaucracy of Oriental Despotism: A Phenomenon That Paralyzed Marx," in *The Review of Politics*, vol. 15, no. 3, pp. 350–359.

points. First of all, he claimed that nationalization could be either a consequence of highly developed capitalism or a condition for its further development, the latter case to apply in countries where capitalism is still young. In such backward societies, where the rural bourgeoisie was still weak, nationalization could be accomplished at an early stage and would contribute to the development of mature capitalism. "To relate nationalization to an era of highly developed capitalism means to deny it as a means of bourgeois progress. And such a denial directly contradicts economic theory," he wrote.[40]

And why would this measure further the development of capitalism? What has nationalization, customarily thought of as an anticapitalist measure, to do with the promotion of individual farming? Quite simple, said Lenin. The nationalization of land would with one stroke convert all rural social relationships into capitalist relationships. "Nationalization (in its pure form) entails the receipt of rent by the state from the entrepreneurs in agriculture, who pay wages to hired workers and receive a medium profit on their capital." [41] For the revolutionary democracy which would nationalize the land could not use its state apparatus to till the soil and grow the crops. Farmers would still be required to put the land to use. The state would therefore have to make land available to individual farmers on conditions imposed by the state.

Nationalization is the transfer of all land into state property. Property means the right to a rent and the determination on the part of the state authority of the rules concerning possession and use of the land, which are valid for the entire state. . . .* If there are still misunderstandings about this, then they originate either from

* Such rules might concern, for instance, the abolition of all rights to sublease land, the elimination of the middleman dealing in land, the prevention of large accumulated holdings, and the creation of local and regional organs of self-government to dispose over the nationalized land. The nationalization of land would thus create a complex hierarchy of rights and duties vested in a number of individuals and authorities. To a certain extent the present rules of land tenure and use in the Soviet Union conform to Lenin's vision, and the entire notion of property in Soviet law can be understood only if his differentiation between ownership, disposition, and use is clearly kept in mind.

failure to understand the difference between the concepts of property, disposition, and use, or from demagogical flirting with provincialism and federalism.[42]

Lenin readily admitted that the nationalization of land might well lead to a firmer consolidation of capitalism in Russia than he thought desirable. He conceded that the arrangement proposed by him would lead to the peasants' demanding the perpetuation of their right to use the land, and thus to the gradual transformation of state property into private property; for there is always a tendency for new privilege to entrench itself by law. But he emphasized that the mere measure of nationalization would be no less capitalistic than the possible consolidation of individual holdings. He wrote in 1908:

> The abolition of private property in land in no way changes the bourgeois foundations of commodity and capitalist agriculture. There is nothing more erroneous than the opinion that the nationalization of land has anything in common with socialism or even with the equalization of the use of land. As regards socialism, it is well known that it consists in the abolition of commodity economy. Nationalization, on the other hand, is the transfer of the land into the property of the state, and such a transfer in no way touches private cultivation of land. . . . As long as exchange remains, it is ridiculous even to talk about socialism.[43]

For this reason he was willing even to accept the so-called Black Partition as an alternative to the policy of nationalization. The term "Black Partition" signifies that spontaneous and extralegal seizure of all land by the peasantry, and its subsequent distribution among them, which actually did take place in 1917. Lenin viewed the prospect of such an agrarian revolution with the same ambivalence with which he viewed all presocialist phenomena. On the one hand, it would be reactionary, in that it would establish small holdings as the prevalent type of property in land. Moreover, it was utopian, insofar as its advocates spoke of it as a socialistic measure. But on the other hand, it would deal a final blow to the old order and was therefore considered preferable to Junker capitalism. It would, finally, make the contradictions of capitalism in the rural economy appear sharper and clearer, so that the peasants' class consciousness would grow.[44] In short, Lenin accepted the Black Partition as a variant to his minimum program.[45] He regarded it as at least a transitional step, which would lead inevitably to the nationalization of all land. For, as he put it dogmatically, "it is not possible to take the land and hold on to it for yourself without new political gains, without delivering a new and even more decisive blow *against all private ownership of land as such.* In politics as in all social life, not to go forward means to be thrown back." [46]

To sum up, we might quote a lengthy statement from a report Lenin read at the Fifth Congress of the Russian Social Democratic Labor Party:

Objectively, that is, not from the point of view of our desires but from the point of view of the given economic development of Russia, the fundamental question of our revolution can be reduced to whether the development of capitalism will be expedited by means of the complete victory of the peasants over the landlords or by means of the landlords' victory over the peasants. The rapid bourgeois democratic transformation in Russia's economy is absolutely inevitable. No power in the world can stand in its way. But this transformation is possible in two forms: In the Prussian manner, as it were, or according to the American pattern. . . . The complete victory of the peasant revolt, the confiscation of all gentry land, and its equal division mean the very fastest development of capitalism, the form of the bourgeois democratic transformation most advantageous for the peasants.

And not only for the peasants is it more advantageous. The same is true also for the proletariat. The conscious proletariat knows that there is and cannot be another way toward socialism than through a bourgeois democratic transformation.

That means that the less complete and the less decisive this transformation is, the longer and the heavier will nonsocialist tasks weigh on the proletariat, not tasks of the proletariat as a class, but general, democratic ones. The more complete the victory of the peasantry, the faster the proletariat will definitely emerge as a class, and the more clearly will it develop its own purely socialist tasks and aims.

Hence you see that the peasant ideas of equal parcellization are reactionary and utopian from the point of view of socialism, but revolutionary from the point of view of bourgeois democratism.[47]

The name that Lenin gave to the regime he wished to see established in this manner was the "revolutionary democratic dictatorship of the proletariat and peasantry." [48] A regime of a

"democratic class" and a "socialist class," this was to be a
"dictatorship (that is, with power in no way limited) of the mass
over the few, not the other way around." [49] Since in his eyes
all political systems were, basically, dictatorships of one class
over another, he was never greatly concerned with the political
forms this mass democracy of workers and peasants might
assume, except when he was thinking about them in terms of
efficiency or tactical usefulness. Even so, he could not refrain
from claiming that the soviet type of organization, which appealed to him in both 1905 and 1917 as the most convenient
form for the revolutionary democratic workers' and peasants'
dictatorship, was a higher form of government than constitutional
democracy, and a step toward the withering away of the state.[50]
As we shall see, during 1917 his judgment of the soviets swung
between enthusiasm and disappointment.

Lenin did not expect, either in 1905 or 1917, that the revolutionary masses would form soviets or any other kind of organization. Once, however, soviets had sprung up, Lenin proposed to
use them as "organs of *immediate* mass warfare of the proletariat." [51] He preferred them to parliaments, not because they
were more efficient, but because they were mass organizations,
whereas parliaments were, historically, bourgeois institutions.[52]
"The Soviet of workers' deputies," he wrote in 1905, "is not a
workers' parliament and it is not the organ of proletarian self-
government; it is not an organ of self-government at all, but a
fighting organization *for the attainment of specific aims.*" [53] A
good deal of additional evidence could be cited to show that
Lenin judged the soviets wholly pragmatically and with considerable reservation. In 1905 he tended to think that the
proper and expedient organization of the party itself would make
them superfluous. Lacking this ideal organization, he conceded
their value, even though he warned against their anarcho-
syndicalist tendencies.[54] In the fall of 1917, during the period
when he himself became involved in anarcho-syndicalist dream-
ing, he tended to judge them much more favorably. After the
October Revolution, the soviets lost most of their significance.

The coming revolution, Lenin thought, would begin with an
armed uprising in an important city or in a province. The im-

mediate task in a successful uprising of this kind would be to proclaim a provisional revolutionary government, because "immediate political leadership over the people is no less essential for the complete victory of the people over tsarism than is military leadership of its forces." [55] This provisional government would then have to proclaim laws codifying the new political and social order, and would have to do so at once, without waiting for more formal action by a legislature or constituent assembly. These laws would not be accepted by the ruling classes. Consequently, the rebellion would lead directly to "the higher and more complex form of a long-lasting civil war, embracing the entire country, an armed struggle of one part of the people against the other." [56]

PERMANENT REVOLUTION

Throughout the period between the two revolutions Lenin sought to make it clear beyond any doubt that he was not capitulating to the peasantry, or in any way making the party dependent on it.

The actual petty bourgeois character of the contemporary peasant movement in Russia is beyond doubt; we must make this clear with all our vigor and without mercy, and we must fight a never ceasing battle against all illusions . . . on this account. The organization of an independent proletarian party, which will through all democratic revolutions strive toward the complete socialist revolution, must be our constant aim, which we must not lose sight of for a minute. But to turn away on those grounds from the peasant movement would be the most hopeless Philistinism and pedantry. No, the character of that movement is without doubt revolutionary democratic, and we must support it with all our power, develop it, make it politically conscious and class-determined, push it further, and go together with it, hand in hand, to the end — for we ourselves are going much further than the end of any peasant movement; we are going up to the complete end of the very division of society into classes.

He called on his followers to support the peasant revolution, "in order that it leave not one stone of the old, cursed, feudal-aristocratic slave society which is Russia on top of another, in order that it create a new generation of free and daring people,

that it create a new republican country in which our proletarian
fight for socialism can develop freely." [57]

Seldom has a political leader fought more energetically for a
program that he endorsed only with the strongest reservations,
for a program that was not really his own at all. Lenin's argument in favor of his minimum program was that first things have
to come first, and that the proletarian revolution could be undertaken only after conditions favorable for the proletariat's class
struggle had been created. One implication of this was that
Lenin would like to see the "revolutionary democratic workers'
and peasants' dictatorship" disintegrate and disappear as fast as
it has been created. "We can not," he wrote with apparent satisfaction, "take upon ourselves any guarantees for the durability
of any conquests — whatever they may be — on the part of the
bourgeois revolution; for the lack of durability, the intrinsic contradictory character of *all* its conquests is an immanent attribute
of the bourgeois revolution as such." * But still, a liberal capitalist Russia had to be created before it could be allowed to disintegrate. Nothing but vague thought should be given to the steps
that the party would take immediately after the coming bourgeois revolution.

This Leninist insistence on "first things first" differs slightly
from the conception of proletarian strategy in Russia that has
become known as "the theory of permanent revolution." This
theory was conceived by A. L. Parvus and L. D. Trotsky, two
leaders prominent in the Russian Marxist movement. Lenin did

---

* "The Agrarian Program of Social Democracy in the First Russian
Revolution, 1905–1907," Lenin, vol. 11, p. 496 (translation in *Selected
Works,* vol. 3, p. 283). After 1917 Lenin undertook to help speed up this
process of dissolution. He proclaimed to the Russian peasants, "We shall
help you attain 'ideal' capitalism"; for, he added, equality of land tenure
and equality of land use is "the idealization of capitalism from the
small producer's point of view." "At the same time we shall show you its
inadequacy, the necessity of the transition of the social cultivation of the
land" (*The Proletarian Revolution and the Renegade Kautsky,* New York,
1934, pp. 87–89; Russian text in Lenin, vol. 23, pp. 398–399).

Similarly, in the People's Democracies of Eastern Europe, communist
policy has been to back up the peasants' demand for the distribution of
land, but see to it that the land was distributed in small, uneconomical lots,
so that subsequent co-operative and collective methods of organization in
agriculture might be hailed as a remedy for an untenable situation.

not consider their views to be of great importance. In retrospect, however, they appear to us highly significant. Not only did Trotsky become Lenin's first lieutenant in the revolution of 1917, while Parvus was in close touch with both, but together with Trotsky a large group of influential intellectuals entered the party in the summer of 1917, who subscribed more or less formally to the theory of permanent revolution. And as its proponents swelled the ranks of the party's leadership, the ideas themselves gradually found their way into Lenin's own scheme of thinking and acting. The term "permanent revolution" had been used by Marx to express the need for unceasing radicalism until communism was achieved. It has a similar meaning for Trotsky and Parvus. The gist of their ideas is the assertion that the purely proletarian revolution should not be relegated to some future time, but is a current problem and should be the center of the party's strategy, even before the bourgeois revolution has been won. The theory of permanent revolution pays full recognition to the Russian peasantry as a cardinal force in this coming bourgeois revolution. But its authors demanded immediate steps leading beyond it. Instead of advocating the creation of a capitalist society on the American pattern, Trotsky and Parvus asked for permanent revolution-making. The dictatorship of the proletariat should be set up during the bourgeois revolution itself. As Trotsky wrote, "Thus the perspective of the dictatorship of the proletariat here grows precisely out of the bourgeois democratic revolution. . . . But the dictatorship of the proletariat appears not *after* the completion of the democratic revolution, . . . for in that case it would simply be impossible in Russia, . . ." *

The reason why the proletarian revolution should begin before the bourgeois revolution was completed is that "in a backward country, the proletariat, small in number, could not come to power if the problems of the peasantry were resolved in the pre-

* Trotsky, *Permanentnaia Revoliutsiia* (Berlin, 1930), p. 58. These views were formulated for the first time shortly after the Revolution of 1905, in a book devoted to the lessons this revolution had taught. The pertinent chapter from this book can be read in English, under the title "Prospects of a Labor Dictatorship," in Trotsky, *Our Revolution: Essays on Working-Class and International Revolution, 1904–1917* (New York, 1918), pp. 69–137.

ceding stage." [58] Trotsky dreaded having the peasants' problems
solved before the proletariat could make use of them for the
purpose of seizing power. He further implied that the peasantry
would betray the revolution just as surely as the liberal bourgeoisie did in 1848 and 1905. His conclusion was therefore that
the "revolutionary democratic dictatorship of proletarians and
peasants" must be prevented from consolidating itself. The bourgeois order which the coming revolution would seek to establish
must be nipped in the bud lest it become too strong to defeat.*
The authors of this theory thought of Russian history as a development in which one important stage in the Marxian scheme
should be skipped altogether, so that, taken literally, Marx's
prognosis did not apply to Russia at all. Trotsky rationalized this
lack of respect for the Marxist outline of history:

> It is nonsense to allege that it be entirely impossible to skip stages.
> Over individual "stages" resulting from a theoretical dissection of the
> process of development taken as a whole, that is, in its maximal
> completeness, the living historical process always makes jumps, and in
> critical moments demands the same of revolutionary politics. It can
> be said that the first characteristic trait distinguishing the revolutionary
> from the vulgar evolutionist is the ability to discern such a moment
> and to make use of it.†

When this theory was first developed, Lenin did not consider
it important enough to make elaborate comments. Instead of
"refuting" Trotsky's "original" theory, as he sarcastically called

* Another argument advanced by Trotsky in favor of a telescoping of
the two revolutions was the theory of imperialism. Imperialism, he asserted,
had completed the bourgeois transformation of Russia, the tsarist superstructure notwithstanding. Hence the struggle in Russia was no longer
that of a "bourgeois nation against the old regime," but of the "proletariat
against a bourgeois nation" (quoted by Lenin in his article, "Two Lines
of Development of the Revolution," vol. 18, p. 317; translation in *Collected
Works*, vol. 18, p. 362).

† *Permanentnaia Revoliutsiia*, p. 59. Trotsky expressly links this with
Lenin's theory of imperialism and the concept of uneven development
(*ibid.*, p. 125). The notion of skipping stages is to be found also in
Narodnik writings and is indeed one of the perpetual issues of nineteenth-
century Russian social thought. An even closer similarity with *narodnichestvo*
is even more remarkable: the populists also feared that the development of
capitalism in Russia and its consolidation would destroy all hopes for
socialism.

it, he merely reasserted his own strategic plans and criticized Trotsky for forgetting the "fact" that the bourgeois revolution still remained to be fought in Russia, and for neglecting the role that remained for the peasantry to play. By denying the role of the peasantry, Lenin argued, Trotsky gave at least the appearance of not wishing to draw the peasantry into revolutionary action. "But that is today the crux" of the party's strategy.[59] Here Lenin insists once more on going whole hog on strategic alliances, and not alienating allies by speaking about more long-range aspirations. He clinched the argument by asserting that, if Trotsky were right, Russia would now be at the threshold of its socialist revolution, and the coming revolutionary regime would have to call itself a socialist government. This is, of course, precisely what Lenin's government did call itself in 1917, but when these lines were written, two years earlier, the idea seemed ludicrous to him.[60]

Even while he engaged in such marginal polemics, however, Lenin himself thought about the problem of how to chart the way from the bourgeois revolution to the proletarian revolution. The word that was chosen for this speculative development shows the gradual transformation of Lenin's thoughts in the years immediately preceding the October Revolution. The word he chose was *pererastanie,* which signifies an organic process of transformation, literally, a "growing into." The word is significant because it marks the distance that Lenin had traveled, by around 1915, from his earlier thoughts about the revolutionary democratic workers' and peasants' dictatorship toward Trotsky's ideas on permanent revolution. In reading Lenin's arguments in favor of American capitalism, we gain the impression that he wished this type of democratic society to be established firmly, and for an appreciable time, in Russia. But the use of "pererastanie" indicates a cautious approach toward Trotsky's idea that the two revolutions should merge and that the democratic regime must not be established.

This merging of two revolutions — "telescoping" is the word Trotsky used — would, of course, pose problems of its own. Lenin, like all other Russian Marxists, admitted that the Russian proletariat was not, in the foreseeable future, going to be strong enough to fight "its own" revolution all by itself. Just as it would need the peasantry as an ally in the bourgeois revolution, so it would need an ally in the later proletarian revolution. But who would this ally be? Lenin's answer is related to his oft repeated assertion that, while bourgeois revolutions are national events, the proletarian revolution would have world-wide proportions. He came to believe in the years of the First World War that the two revolutions might indeed "grow together," for he thought that the bourgeois revolution in Russia might furnish the spark to touch off the world-wide proletarian revolution, which in its turn would enable the Russian proletariat to establish its dictatorship at home. By pursuing their minimum aim, the Russian workers would thus create the conditions for the immediate pursuit of their maximum aim. Wrote Lenin: "The task of the Russian proletariat is to carry the bourgeois democratic revolution in Russia to its conclusion, *in order* to kindle the socialist revolution in Europe. This second task has today come very close to the first, but it nevertheless remains a separate and second task; for *different classes* are to co-operate with the Russian proletariat: for the first task our ally is the petty bourgeois peasantry of Russia; for the second, the proletariat of other countries." [61] Lenin here makes considerable efforts to differentiate between his idea of pererastanie and the Trotsky-Parvus idea of permanent revolution. Nevertheless, his theory of the Russian revolution as the spark which would kindle the world-wide conflagration and lead to socialism even in Russia comes very close to it.

Chapter 7

Nationalism

At a time when the rapid rise of "national industry" was the pride and the hope of the intelligentsia in western and central Europe, the Russian intelligentsia regarded the fight of the proletariat against foreign capital, which was dominating Russian industry and was making Russian absolutism its tax collector, as the Russian nation's fight for liberation from foreign oppressors.

BAUER

NATIONAL SELF-DETERMINATION

The Marxist movement has traditionally professed internationalist leanings. For one thing, its members have tended to assume that nations were obsolete. Nations, they believe, are the creation of a "feudal" or precapitalist past; and, by serving as the political framework of modern capitalist societies, they hinder, obstruct, or retard the development of industrial production, which was made possible by capitalism but which will develop its greatest potentialities only after capitalism has been destroyed. Nations are considered to be a form of political organization that in the past may have been a positive and progressive "force of production" necessary for the growth of mercantilist capitalism. But now that industrialism can stand on its own feet on a global scale, the nation has lost all justification for its continued existence. It is therefore doomed to be abolished. All this may be merely the expression of a wish. Marxist theory, however, maintains that the nation will inevitably vanish, primarily because Marxism looks at the modern world as a single society, in which all local, regional, or national differences are negligible compared with the leveling and equalizing effects of capitalism. In essence, conditions are the same everywhere. In particular, the working class has, all over the world, been reduced to essentially the same status of wage slavery, exploitation, and misery. To a worker, the fellow proletarian across the border is closer than the bourgeois at home; he lives under the same conditions, he suffers the same evils, and he fights the same enemy. Marx and most of his followers therefore believed that as soon as the proletariat had assumed power over society, the system of nations would be revealed in its obsoleteness, and would wither away just as the state would wither. Not only that, they also thought that this one-world character would find expression in the proletarian movement long before the seizure of power. The working class, having no fatherland, would fight as one international army of world revolution.

Marxism, however, is not only a particular way of viewing reality and trends inherent in the world, it is also a program of practical strategy. As such it attempts to have as firm a footing as possible in the political and social actualities of the current moment. Part of that actuality is the nation, both as the social, ethnic, or ideological "content" of existing states and as the political aspiration of dependent national groups.* Since national states are the universally accepted form of political organization, revolutions will take place within their bounds. As Lenin put it, the proletarian revolution, even though it should not be a national revolution, would nevertheless take the form of a nation-wide revolution,[1] and it would establish, at first, socialist regimes within national bounds.[2] Marxist strategy, he argued, should take all available forces into consideration, including the force of nationalism. When translated into political strategy, therefore, its internationalism was bound to take "national forms."[3]

The strategic rule developed from this by Lenin was that the

* Lenin expressed this idea by writing that "the fatherland, i.e., the given political, cultural and social environment, is a most powerful factor in the class war of the proletariat" ("Aggressive Militarism and the Antimilitarist Tactics of Social Democracy," Lenin, vol. 12, p. 314; translation in *Selected Works,* vol. 4, p. 327).

proletariat, an international class, should nonetheless hitch its wagon to those "parties" in the national struggles that represented relative progress or would somehow further the Communist Party's causes. We might say that Marx and Engels conformed to this implicit rule when they tended (with some notable lapses) to pin their hopes on England and therefore to favor English national causes. For, according to their theory of capitalist development, the higher the state of the forces of production, the sooner and faster the revolution would develop. Even if the revolution should break out first on the continent, it could be considered secure only after the English working class had joined its brethren in the European countries. England, in short, would be the lever of international socialism; once she had gone through the revolution, the whole world would have to follow suit.[4]

Lenin's thoughts about the national problem developed, as did most of his views, in the course of bitter polemics with other Marxist leaders.[5] The problem of how to relate national aspirations to the socialist movement had been discussed with considerable heat from the very beginning of the twentieth century. In the Russian Empire, Marxist groups among such minorities as the Jews, Georgians, Armenians, and Ukrainians, contributed the first arguments, but the first systematic treatises on the subject were written by two Austrian socialists, Karl Renner and Otto Bauer, who developed a pronouncedly positive attitude toward the national and cultural heritage of the various peoples composing the Austro-Hungarian empire. In their eyes, the socialist cause meant a fight against capitalism, but not against national cultures. In order to justify this exception in terms of Marxist theory, they had to argue that culture was not part of the capitalist superstructure. The reason why so positive an attitude toward national culture could develop in the Austrian social democratic movement was that it expressed their opposition to the supranational dynasty and the supranational Habsburg state. Nationalism could be regarded as a rebel movement in Austria-Hungary, therefore as something progressive. Hence not only did the Marxist movement in the empire incorporate in its platform demands for national autonomy within a socialist Austria; it even organized itself on a national basis, so that it turned into a loose federation of nationally autonomous social democratic parties. To Lenin this and similar tendencies among Russia's national minorities seemed to be a fantastic bourgeois aberration.

Another viewpoint with which he contended was that of the Polish Socialist Rosa Luxemburg, whose radical impatience with nationalism he considered to be utterly utopian. Luxemburg denied nationalism and nations all significance in the struggle of the proletariat. She viewed nationalism as an ideology belonging to preindustrial societies, which should be of no interest to classes fighting either the bourgeois or the proletarian revolution. Her staunch opposition to the incorporation of any nationalist demands or aspirations kept her following in Poland from becoming larger. In her major economic work, *Die Akkumulation des Kapitals*, capitalism was presented as a virtually integrated world-wide system. Between her impatient denial of nationalism as a force with which to reckon and the tendency of Bauer and Renner to demand national cultural autonomy, Lenin took a middle position, characterized mainly by a realistic appraisal of the force of modern nationalism, which was, however, coupled with a thoroughly negative attitude toward the national principle. As in everything else, Lenin's position was strongly ambivalent.

In fitting nationalism into the strategy of revolution, one question that Lenin often asked himself might serve as point of departure: Where is the world revolution going to begin? In early formulations of his strategy, he adopted the Marxist axiom that it would begin in one of the advanced countries of the West. As late as 1916 he maintained, in a polemic against Rosa Luxemburg, that "the social revolution cannot be the combined act of the proletariat of *all* countries, for the simple reason that the majority of countries and the majority of the earth's population do not, so far, stand on a capitalistic or even at the beginning of a capitalistic level of development. For socialism, *only* the advanced countries of the West and of North America have ripened" — and Lenin specifically named England, France, and Germany.[6] This view was shared, explicitly or tacitly, by most other European Marxists. If there were differences between him and the majority of his comrades in Russia as well as in the West, they lay in the conclusions drawn from this view, or in the implications Lenin saw in it. According to his angry comments, the moderate socialists of the West, in asserting that the revolution would start in the West, were implicitly condemning the proletariat of backward countries to inaction; in effect, therefore, they were contributing toward keeping the backward nations in bondage to their advanced neighbors. As for the Russian Mensheviks, Lenin interpreted their agreement with the proposition that the revolution would begin in the West as weak-kneed submission to Western imperialism and its financial domination of Russia. His own acknowledgment of the West as the probable starting point was coupled with a militant spirit of action. Socialism, he argued, might be possible only in the advanced nations; but this need not condemn the proletariat of Russia to inaction. On the contrary, Russian workers could help their brothers in Europe by making as much trouble within Russia as possible and by stirring all the backward and exploited nations of the world into revolt against the West, so that the foundations on which the European bourgeoisie had based its power would be shaken. The sentence quoted earlier in this paragraph is therefore not all that Lenin had to say on the subject. He went on to state that movements of national liberation in underdeveloped areas should come to the assistance of the proletarian revolution in the West: "The social revolution can not take a form other than an entire era combining the civil war of the proletariat and the bourgeoisie in the advanced countries, with *quite a number* of democratic and revolutionary movements, including movements of national liberation, in the undeveloped, backward, and oppressed nations." [7] This rising tide of national revolts would strengthen the movement of the Western proletariat by weakening the position of the Western bourgeoisie.*

The strategic problem entailed by supporting movements of

* With this, Lenin picked up a strand from the fabric of Marxist thought which had been forgotten or neglected by Marxist theorists in the West, but which was of great importance to Marx and Engels themselves. Witness their support of the Irish movement of rebellion against England, the Polish movements of liberation, and similar currents in the world politics of their day. See also note 4 to this chapter, and Chapters 11 and 12.

national liberation stems directly from the Marxist appraisal of such movements as bourgeois in origin and in aim. The crucial issue for Lenin was how much and what kind of support the conscious leader might give to bourgeois nationalist revolts. Another equally baffling problem arose in the effort to co-ordinate the strategies of the various national proletarian parties by reconciling them both to each other and to the over-all strategy attributed to the world proletariat as a whole. For Leninist "internationalism," when applied in practice, came to mean different and sometimes conflicting policies for the various national units of the international proletarian army.

The policy Lenin devised to resolve dilemmas and difficulties of this kind was a sweeping advocacy of "national self-determination." Behind this all-too-simple Wilsonian slogan, far more radical than the modest demand of the Austrian Marxists for cultural national autonomy, a complex array of theoretical and practical considerations was hidden. As soon as they are reviewed, it appears that the slogan itself, far from resolving difficulties, merely reflects Lenin's problematic attitude toward the question. The slogan epitomizes all the problems which it was designed to settle, so that in every new situation concrete decisions still had to be made. The strategic problem may have been solved on paper, but tactical execution of the solution pose problems anew.

Lenin's radical demand for national self-determination expresses his well-known conviction that the first step of the proletarian revolution should be the sweeping fulfillment of the bourgeois revolution and all the demands attributed to it. By clever analysis of Wilson's war aims, and of similar proposals made in liberal and moderate socialist circles within the countries participating in World War I, Lenin tried to show that the bourgeoisie would never be able or willing to comply with its own ideals of national self-determination for all, because such compliance would mean self-liquidation. Radical execution of these ideals would contribute to the downfall of world capitalism; hence the national aspirations of, say, the Chinese people (directed against world imperialism), but also of the Poles (directed against Germany, Austria, and Russia), and even of the Jews (directed against the very principle of exploitation and oppression) were all seen as revolts against the existing social system, hence as revolutionary forces deserving the support of the proletariat.

Lenin had an additional motive for his strong advocacy of national self-determination. He seems to have been loath to antagonize his temporary allies (the bourgeois movements of national liberation) before it was necessary. Just as he argued against Trotsky for not giving the revolutionary tasks of the peasantry their proper attention, so he sought to nurse national movements of revolt in order that they might attach themselves to his party and follow its leadership.

Finally, his strong arguments in favor of his slogan make full sense only if they are recognized as parts of the program, not of world communism, but of the Russian Communist Party. In advocating national self-determination for all peoples, Lenin spoke as a Russian communist first, and he exhorted his comrades to think as such. "There is one absolute demand," he wrote in a polemic against Luxemburg, "which Marxist theory makes in connection with the analysis of any social problem whatsoever: that is to place it within its *specific* historical framework and then, if the problem concerns one particular country (for example, the national program for that given country), to take account of the concrete particular traits distinguishing that country from others within the framework of the same historical period." [8] Hence it is significant that the sharpest conflict over his slogan arose in the revision of the platform of the Russian Communist Party, in 1919. Lenin told his comrades that a firm stand in favor of national self-determination was the only proper internationalist thing for a Russian proletarian to do. His conception of "internationalism" was starkly simple: the proletariat of any one nation must first of all seek to bring about the weakening, defeat, and downfall of "its own" bourgeoisie. It should work with all its vigor against "its own" national interests as conceived by the ruling classes. As Lenin wrote in 1918, "Internationalism consists in breaking with *one's own* social chauvinists (that is, defensists)* and with *one's own* imperialist government; it consists in a revolutionary struggle against it, in its overthrow, in the readiness to make the greatest national sacrifices (even as far as a peace of Brest) if they are useful to the development of the *international* workers' revolution." [9] In wartime the proletarian should work for, and rejoice in, the defeat of his own government, just as the Russian proletariat, and, indeed, the broad masses of the Russian people, rejoiced in the defeat of tsarism at the hands of the Japanese in 1905.[10] At the last prewar congress of the Second International, Lenin and Luxemburg proposed a resolution to the effect that in any future war between capitalist nations the representatives of the working class should adopt a defeatist attitude; they should not vote for war credits or any other war measures; they should try to evade military service; and, if they were pressed into uniform and given weapons, they should turn these weapons against their own ruling classes, thus transforming the international war into a revolutionary civil war.†

As far as the Russian proletariat was concerned, Lenin held that not only should it be defeatist, but that it had a duty to support all separatist strivings on the part of any subjects of the tsar, or of any national minority oppressed and exploited by Russian imperialism. Any other attitude, he claimed, would be tantamount to chauvinism and would implicitly condone tsarist policies of national oppression. Lenin was suspicious of his own comrades on this score and was convinced that national loyalties had not been eradicated among them as yet. "Scratch a communist — and you will find a Great Russian chauvinist," he thundered angrily at the Eighth Party Congress in 1919.[11]

---

* Lenin labeled those social democrats "defensists" who declared themselves ready to fight for the defense of their country instead of adopting a strategy of "revolutionary defeatism." "Social chauvinists" is another epithet for the same group of people.

† The resolution was shelved at the time, though Lenin tended to overlook this and to rejoice over the fact that it had been supported by at least some of the delegates. Five Years later, at the Basel Congress of the Second International, a somewhat watered-down resolution against war was passed. For the text of the resolution submitted at Stuttgart, see Merle Fainsod, *International Socialism and the World War* (Cambridge, Mass., 1935), p. 16.

Exactly here lies the source of conflict: in Lenin's demand that any given national proletariat strive to frustrate the efforts of "its own" bourgeoisie. Applied to the workers of any one of the nationalities oppressed and exploited by Russian imperialism, this means that the local proletarian parties should with the utmost determination oppose "their own" movements of national liberation and thereby work at cross purposes with the Russian communists. It is significant that the most conspicuous and most consistent "Great Russian chauvinists" in Lenin's party were men from Russia's subject nationalities, who, as internationalists, had joined the Russian social democratic parties and were thus opposing the separatism of "their own" bourgeoisie.* Their conflict with Lenin stemmed from the fact that they found themselves in the Russian party; and, in denouncing their Russian chauvinism, Lenin by implication encouraged local proletarian parties to ally themselves temporarily with "their" bourgeoisie, in the interests of the larger struggle to defeat the great and important imperialist powers. Similarly, Rosa Luxemburg's fight against the Leninist slogan of "national self-determination" is but a logical corollary of Lenin's own views. Her refusal to join "her own" bourgeoisie in fighting for the resurrection of a national Polish state, and her advice that Poland should merge with Russia, the country to which strong economic ties were binding her, is perfectly compatible with Lenin's arguments, and Lenin seems to have understood this, too. Still, for tactical reasons he denounced her views as false. We can understand his unstated motives if we realize that tsarism had been conspicuously guilty of trampling on the rights of Russia's numerous national minorities. Lenin's belief, therefore, that Russian Marxists must be particularly tolerant of national minorities and their aspirations appears to be both an act of defiance against the old Russia and also, perhaps, the voice of a guilty conscience that wanted to atone for Russia's sins. Typically, Lenin argued that any denial of the minorities' rights to full self-determination would mean a continuation of the injustices of tsarism.

Nevertheless, there is a danger of lag in this policy. The ques-

* For instance, the Pole Dzerzhinsky and the Georgians Stalin and Ordzhonikidze.

tion is how long and to what extent a local proletariat can support "its own" struggle for national liberation without becoming infected with the virus of nationalism. Might not the national orientation of a local proletariat perpetuate itself beyond its usefulness to the revolution? Lenin never understood the formula of "national self-determination" in any but a strictly negative sense; he recognized nationalism not as a principle of political organization for the future, but only as a destructive force. And even for the stages preliminary to socialism, Lenin was clearly in favor of the largest possible political units. "We social democrats," he wrote a few months before the outbreak of World War I, "are enemies of *all* nationalism and are for democratic *centralism*. We are against particularism, being convinced that, *other conditions being equal,* large states can solve the tasks of economic progress and the tasks of the proletariat's struggle with the bourgeoisie much more successfully than small states." *

After the October Revolution, he became somewhat alarmed at the prospect that national socialism might be derived from his formula. At the Baku congress, he felt it necessary to warn the communist organizations of the Eastern nations that national stirrings in backward nations, although desirable as a destructive force, should never become aims in themselves.[12] In the preceding year (1918) he had been deeply shocked by the chauvinism of the short-lived Finnish Socialist Workers' Republic, which was manifested by that government's demands for several pieces of territory during peace negotiations with Lenin's Russia. Here was one socialist government bargaining with another over bits of land and over boundary questions, very much to Lenin's amaze-

* "A Contribution to the Question of a National Policy," Lenin, vol. 17, p. 327. Lenin asked for the "unification *only* of those states that have gone over or are in the process of going over to socialism, colonies that have liberated themselves, etc." The communists, he went on to say, "want the largest possible state, the closest possible union, the greatest possible number of working people from the various nations to join in the struggle of the proletariat" ("A Contribution to the Revision of the Party Platform," vol. 21, pp. 316–317). In short, he demanded a free but centralized federation of socialist nations, including "colonies that have liberated themselves, etc." At the same time he tended to assume that such a free federation or fusion of anti-imperialist states would inevitably emerge from socialist and colonial revolutions.

ment and indignation.[13] Finally, there were troubling situations
in the Ukraine, in Georgia, and in other fringe areas of Russia,
where local communist parties during the Civil War were
sharply divided over the problem of their relationship to Russia
and the Russian party. In a very revealing letter that Lenin
wrote "to the workers and peasants of the Ukraine on the occasion of the victory over Denikin," he tried to resolve these difficulties, but at the same time he showed how clearly he recognized them. Modifying his sweeping demand for "national self-
determination," he wrote that, indeed, this slogan must be accepted by every Russian Bolshevik, but that in the mouth of a
Ukrainian Bolshevik it was a betrayal of international principles.
Here at last was a formal recognition of the fact that the "interests" (or at least the slogans) of a given national proletariat
might come into conflict with the interests of parties across the
border.

For this reason, an attempt was made at the Eighth Party
Congress, where much time was devoted to the problem of nationalities, to modify the Leninist slogan. V. V. Osinsky tried to
circumscribe the concept of "self-determination" by specifying
that "genuine" self-determination could consist only in the establishment of a proletarian dictatorship and in voluntary federation
with Soviet Russia.[14] This scholasticism was rejected at the time
but is well in line with subsequent Soviet interpretations. Another group, headed by G. L. Piatakov, submitted a formula from
which reference to "national self-determination" was eliminated.
Their slogan called instead for the "subordination of the interests
of the proletariat of any one nation to the interests of the world-
wide fighting organization of the proletariat." [15] This slogan
made sense, particularly since such a "world-wide fighting organization" was just being set up, in the Communist International; it would have obviated the difficulties of interpreting
Lenin's formula, even though it would still have been necessary
for some central authority to determine the interests of the
world-wide fighting organization. But in Lenin's eyes the Piatakov formula undoubtedly sounded too much like the views of
Luxemburg. In any event, he clung to his own wording and kept
imposing it on the party.

THE THEORY OF THE SPARK

The principal ideas we have outlined here were formulated during the two or three years preceding the outbreak of World War I, when a succession of international crises were heralding the coming cataclysm. In any event, these theories were based on an acute awareness of the imminence of war, the outbreak of which was no surprise to the Leninist group. The breaking of the storm merely served to confirm, not only the prognoses that had been made, but also the strategic demands based on them. In particular, Lenin expected the social democratic parties of the countries at war to act in accordance to the resolutions discussed at the Basel and Stuttgart congresses. He expected, that is, the European workers and their leaders to show international solidary, to declare themselves disinterested in the war and unwilling to shoot at brother proletarians across the trenches; he thought they would be ready to turn the bayonets given them against their own governments and ruling classes. He was sorely disappointed. The majority of the social democratic representatives in all the warring nations did support the war, voted for war expenditures, declared their loyalty, and joined all other parties in swearing to a "civic peace" for the duration of hostilities. This meant the collapse of the Second International, which had rested on the international solidarity of working-class parties.

The news of this development came as such a surprise and such a shock to Lenin that it took him quite a while to be convinced that it was genuine. It left him with a profound and lasting bitterness against the moderate leaders of the European Marxist movement, who had, he felt, sold out to the bourgeoisie and were now irrevocably on the other side of the barricades; and it strengthened his stubborn determination to pursue his strategy of revolutionary defeatism nevertheless, with the aim of converting the imperialist war into a civil war. More than ever he was convinced that the moderation of European Marxist leaders was not representative of the true feelings of the workers, who he thought were far more revolutionary and far more defeatist in sentiment than their "betrayers."

As we have already mentioned in brief, the coming bourgeois revolution in Russia was a possible key, for Lenin, to the transformation of the international war into a world-wide civil war. He thought that it might develop immediately into a proletarian revolution, given certain favorable circumstances. This is what we have called his "theory of the spark." Lenin admitted that the Russian proletariat by itself would never be able to achieve socialism, which, after all, could only arise on the basis of the most advanced industrial economy. He went so far as to acknowledge that not even a national democratic revolution could succeed in Russia unless it were supported by a simultaneous revolt of the Western proletariat against Western imperialism. His view of the Russian revolution as the spark that would ignite the fire of a world-wide (this really means European) proletarian revolution was the means by which this seemingly vicious circle could be broken. The Russian revolution, a democratic one, would set off a world-wide chain reaction of proletarian revolutions, and the inevitable victory of socialism in the West would compel Russia to adjust herself to a socialist world by becoming socialist herself. Moreover, she would be economically helped by the friendly socialist regimes of Europe.*

Our task is to discover the reasoning behind this theory of the spark, which is of such crucial importance in the understanding of Leninism. Unhappily, this theory, like so many of his cardinal concepts, he never developed systematically. Its formulation

---

* In this form the idea was first expressed in 1907 (see "The Agrarian Program of Social Democracy in the First Russian Revolution, 1905–1907," Lenin, vol. 11, pp. 418–419; translation in Selected Works, vol. 3, pp. 237–239). As a desideratum, however, Lenin had conceived it earlier. Thus in 1906 he wrote that a revolution in Europe would serve to strengthen reaction in Russia, and because of Russia's great influence as the major bastion of reaction this was considered extremely dangerous. The danger could be obviated if the Russian workers could lead the proletariat of the more advanced nations in making revolution. In this sense, the proletarian revolution in Russia would be the precondition for a proletarian revolution in Europe ("Two Tactics of Social Democracy in the Democratic Revolution," vol. 8, pp. 83ff; translation in Selected Works, vol. 3, pp. 97ff). Marx and Engels had stated that a revolution could create socialism in Russia only "if the Russian revolution becomes a signal for the workers' revolution in the West, so that the one supplements the other" (Marx and Engels, Selected Correspondence, New York, 1936, p. 355).

must therefore be distilled from innumerable scattered pronouncements in books, pamphlets, speeches, letters, and conver-
sations. The main arguments can be found in the cluster of articles and speeches grouped around his famous book on "imperialism" and written between 1915 and 1917. In them, Russia was
seen as a "semicolonial" country, exploited by Western imperialism. Russian industrial enterprise was in fact largely financed by
the West; to a great extent it represented French, Belgian, German, and British investments. The tsarist government, furthermore, had been able to meet its financial obligations only with
the help of foreign loans, mostly French and Belgian. In the eyes
of Lenin, both tsarism and Russian capitalism were thus heavily
in debt to the West, and had become agents and tools of Western
imperialism. A rebellion against tsarism would therefore be not
only a strike against an important ally or satellite of the so-called
imperialist nations, but also a direct economic blow against
Western capital. In both aspects, it would be an attack against
world imperialism, through its "weakest link."

Another argument underlying the theory of the spark was this:
Lenin and his followers saw tsarist Russia as the protector of
reaction in Europe. The overthrow of this reactionary regime
would therefore be a death blow to those forces in Europe which
Marxists classified as reactionary, and would by the same token
free the Western proletariat for the socialist revolution. The conception of Russia as the bastion of reaction was familiar to all
liberals and radicals in nineteenth-century Europe. It dates back
to the time of the Holy Alliance, when Alexander I and later
Nicholas I became Metternich's most faithful allies, when liberal
and national movements throughout Europe were crushed under
the powerful heel of the Russian soldier, and the Russian emperor was known as the "gendarme of Europe." With the wisdom
of hindsight we can say today that this view of Russia was erro-
neous, because it was based on an overestimation of her power.
The Russian state was weak internally, and could ill afford frit-
tering away its forces in foreign adventures. Yet the legend of its
invincible strength was kept alive for decades by the memory of
Russian victories over Napoleon, and it persisted even after the
Crimean War, which certainly should have revealed the feet of

clay on which the Russian colossus was standing. We see it crop
up in the writings of Marx;* traces of it can be found in Lenin's
earliest works;[16] and it is expressed most clearly in a passage
written by Trotsky for the first issue of the journal *Communist
International,* where he proclaims triumphantly: "The working
class of the entire world has conquered *the most impregnable
fortress — former tsarist Russia —* from its enemies. With that as
its base, it is uniting its forces for the last decisive battle." [17] This
view of Russia obviously contradicts Lenin's concept of Russia
as the weakest link of imperialism. We have here one of the
many examples of how Lenin found a number of conflicting
arguments to support a position that may, in fact, have been
derived from none of them.

The outbreak of World War I had, in Lenin's eyes, created a
revolutionary situation. Given such a situation, he firmly believed
that an immediate chain reaction would follow a Russian revolution. For, as he wrote in 1918, "it is obligatory for a Marxist to
count on a European revolution if a *revolutionary situation* is at
hand." [18] The endorsement of war aims and war measures by the
European socialist leaders did not convince him of the contrary.
Instead, he differentiated sharply between the European proletariat and its leaders: The former, he maintained, had not lost
its revolutionary spirit; on the contrary, the war had made it
more acute. It was only the upper layer of the party and trade-
union hierarchies which had turned bourgeois and betrayed the
movement. Fifteen months after the collapse of the Second International, Lenin could therefore write with confidence:

To the question what the party of the proletariat would do if a
revolution were to put it in power during the current war, we
answer: We should propose peace *to all* countries at war on the
condition that the colonies and *all* dependent, oppressed, and under-

---

* For instance, it is the argument behind his enthusiastic support of the
Polish revolt of 1863, in which he saw a chance of isolating Russia from
Europe and thereby freeing the European workers' movements from Russia's
reactionary influence — a *cordon sanitaire* concept that was applied far
more successfully *against* the revolution when finally it broke out in Russia.
For a collection of Marxian pronouncements on Russia as the bastion of
reaction, see Marx and Engels, *The Russian Menace to Europe,* edited by
Bert F. Hoselitz and Paul Blackstock (Glencoe, Ill., 1952).

privileged peoples be liberated. Given their present governments, neither Germany nor England nor France would accept that condition. In that case we should have to prepare and undertake revolutionary war, that is, not only should we fully carry through in the most decisive ways our entire minimum program, but we should systematically begin to draw into revolt all peoples now oppressed by the Great Russians, all colonies and dependent countries of Asia (India, China, Persia, and so on), and also — and primarily — the socialist proletariat of Europe, against its governments and in spite of its social chauvinists. Beyond any doubt, the victory of the proletariat in Russia would provide unusually favorable conditions for the development of the revolution in Asia as well as in Europe. *Even* the year 1905 has proven that. And the international solidarity of the revolutionary proletariat is a *fact*, the dirty scum of opportunism and social chauvinism notwithstanding.[19]

At the very moment of the seizure of power in Russia, Lenin justified the October Revolution by just these arguments. The world revolution was approaching. Until its consummation, the revolutionary regime of Russia would have to hold out against a momentary onslaught by the entire world. But this would collapse at once, and the regime would survive. "The congress of Soviets is convinced that the revolutionary army will be able to defend the revolution against all and any encroachments of imperialism, until the new government succeeds in bringing about the conclusion of that democratic peace which it will at once offer to all nations." [20] This democratic peace was to be concluded with the regimes set up by brother proletarians in the West. Today, almost forty years after the words were spoken, it has not yet transpired.

Chapter **8**

Eight Months of Revolution

The overthrow of bourgeois counterrevolution can be accomplished by nothing and by no power except the revolutionary proletariat. The revolutionary proletariat . . . by itself must seize the power of state in its own hands — outside of that the victory of the revolution is impossible.

LENIN

During the war Lenin lived in exile in Switzerland, and although he tried to keep busy in revolutionary organization and congresses, his isolation from Russia and the smallness of the number of social democrats who joined him in his fight against "defensism" convinced him at times that he was swimming against the stream, that his followers constituted but a small and powerless sect, and that the likelihood of his ever seeing another Russian revolution was small indeed. But then the revolution did break out. When the first news of it reached Lenin, he hailed it as the bourgeois revolution which he had for so long demanded and predicted. The overthrow of tsarism, he thought, had been accomplished by the revolutionary wing of the bourgeoisie, led by the industrial proletariat, and against the will of the reactionary bourgeoisie, who would have preferred to save the monarchy.[1] In Lenin's opinion, the course of the revolution in its first days conformed to his more recent pessimistic prognoses: the masses had revolted, and the capitalists had reaped the benefits of the workingmen's efforts, only to betray the revolution forthwith. "Dear A. M.," he started his first comment on the news, a letter to Alexandra Kollontai, "We have just received the first government telegrams about the revolution of March 1 (14) in Peter [slang for St. Petersburg]. A week of bloody battles on the part of the workers, and Miliukov plus Guchkov plus Kerensky* in power!! True to the 'old' European pattern . . ." And, a short paragraph later: "All our slogans remain the same. In the last issue of the *Social Democrat* we spoke directly about the possibility of a government of Miliukov with Guchkov, if not Miliukov with Kerensky. The one as well as the other has come true: it is all three together. Charming!"

"All our slogans remain the same." This was no less than a command directed to the party's underground organization in Russia. In his subsequent comments[2] Lenin buttressed this command with as good an analysis of the events and their consequences as his information permitted him to make. What had happened in Russia in the past few days, he wrote, was the bourgeois revolution. Although the bourgeoisie was still dickering with the dynasty in an effort to restore it to power, tsarism had been overthrown, at least for the time being. The forces now operating in Russian society were three. First of all, there was tsarism and the old bureaucracy, striving for a restoration. Then there was the bourgeoisie, represented by the Octobrists and Cadets, whose chief aim was to maintain "order," which really meant the maintenance of their property and privileges. To this end they were ready, he thought, to come to agreements with tsarism, as long as there was any hope of restoring it. Third, there were the masses, spontaneously organizing themselves into soviets. Their aim was the radical democratic revolution, or, to put it differently, they were striving to carry the accomplished revolution to its logical conclusion. Lenin realized that the revo-

---

* P. N. Miliukov was a leader of the Cadet party and Foreign Minister in the Provisional Government until his resignation in May 1917. A. I. Guchkov was a leading Octobrist and War Minister in the Provisional Government until his resignation in May 1917. A. I. Kerensky was a prominent spokesman of the "Toilers" group, a peasant party forming the right wing of the socialist revolutionaries. He was the only member of one of the revolutionary parties who joined the Provisional Government at once. From the Ministry of Justice he moved to the War Ministry and became Premier in July.

lution had barely begun its course, that the swift overthrow of the Romanov dynasty was but a prelude. For the time being, the bourgeois parties had come to power, but, simultaneously with the establishment of the Provisional Government, another force had emerged representing a potential alternative government. This force was the soviets, the revolutionary organization of the masses. To organize and strengthen this prospective government, with a view toward overthrowing the Provisional Government, was the first task of the proletariat. Undoubtedly, the capitalist regime could not last.

Under certain circumstances, those most favorable to it, the new government can delay its collapse somewhat if it marshals all the organizational means at the disposal of the entire Russian bourgeoisie and the bourgeois intelligentsia. But even in that case it is *in no position* to escape collapse, for it is impossible to tear ourselves out of the claws of that terrible monster begotten by world capitalism — the imperialist war and the famine — without leaving the soil of bourgeois relations, without going over to revolutionary methods, without appealing to the greatest historical heroism of the proletariat in Russia and the whole world.

Hence my conclusion: we shall probably not be able to overthrow the new government with one stroke; but if we are able to do so (in times of revolution the bounds of the possible are extended thousandfold), then we can not hold on to power *without putting up* against the magnificent organization of the entire Russian bourgeoisie and bourgeois intelligentsia an equally magnificent *organization of the proletariat,* which is to be the leader of the entire vast masses of the urban and rural poor, the semiproletarians and small landholders.[3]

Lenin thought that the next step in the Russian revolution should be the establishment of his long-advocated "revolutionary democratic workers' and peasants' dictatorship," a "people's state," as he more and more preferred to call it, or, a state run by "all the poorest sections of the population" under the effective leadership of the proletariat.[4] This "people's state," he emphasized, would be that democratic regime which precedes the dictatorship of the proletariat and is but a necessary means to the attainment of the latter. In short, it was still the minimum program,[5] a thoroughly negative objective in that it meant nothing but the complete and irreversible smashing of the old order. During this interim state, the masses would be sovereign, though only for a while. For, he added shortly after his return to Russia, the people's state would give way immediately to newly developing contradictions.[6]

Lenin obviously wished to point out the ephemeral nature of the people's state in order to remind his followers of the larger tasks that would follow immediately upon its establishment. While still in Switzerland, he had sketched some of the features that would characterize the mass regime. These features were copied from the Paris Commune of 1871, or, rather, from the comments on this commune written by Marx and Engels.[7] Lenin demanded the establishment of a workers' and peasants' militia to take the place of the regular army and police. He called for the abolition of all privileges due to property differences: the rich, he wrote, should not drink milk so long as a single poor child went without; they should not have spacious quarters so long as any one of the poor still needed shelter. Measures of this sort would lead directly toward socialism.

In connection with the peasant revolution and on the basis of it, further steps of the proletariat, allied with the *poorest* section of the peasantry, are both possible and necessary, steps which are directed toward the *control* of production and of the distribution of the most important products, toward the introduction of a "universal labor service," and so forth. These steps are quite inevitably prescribed by those conditions which the war has created and which the postwar aftermath will make even more acute in many respects; and, in their totality as well as in their further development, these steps would be a transition to socialism, which cannot be realized in Russia immediately, with one stroke, without transitional measures, but which is perfectly feasible and scientifically necessary as a result of such transitional measures.[8]

At the same time, Lenin warned against attempts to classify actual events and untested strategies with any amount of theoretical rigidity. The situation was so fluid that theory could easily become a hindrance to courageous action. Why squabble about a strict definition of the coming revolutionary measures? "It is not our concern now how to classify them correctly. It would be the biggest mistake if we started to put complex, urgent, and swiftly developing practical tasks of the revolution on the Procrustean bed of narrowly conceived 'theory,' instead of seeing in theory primarily a guide to action." [9] With this passage, written a few days after the beginning of the revolution, Lenin abandoned himself to the unconditional quest for power. He no longer troubled to ask for what purpose that power was to be used; this question could wait until it had been secured. In the meantime, preoccupation with such theoretical problems was considered a waste of time and an intellectual burden with which the revolutionary activist should dispense. This strong aversion to theory at a time when the party could *act* prevailed throughout the revolutionary months of 1917. Lenin did indeed continue to talk in theoretical terms, inventing new slogans, analyzing and again analyzing the shifting constellations of the current moment. But as soon as his thoughts went beyond the immediate situation and the momentary strategy, his ideas were marked by a utopian character, a lack of political realism, which is quite untypical of Lenin and sets off the months of revolution in 1917 as an unprecedented period in the development of his thought. Quite obviously he was carried away by the glorious opportunity to act and to seize power. On the one hand, this made him impatient with theory; on the other hand, it caused him to surrender to the most fanciful notions about the coming world revolution and the immediate dawn of a new Golden Age. His ideas, usually marked by a good deal of realism, both in assessing the "current moment" and in making plans for the future, now became both utopian and ideological — witness his fanciful dreams about the coming "people's state" (to be discussed later) and his theory of the spark, which, based on little evidence, was an ideological justification for the seizure of power.

Lenin's preoccupation with the problem of seizing power caused him to be absorbed in political problems per se. He seemed to think that political action solved all problems, and, for the first time, he wrote a book dealing with the Marxist theory of the state.[10] Even where he seemed to discuss the problem of how power should be used, he evaded it in fact. In April 1917, his report on the current moment contained the following remarks:

We are all agreed that power should be in the hands of the Soviets of Workers and Soldiers Deputies. But what can and should they do in case power goes to them . . . ? And if we are talking about the transfer of power, there appears a danger that has played a large role in previous revolutions: the revolutionary class takes state power into its own hands and does not know what to do with it.

But, in discussing what the soviets should do once power fell into their hands, he did not discuss the changes (if any) in the relations of production which the soviet regime should wreak; instead, he talked about the commune-type state, with its popular militia and other much-discussed features. He expressly dismissed any talk about "introducing socialism," and was concerned only with the replacement of old state organs with new, proletarian institutions. "Marx has said that this constitutes a very big forward step of the entire world movement of the proletariat." *

An additional reason for Lenin's impatience with theory was, perhaps, the fact that not all events of the early revolutionary days had conformed to his previous expectations. Lenin had believed in the revolutionary radicalism of the Russian petty bourgeoisie. He could hardly believe that the soviet which had sprung up in Petrograd was not attempting to overthrow the Provisional Government, that it had, on the contrary, made an agreement — however shaky and conditional — with the latter,

---

* Lenin, vol. 22, p. 248 (translation in *Collected Works*, vol. 20, book 1, p. 281). Lenin went on to say that the soviets should "seize power not for the creation of the usual bourgeois republic nor for the immediate transition to socialism. That cannot be. For what then? They must seize power in order to take the first concrete steps to that transition which can and must be taken. Fear is the main enemy in this respect. We must preach to the masses that these steps must be taken now, or else the power of the soviets . . . will be meaningless and will give nothing to the people." And what steps did Lenin suggest be taken? They consisted of nationalizing land and the sugar syndicate, preaching socialism through practical methods, such as aid to the peasants by socialist state banks, and giving the soviets administrative tasks to do. As long as the soviets survive, he said, they will develop. On the other hand, "if a bourgeois republic were required, that could be done by the Cadets too." Lenin concluded with the following words: "The full success of these steps is possible only in connection with a world revolution, if that revolution will end the war, and if the workers in all countries support the revolution; therefore [sic!] the seizure of power is the only concrete measure and the only way out."

by which it had, in Lenin's opinion, relinquished power to the bourgeoisie voluntarily. This seemed so preposterous to him that he thought at first it might be the fabrication of bourgeois propaganda.[11] Confirmation came soon, however, and Lenin, as was his custom, attempted to make a new estimate of the situation and to formulate a new strategy befitting the changes that had taken place. He now characterized the situation as a curious merger of two revolutions, something akin to Trotsky's idea of the telescoping of both. Two revolutions had occurred at the same time, and each had created its own organ of government. The old Duma parties, representing property, had created the Provisional Government, while the democratic dictatorship of the masses had its organ in the soviet. These two governments existed side by side in what Lenin called a "diarchy." Prussian democracy and American democracy (which he was gradually coming to call the "commune state") had been created simultaneously. As he put it, "in the measure as these soviets exist, and *in the measure* as they constitute authority, in that measure a state of the Paris Commune *type* does exist in Russia." [12] But the forces behind that commune state had voluntarily, and, Lenin thought, without any reason, capitulated to the Duma bloc. Instead of seizing power and ousting the capitalists, the soviet was lending its power to the maintenance of an actually powerless group of liberal politicians, whose main interest lay in taming the revolution as quickly as possible. Hence Lenin continued the passage just quoted by writing, "I emphasized 'in the measure.' For what we have here is only the promise of authority. It itself *has betrayed and still is betraying* its position to the bourgeoisie through outright agreements with the bourgeois Provisional Government as well as through a number of practical concessions." [13] He then went on to search for the reasons behind this development. Why, he asked, had the petty bourgeoisie betrayed the revolution? "Because Chkheidze, Tsereteli, Steklov & Co.* are making 'mistakes'?

---

* N. S. Chkheidze was a prominent Georgian Menshevik, Chairman of the Petrograd Soviet, and Minister of Labor in Kerensky's cabinet. Irakli Tsereteli was another prominent Georgian Menshevik, and also Minister for Post and Telegraph in Kerensky's cabinet. Y. M. Steklov was a less important Menshevik, who soon after the October Revolution joined the Bolsheviks and rose to high party offices.

Nonsense! Only a Philistine thinks that way, not a Marxist. The cause is the *insufficient consciousness* and state of organization of proletarians and peasants." The "mistake" or, rather, misdeed of the Menshevik and socialist revolutionary leaders, he concluded, consisted only in that they had befogged the consciousness of the masses instead of awakening it.[14]

The practical conclusion to be drawn from this seemed obvious. It amounted to the abandonment, henceforth, of all faith in the petty bourgeois masses.* They deserved the trust of the proletariat no longer. In Switzerland, Lenin had already asked himself whether the masses would marshal enough consciousness, heroism, and energy for the task of organizing the next revolution. He had answered that it would be idle to make a guess about it, since practical experience would have to answer that question.[15] Yet his strategy then had been based on the implicit assumption that these qualities were present in the masses. Only failure would convince him that his premises had been overly optimistic, and this failure had now occurred.

Hence optimism was abandoned for the time being. With this step, the old Marxist and Leninist argument that the bourgeoisie was unable to carry out the bourgeois revolution in Russia was carried further: the petty bourgeois masses, hitherto deemed a revolutionary force, were now regarded as an unreliable ally, unable or unwilling to revolt. By thus betraying its own cause, the petty bourgeoisie had, Lenin thought, compelled the proletariat to take up the cause of the radical bourgeois revolution alone. The working class, he maintained, should now cancel its alliance with the peasantry. It should make a sharp separation in strategy and in organization, in order to manifest its own unerring revolutionary aspirations. In place of the old constellation of classes that Lenin had claimed constituted Russian society

* It would be impossible to say precisely whom Lenin had in mind at this time when speaking of the petty bourgeoisie. In general, he meant the peasantry. But, certainly, he also included all the moderate leaders of the "soviet" parties. Consequently it appears that by 1917 the term "petty bourgeoisie" vaguely included all socialists (whether workers, peasants, or intellectuals) who disagreed with him, whereas the term "proletariat" referred to the party which in his opinion was the only true representative of the working class, namely, his own Bolsheviks.

(the tsarist reactionaries, the bourgeoisie, and the revolutionary masses), a new constellation was formed, composed of four distinct political groups: (1) the group to the right of the Cadets, representing the most reactionary classes; (2) the Cadets, the party of the bourgeoisie; (3) the "soviet" parties, representing the petty bourgeoisie "and also sections of workers who have submitted to the influence of the petty bourgeoisie"; and (4) the Bolsheviks, the party of all class-conscious proletarians, wage slaves, and rural semiproletarians.[16] Lenin thus wished to demonstrate and dramatize the gulf that had opened between the "soviet" parties and the "class-conscious proletariat." For the same reason, he insisted on scrapping his own slogan calling for the revolutionary democratic dictatorship of workers and peasants. Since this slogan presupposed revolutionary activism on the part of the peasantry, it had now become illusory. For, as he said at the party's stormy April Conference, at which he tried successfully to have his new views adopted as the official party line, "we cannot be convinced that the peasants will go further than the bourgeoisie; and it would be without foundation if we were to express our faith in the peasantry, especially now that it has turned toward imperialism and defensism . . ." [17]

Lenin shocked the party leaders by stating flatly that "the bourgeois or bourgeois democratic revolution in Russia has been completed," [18] even though the agrarian revolution, supposedly inseparably connected with it, had not yet taken place. He pleaded for flexibility as a Marxist virtue and philosophized that life is stronger than abstract formulas. With all the sarcasm he could muster he blasted those "old Bolsheviks" who lived in the past and could not adjust their strategy to new developments. In the old scheme, he summed up, the revolutionary democratic dictatorship of the masses was supposed to follow the reign of the bourgeoisie. Actually, the two had occurred together, and the former had voluntarily relinquished its power to the latter. Hence, even though the agrarian revolution was still possible, the party could no longer rely on it as an aid to the proletarian struggle; instead, it should beware of possible deals between the peasantry and the bourgeoisie, even in case of an agrarian revolution.[19]

These arguments, voiced in March and April of 1917, immediately after his dramatic return from Switzerland, came as a rude shock to the vast majority of Bolshevik leaders. Prior to his return, the party line they formulated had hardly differed from that of the Mensheviks, especially in its attitude to the Provisional Government, to the soviets, to the further pursuit of the war, and to the immediate objectives of the revolution in general. Vigorous efforts were required of Lenin, who hammered his own views into the minds of his followers through a whole series of stormy debates, to convince his comrades that ten-year-old slogans had suddenly become obsolete.

In theory, the deep rift in the party symbolized a contest between Lenin's old views and the radical theory of permanent revolution; in strategy, between the caution of the old party organizers and the incoming militants. Still, if the new slogans are compared with Lenin's former views, the issue can also be seen as a petty squabble over terminology. The slogan "All power to the soviets" still meant no more than a demand for the completion of the bourgeois revolution, for the establishment of mass democracy, which could then be followed by a state in which the proletariat would eliminate the influence of the petty bourgeoisie.[20] True, Lenin's assumptions concerning the revolutionary spirit of the peasants had been revised, and only the proletariat remained in his revolutionary order of battle. But, then, he had never believed the petty bourgeoisie to be fully reliable, and he had always advocated firm proletarian leadership over it. Nor did his cancellation of the alliance with the peasantry mean that he gave up his belief in the necessity for an agrarian revolution. "We do want the peasantry to go further than the bourgeoisie, and to take the land from the squires, . . ." he said at the April Conference,[21] because "the conscious workers must win a majority over to their side if they want to come to power." [22] The call for "all power to the soviets" was therefore nothing but a demand that the petty bourgeoisie reverse its action of February and renounce its surrender to the bourgeoisie. In spite of the fact that his optimistic assumptions had proven fallacious, Lenin still believed that, given a good party organization, the swing of the peasant toward renewed political activism

would be only a matter of time, since time would confound the
masses' petty bourgeois illusions. All that was needed to win the
sympathy of the masses was an agitation and propaganda fight
by the Bolsheviks. Let us be careful, Lenin warned his comrades, lest we plunge into revolutionary adventures before the
masses are behind us. The soviets must seize power, but, as long
as they are dominated by moderate leaders, "there is nothing we
can do about it. We can only patiently, insistently, and systematically explain the error of their tactics. As long as we are
in the minority, we perform the work of criticism, in order to
save the masses from their error. We do not want the masses to
believe us on our word. We are no charlatans. We want the
masses to save themselves from their mistakes, through *experience*." [23] In essence, he felt that the deal between the peasantry
and the bourgeoisie, disturbing as it was, could not last long;
and he proposed to do his utmost to speed the break-up of their
alliance.

As Lenin had always hoped and expected, the bourgeois Provisional Government and the moderate soviet leaders did much
to accelerate this break. By their insistence on pursuing the unpopular war to the bitter end, and by their policy of inaction or
procrastination in matters of undisputed urgency, such as the
convocation of a constituent assembly and the long-overdue land
reform,* the forces of moderation contributed to the growing
Bolshevization of the masses, who were impatient for radical
action and demonstrated this impatience by taking matters into
their own hands. The peasants began to seize the squires' estates
and divide the land among themselves. The peasant soldiers,
fearful lest they be left out, voted for peace "with their feet" in
a growing wave of desertions. They showed themselves unim-
pressed by faithfulness to democratic principles, on the grounds
of which the Provisional Government hesitated to take action.
Instead, they were ready to follow any leader who professed a
willingness to act, and they found such leaders in Lenin's party,

* In part, the hesitation and procrastination of the Provisional Government
reflected their unwillingness to violate principles of legality, constitutional
procedure, and democracy. At the same time, it was without doubt also a
matter of political fence-sitting.

which incorporated all the most sweeping demands of the urban and rural masses in its platform of slogans. Indeed, by the early summer months, Petrograd had grown more radical, or at least more impatient for radical action, than Lenin himself desired. During the first days of July, spontaneous riots and disorders broke out in the capital, in which the slogan "All power to the soviets" was shouted most persistently. These "July Days" came on the heels of the abortive Brusilov offensive in Galicia; they were in part provoked not by the failure of the offensive itself, but by the transfer of troops to the front which had preceded it. A cabinet crisis in the Provisional Government helped to precipitate the disorders.[24]

An utter lack of direction in the riots was chiefly responsible for the failure of what Lenin called this "play at revolution." In addition, some regiments remained loyal to the Provisional Government, and, finally, a timely propaganda campaign designed to "smear" Lenin as a German spy assured the immediate collapse of the revolt by turning public opinion decidedly against the Bolsheviks. The riots had been undertaken against the advice of the party, which feared that premature actions of this sort might only provoke counterrevolution and which would, rather have chosen a more propitious moment for the overthrow of the Provisional Government. But, true to the tradition of 1871 and December 1905, Lenin, against his own better judgment, placed his party at the head of the revolt though it appeared doomed to fail. Yet the very failure of the July uprising may have sped up the revolutionary process and turned it in an even more radical direction. For the counterrevolutionary currents that rose up in reaction to the revolt, taking the form of an abortive *Putsch* by General Kornilov, were not strong enough to crush the masses' radicalism; they were only sufficient to drive even more workers and peasants into the arms of the Bolsheviks.

In the aftermath of the riots, the Provisional Government took repressive measures designed to curb the activities of Lenin's party. Workers were shot, Bolshevik establishments were raided and looted, party leaders were thrown in jail, and the party itself was outlawed. At the time these measures were taken, the members of the moderate left (Mensheviks and socialist revolutionaries) who were members of the cabinet remained in the government. In the eyes of Lenin and his followers they thereby identified themselves with these measures, and the moderate left was therefore, from that moment, identified with counterrevolution. This, Lenin concluded, gave the entire revolution a new turn, and this turn was more radical than were his previous policies. In brief, Lenin after the "July Days" called for the establishment of the dictatorship of the proletariat.

In arguing for this new policy, he began by reviewing previous developments. From February to July of 1917, he wrote, power had been in the balance.

It was divided, by common, voluntary agreement, among the Provisional Government and the soviets. The soviets constituted delegations from the masses of free (that is, not subject to any external coercion) and armed workers and soldiers. Arms in the hands of the people and the absence of external coercion over the people — that was the *essence* of the situation. That was what guaranteed a peaceful road of progress for the entire revolution. The slogan "All power to the soviets" was the slogan of the next step, an immediately feasible step, on this peaceful road of revolution. It was the slogan of peaceful development, which from 27 February to 4 July was still possible and, of course, most desirable, and which is now absolutely impossible.[25]

He went on to explain why this situation had promised a peaceful development of the revolution. There were, he claimed, no forces at the time which could have prevented the transfer of all power to the soviets, so that the ouster of the Provisional Government would have provoked neither civil war nor bloodshed. Furthermore, the subsequent class struggle *within* the soviets would have taken on a more peaceful character after such a coup. "The soviets . . . were organs of the movement of workers and peasants. Once in power, the chief deficiencies and the chief sin of the petty bourgeois sections, their trustful attitude toward the capitalists, would have been eliminated through practice, would have been criticized by the experience of their own measures."[26]

But after July 4, 1917, continued Lenin, power could no longer be seized peacefully; now there would have to be an armed up-

rising. The slogan "All power to the soviets" was dated. For the
soviet parties, as parties, had played the last of their revolutionary role. They had completed the cycle from democratic
revolutionism to silent or open support of the military counterrevolution. Hence the class-conscious proletarian could no longer
collaborate with them in the peaceful transfer of power to the
masses. The actual seizure of power, Lenin insisted, could of
course be accomplished only with the support of the masses, and
the task of weaning them away from their counterrevolutionary
leaders faced the proletariat as before. But the coming mass
uprising should not give power to the masses, as previous slogans
had envisaged, but to the proletariat alone. "The overthrow of
bourgeois counterrevolution can be accomplished by nothing and
by no power except the revolutionary proletariat. The revolutionary proletariat . . . by itself must seize the power of state
in its own hands — outside of that the victory of the revolution
is impossible. Power to the proletariat, support of it by the
poorest peasantry or semiproletariat — that is the only way
out . . ." * When the time for this new uprising approached
(and he warned that the moment for it must be well chosen, to
coincide with the peak of the revolutionary enthusiasm of the

---

* "On Slogans," Lenin, vol. 21, pp. 37–38 (translation in *Collected Works,*
vol. 21, book 1, pp. 48–50). At the same time Lenin admitted even as
late as October 10 that a more peaceful form of proletarian revolution was
still possible, if the moderate parties would agree to the overthrow of the
Provisional Government. The alternative, he wrote, would be civil war; for
the proletariat "will not halt before any sacrifices to save the revolution"
("The Tasks of the Revolution," Lenin, vol. 21, pp. 227–228; translation
in *Collected Works,* vol. 21, book 1, pp. 263–264).

Two months earlier, immediately after the failure of the Kornilov
putsch, Lenin had gone even further. In an article entitled "On Compromises," he had offered the moderate parties an alliance. If you accept
our support, he wrote, we shall honestly aid you in establishing a government composed of your two parties, and responsible only to the soviets —
"honestly" in the sense that we shall not demand the immediate transformation of such a government into a proletarian dictatorship. Here we have the
first precursor of the Popular Front policy pursued by communist parties
in the 1930's. The precursor was stillborn, however. By the time the article
went into print, a few days after it had been written, it was accompanied
by a postscript saying that further developments had made the offer of
such a compromise obsolete (Lenin, vol. 21, pp. 132–136; translation in
Collected Works, vol. 21, book 1, pp. 152–157).

masses), the slogan "All power to the soviets" would once again become acceptable. For the soviets would become the organizational form of the mass uprising as soon as they had cleansed themselves of their moderate leaders. "Soviets can and must make their appearance in that new revolution, but not the *present* soviets. . . . Even then we shall advocate the organization of the entire state according to the soviet pattern, that is true. I am not discussing soviets in general but am talking about the struggle against the *present* counterrevolution and against the treachery of the *present* soviets." [27]

These lines were written in early July, when the riots had failed, when the prestige of the party and its leaders seemed to be at its lowest point, when Lenin himself was hiding from the police and soon to flee across the Finnish border in disguise. Two months later the soviet in Petrograd for the first time carried a Bolshevik motion by a majority, and in Moscow, too, the party was winning over the majority of the soviet. This put the seizure of power on Lenin's immediate agenda. "Having received a majority in the Soviets of Workers' and Soldiers' Deputies in both capitals," he wrote to the Central Committee from Finland, "the Bolsheviks can and must take state power in their own hands." [28] Lenin's urgent demands for immediate action met stiff resistance from those Bolshevik leaders who had remained in Petrograd, living underground, to direct the work of the party on the spot. They tried to disregard the appeals with which Lenin bombarded them from his hideout across the border, and it was only with the greatest difficulty that he made his views prevail. The arguments with which he sought to justify the seizure of power referred both to the dynamics of domestic Russian developments and to the international revolutionary situation that he presumed had been created by the war.[29] He argued that the masses in Russia were impatient for a radical solution of their problems, and that they should not be let down by the bolsheviks as they had been by the bourgeois liberals and by their own petty bourgeois leaders in 1905 and 1917, respectively. He warned that the Allies might at any moment conclude a separate peace with the Central Powers, so as to isolate the Russian revolution and enable the imperialist world to fall upon

Russia and crush her.* He devoted a lengthy article to showing
that the party, once in power, would be able to stay there.[30] His
most important argument, however, was the fact, undisputable to
him, that the seizure of power by the Bolsheviks would be supported by the vast masses of Russia's workers and peasants, and
would not be opposed by any unsurmountable forces. Even the
traditionally conservative Cossacks, Lenin wrote, would not
prevent the party this time from overthrowing the existing
government.

Lenin correctly assessed the revolutionary mood of the
common man. He approved of this mood, and he did not mean
to let it go to waste; instead, he utilized the moment of the
greatest radicalism of the masses for the overthrow of the
Provisional Government. While the population as a whole stood
by inactive, armed detachments of Bolsheviks in concerted action
swiftly moved to occupy strategic places, arsenals, centers of
communication, and strong points in Russia's capital, meeting
only sporadic resistance. In a few hours, and with almost no
bloodshed, Petrograd turned Bolshevik, and the country as a
whole quickly followed suit.

Up to the last moment, sharp warnings against the seizure of
power were raised even by Lenin's closest collaborators. Zinov'ev
and Kamenev, his two chief lieutenants, were so alarmed by
the prospect that they openly violated party discipline by publishing their divergent views in a non-Bolshevik paper.† Their
warnings referred chiefly to the international situation. Would
the Russian revolution fit into the development that the socialist

* The specter of a separate peace was also used by those who warned
against the seizure of power. Zinov'ev and Kamenev warned that it would
be precisely the proletarian revolution in Russia which would bring the
warring imperialists together in a separate peace. The result would be a
world-wide bloc of imperialist powers against a weak and isolated proletarian regime.

† Lenin at the time announced that he was breaking his friendship with
them and demanded that they be removed from the party as "scabs."
However, before very long, he himself had swung back to a more cautious,
"rightist" appraisal of the international situation. During the controversy
over the peace treaty of Brest-Litovsk, he denounced his friends on the
"left," while the "strike-breakers" Zinov'ev and Kamenev were once again
receiving his friendship and trust. For the text of their warning against
the planned seizure of power, see Lenin, vol. 21, pp. 494–498.

world revolution was about to take, or would it be an obstacle to the world revolution? Would the West join the Russian proletariat by overthrowing its own imperialist governments, or would the Russian revolution itself be jeopardized by Western failure to follow suit? Equating the October Revolution with the advent of socialism, one comrade queried, "But, once we have blown up the bridge leading to that shore, will we not remain all alone? We are not yet, after all, receiving any real support from anywhere. Western Europe is shamefully silent. You cannot decree socialism . . ." [31] Lenin angrily replied that all such warnings were unworthy of a true internationalist. For one thing, he argued, they were belied by facts that he thought were obvious: "Only a blind man can fail to see the discontent that grips the working masses in Germany and in the West. . . . The proletarian rank and file, even against the will of their leaders, are ready to withdraw at our call." [32] Whatever the facts, moreover, a true internationalist should also have faith in the world proletariat: "*We believe* in a revolution in the West," he wrote. "We know that it is inevitable, though, of course, one cannot create it by a command." [33] It is as internationalists that the Russian party members were obliged to take fullest possible advantage of the revolutionary situation that had ripened in their own country, he wrote.[34] The revolution was ripening in the West. To doubt it would be a betrayal of internationalism. Moreover, the completion of the Russian revolution would stimulate the revolution in the West.* The spark would kindle the world conflagration.

* In that spirit he spoke at the April Conference: "We are being asked, if the revolutionary class in Russia were to take power into its hands, but in the other countries there were no revolution, what were the revolutionary party to do then? What can it then be like? The following point of our resolution gives an answer to that question:
  'As long as the revolutionary class in Russia has not taken into its hands the entire power of the state, our party will by all means support those proletarian parties and groups abroad which are already during the war waging actual revolutionary warfare against their imperialist governments and their bourgeoisie.' "
(Lenin, vol. 20, p. 266; translation in *Collected Works*, vol. 20, book 1, p. 300.)
  It should be clear to the reader that Lenin here did not give a satisfactory answer to the question he had raised.

We know, of course, that it failed to do so, and we later shall consider the long-range effects that this isolation of the revolution in Russia had on Lenin's views and policies. At this point, we shall deal only with how he coped with the failure of his prognosis, a prognosis which, we must remember, had served as the major justification of his seizure of power. We see with some amazement that only two years after the revolution he had forgotten all about his theory of the spark. He chided those who condemned the seizure of power as a mistake, and said that they

actually represented a radically false and un-Marxian point of view. They forgot under what conditions, after what long and difficult developments during the Kerensky period, after what a price in enormous preparatory work in the soviets, we reached the point where . . . finally, in October, the determination and readiness to overthrow the bourgeoisie had come to full maturity among the vast masses of the working people, and, with it, the material organized force necessary therefor. *It is obvious that at that time there could not have been even a mention of anything similar on the international level.*[35]

Thus Lenin falsified his own arguments of two years before and claimed, by implication, that the revolution was made because an opportunity for it was at hand, not because it made any sense in terms of long-range or world-wide developments. At other times, however, he readily admitted that things had not gone according to expectations. Russia, he wrote in 1918, "put her faith in the international solidarity of the proletariat before the international revolution had fully ripened." [36] And at the same party congress where he denied having based his calculations on the international revolutionary situation, he not only admitted that his calculations had been wrong, but claimed that there had not even been an opportunity to calculate. "We had to grope our way all the time. But that necessity never made us hesitate, even on October 10, 1917, when the question of the seizure of power was decided. We had no doubt that, to use Trotsky's expression, we had to experiment, to make experience." [37] Similarly, five months after the October Revolution, in a speech before a congress of soviets, he surveyed the past months and remarked that the Russian revolution had in effect been a local development that took place in an international vacuum. Its swift and unexpectedly easy progress from March 1917 to March 1918 could, he thought, be explained only by the realization that "all this time it was going on independently, as it were, from international socialism." *

By implication, Lenin is here accusing himself of what he himself would have called adventurism. His actions in October 1917 should be measured against the criticism he later hurled against the left opposition, when he scolded them for their "adventurist" advocacy of revolutionary war. At that time he said that the only criterion of revolutionary action, or of any action whatever, was success. "Could we expect to overthrow world imperialism by a single application of violence, without a corresponding development of the proletariat in those imperialist countries?" he asked at a later occasion. "If we put the problem thus," he continued, "— and as Marxists we have always thought that it would have to be put thus and only thus — then an application of a policy of violence here would have been outright nonsense, an absurdity, and the utter failure to understand the conditions under which a policy of violence brings success." [38] These words could have been applied to the October Revolution. But Lenin was not ready to admit the charge of "adventurism." He claimed that it would have been a betrayal of the revolution to let it cool off. The choice in October had been between waiting for a world-wide spread of the revolutionary situation and risking a premature revolution, with the resulting difficulties. As he said in May 1918:

I know there are, of course, wise guys who consider themselves very learned and even call themselves socialists, who assure us that it was not the right thing to seize power so long as the revolution did not break out in all countries. They do not suspect that by saying so they are turning away from the revolution and are going over to the side of the bourgeoisie. To wait until the working classes make revolution on an international scale means that everybody will cool off while waiting. It is nonsense.[39]

* From a speech at the Fourth Extraordinary All-Russian Congress of Soviets, 14–16 March 1918 (Lenin, vol. 22, p. 390). This frank admission was so incomprehensible or so embarrassing to the editors of Lenin's works that they substituted the word "imperialism" for Lenin's "socialism" in the above phrase, explaining that the stenographer must have made a mistake in taking down Lenin's speech.

In short, Lenin preferred the Russian sparrow in the hand to the world-wide dove in the bush, particularly since he was convinced that it would come out of the bush in any case. Yet, in his concern for seizing power when the seizing was good, the problem of what to do with it once it was won was conveniently forgotten or pushed in the background. Only his preoccupation with the transfer of power can explain Lenin's confusion of slogans during the year 1917, a confusion that shows how impatient he was with theory and how determined on political action. While he used current myths about the probable progress of the revolution (the spark theory) to justify his actions, he was not really interested in the long-range process of revolution. He cared only for the establishment of the proletarian dictatorship, to be carried out by his party. All other bridges could be crossed when he reached them.

Some readers may be tempted to blame the moderate leaders of the peasants and workers for the radical course that the Russian revolution assumed by Lenin's coming to power. Undoubtedly, the moderates of the Provisional Government failed to solve problems that became more and more pressing in the eyes of substantial segments of the population. Political pressures developed that had to be channeled somehow if they were not to cause an explosion. A political tide was swelling which would drown all but the courageous adventurer skilled and ruthless enough to ride the dangerous waves. Yet it would have been unrealistic to expect the Provisional Government leaders to forestall the disaster. For one thing, the heaviest pressures developed in those segments of the population to which these leaders were least attuned, the segments to which Lenin had paid particular attention. Moreover, what has been said about Lenin is also true of the moderate parties: they lacked a realistic program of how to rule Russia after coming to power. This is clear not only from their performance as participants in the Provisional Government, but also from the programmatic statements of their leaders.[40] Last but not least, the adventurism and ruthlessness required of anyone who wished to ride the waves of the revolution were foreign to their pattern of thought and action. The only alternative to a Bolshevik seizure of power was the repression of the radical sections of the population by force and the imposition of some sort of dictatorship, at least for a time. To carry out these measures efficiently and thoroughly was not within the power of the moderate leaders, and it would be foolish to blame them for it. One can not expect politicians to forget the most basic principles in the name of which they fight, and the simple truth is that in the fall of 1917 liberals in Russia were out of place. The choice was between Lenin and some other dictator.

As early as 1853 Engels foresaw such a turn of events. In a letter to his friend Weydemeyer, he wrote: "I have a notion that our party, thanks to the perplexed helplessness and laxness of all others, will one nice morning be forced into government." It would then, he continued, forsake specific proletarian aims for petty bourgeois aims, since it would have to fight for its very life. At the same time, it would have to make premature "communist experiments and jumps" and would promptly "lose its head." Bloody reaction and counterreaction would follow, all to the compromise of Marxism in general. "I cannot very well see how it can come otherwise. In a backward country . . . which possesses an advanced party . . . at the first serious conflict and as soon as real danger sets in, the advanced party will come to power, and that is certainly *before* its normal time." [41]

PART THREE

Leninism in Power

Chapter 9

The Leninist State in Theory and in Practice

Work, discipline, and order will save the Soviet regime.

TROTSKY

The more backward the country in which, by virtue of the zigzags of history, the start of the socialist revolution is ordained, the more difficult is the transition from the old capitalist to socialist relations. To the tasks of destruction are added new ones of unprecedented difficulty — organizational tasks.

LENIN

THE HONEYMOON OF THE REVOLUTION

The October Revolution brought about the overthrow of all remnants of the old order. It radically destroyed the last shreds of tsarism and the old bureaucracy and relegated the landowner to the realm of dead institutions. The distribution of all gentry land among the peasants, which the Leninist seizure of power guaranteed, was as thorough as it could possibly have been. This was indeed the "bourgeois revolution" of which Lenin had spoken. It carried with it all those changes usually attributed to the complete abolition of the precapitalist order. National self-determination of Russia's many nationalities was, at least for the moment, carried to its logical conclusion, so that at first only the rump territories of Old Muscovy belonged to the new Soviet state. Legal separation of church and state, removal of the old judiciary, reform of the calendar — all these measures were within the European liberal tradition, as part of the "bourgeois revolution." This revolution was also expressed in the social institutions, in science, art, and education — in virtually all functions of public and private life. Everywhere — and this development had already begun with full vigor in the spring of 1917 — the revolution carried with it maximal freedom of expression and experimentation. Even where political liberties were soon curtailed, a certain degree of personal freedom was not extinguished for several years.

In addition, the cancellation of all foreign debts incurred by the tsarist regime was an act designed to declare the new Russia's independence from imperialist oppression. The principle of economic self-determination embodied in this defiant gesture was at once a part of the "bourgeois revolution" and something beyond it — a revolt against the old "bourgeois" order of imperialism. Here the bourgeois revolution merged with a simultaneous antibourgeois revolution. Clearly, the simple set of class labels with which Marxist historical materialism had sought to operate approached a point of collapse at this juncture. Another illustration of this is the fact that the almost anarchical liberties of the first revolutionary weeks manifested themselves in a spontaneous wave of workers' communism or syndicalism. "The destruction of all defense organs of capitalist exploitation and the appearance in their stead of organs of proletarian dictatorship unleashed the class will of the proletariat, which had up to that time been suppressed, and led to *spontaneous chaotic* moves to overcome capitalist exploitation, to a *spontaneous chaotic* proletarian *nationalization from below, . . .*" [1] The workers, without waiting for decrees, were taking over the factories of the capitalists. As a matter of fact, all order and government in Russia had collapsed, giving way to local and sectional anarchy, a naked struggle of interest groups. Thus the bourgeois revolution was accompanied not only by a number of official measures designed to lead the country toward socialism, but also by a real anarcho-syndicalism, uncontrolled, and undesired by the party. This was one factor that led to a tightening of controls and to the abandonment of anarcho-syndicalist phrases, which Lenin himself had used for a short time. Even as the threat of proletarian radicalism had driven the European bourgeoisie into the arms of the counterrevolutionary monarchy in 1848, so the ultraradicalism of Russia's urban masses now contributed to a swing to the right of the Bolshevik leaders.

Lenin's intellectual development after the October Revolution went through three principal phases of very unequal length. The phases overlap considerably; in fact, they are often nothing else than conflicting patterns of ideas running concurrently through his mind, with the emphasis shifting now to one and now to another pattern. Nonetheless, we can distinguish three phases. The first was an exuberant optimism, which saw the socialist Good Society just around the corner and expressed itself in maximal demands. The period of almost complete optimism was brief. But, even though it became severely tempered as early as the spring of 1918, and continued to be tempered more and more, optimism was never given up in principle; otherwise Lenin would have ceased being a communist. It is possible to mark off a fairly distinct second phase: a period of emergence from utopian dreams, in which a relatively realistic appraisal of trends led to ruthless terror against political opponents even within the movement, coupled with desperate and painful attempts to reconstruct the ruined country. The identity of this second phase in Lenin's ideological development is obscured by the fact that a decisive change in policy sharply divides it into two periods. This change was the abandonment of War Communism and the introduction of the New Economic Policy (NEP) in the early months of 1921. The third postrevolutionary phase can easily be overlooked, because it seldom dominated Lenin's thoughts and he rarely expressed it. It was an attitude of objective self-criticism. Not as distinct as the first two phases, this one was, admittedly, brief; it was a period of stock-taking that hinted at potential new policies. But the third phase coincided with the end of Lenin's political life. A semi-invalid, and in semiretirement from public life for the first time, Lenin in his last months began to review his own achievements with detachment. Not all he found was to his liking. Evidence that he basically reformulated his strategy is, however, only fragmentary and, at times, inconclusive.

In his pronouncements shortly before and after the October Revolution, Lenin proposed to reorganize the country into a socialist society. Political and economic tasks were to be tackled by the masses directly and collectively. The workers and poor peasants were to plan production, and, through a system of accounting and controls, supervise the execution of their plans. As he put it,

In bourgeois revolutions, the main task of the working masses consisted in doing the negative or destructive work of annihilating feudalism, monarchy, and the Middle Ages. The positive or creative work of organizing the new society was done by the property-owning bourgeois minority of the population. . . . In contrast, the main task of the proletariat and (under its leadership) the poorest peasantry in any socialist revolution — and consequently in the socialist revolution which we started in Russia on 7 November [25 October] — is the positive or creative work of laying down an extremely complex and fine network of new organizational relations, comprising the planned production and distribution of products necessary for the existence of tens of millions of people. Such a revolution can be realized successfully only with the help of the independent historical creative power of the majority of the population, especially the majority of the working people. Only if the proletariat and the poorest peasantry can muster enough consciousness, idealism, selflessness, persistence — only then will the victory of the socialist revolution be guaranteed. By creating the new soviet type of state, by thus opening the possibility for the working and oppressed masses to take an active part in independent construction of the new society, we have solved only a small part of the difficult task. The main difficulty lies in the economic sphere: socializing strictest accounting and control over the production and distribution of products everywhere, raising the productivity of labor, socializing production in fact.[2]

Whatever the difficulties of teaching socialist habits and principles to the masses, the road was nevertheless open to socialism, Lenin thought, and so he continued to think as long as he lived. In one of his last articles, he asserted this again:

What constitutes the utopian character of the plans of the old advocates of co-operation, beginning with Robert Owen? It is the fact that they dreamed of a peaceful transformation of contemporary society to socialism, without taking into account such basic questions as the class war, the conquest of political power by the working class, and the overthrow of the rule of the class of exploiters. And therefore we are right when we see in that "co-operative" socialism nothing but utopia, when we see something romantic or even stupid in the dreams of converting class enemies into class allies, and class war into class peace (so-called civic peace) merely by inculcating principles of co-operation in the population.

Without doubt, in the light of the basic task of our era we were right, for without class war for political power in the state, socialism cannot be realized.

But look how the matter has changed today: as soon as state power is in the hands of the working class, the political power of the exploiters is overthrown, and all means of production . . . are in the hands of the working class.

Today we are correct in asserting that the mere growth of co-operation is, for us, identical . . . with the growth of socialism. . . . Formerly we emphasized and had to emphasize the political struggle, revolution, the conquest of power, and so on. Today, however, the emphasis has shifted to the peaceful work of organization and "culture." [3]

In tune with his general feeling of triumph and optimism during these months, Lenin emphasized those features in the proletarian dictatorship that promised a speedy withering away of the state as an agency of class war and coercion. The beginnings of this mood can be traced back to the spring of 1917, when he viewed the coming soviet state as a new example of the Paris Commune type of state. Under the dictatorship of the masses, he wrote then, there would be more personal and political liberty than there had ever been or ever could be in the most liberal kind of bourgeois constitutional democracy. In fact, the commune state transcended the bounds of political democracy as such, being a higher sort of freedom. Lenin referred to the coming soviet state as a "new democracy," and wrote that it would "cease to be democracy, for democracy is the rule of the people, but the people-in-arms itself cannot rule over itself." [4]

By July of the same year, he had ceased to demand the

democratic dictatorship of the urban and rural masses and began, instead, to call for the establishment of a purely proletarian dictatorship. The relatively small size of the proletariat in Russia made it difficult to claim that this state would still be the epitome of democracy; and, as we have seen, Lenin himself insisted that the dictatorship of the proletariat must be called a state, for it would use force, it would organize, control, check, and punish the population, and would be an instrument of political coercion. To speak of a "free people's state" is un-Marxian nonsense, he wrote at that time. A state is a state; and so long as any state exists, a Marxist has no right to speak of freedom.[5] "The state is an institution for coercion," he wrote a few days after the seizure of power. "Formerly this was the oppression of the entire nation by a bunch of moneybags; we, however, want to transform the state into an institution for the coercion of all to act according to the will of the people. We want to organize coercion in the interests of the working people." [6]

This class content of the new dictatorship would be its justification. What counts, Lenin implied, is not the fact that the coming regime would be coercive; what counts is that this coercive state would for the first time be under the control of the vast majority of workingmen and would therefore never become bureaucratic; it would always remain an instrument to be wielded for rational purposes, and not become an end in itself. Here Lenin wrote about his bold vision of a dictatorship controlled and run by the population as a whole. In the bourgeois state, he wrote, "the civil servants, the *servants of society,* are transformed into *masters* of society." [7] But this would never happen in the proletarian dictatorship. There everyone, high or low in the civil service ranks, would be a worker receiving a workingman's salary; the workers themselves would perform the bureaucratic functions. The civil servants would be fully accountable to the people, through the device of recall and through the law making the mandates of the electorate binding upon the people's representatives. Through the device of rotation in office, everyone would get his chance to be a bureaucrat for a while; hence no one could ever become a professional bureaucrat. Lenin based these predictions on the

explicit conviction that the socialist state would entail the
utmost simplification of the functions of control, command, and
administration. It would be a push-button state, and every female
cook would get a chance to push the buttons at times.*

The proletarian dictatorship, even though designed as an
instrument of coercion, would actually coerce only a small
minority of exploiters; its institutions would be run by the
common man.

The crux of the matter is that the bourgeois state, embodying the
dictatorship of the bourgeoisie through the means of the democratic
republic, can not admit before the people that it is serving the
bourgeoisie, can not tell the truth, and is forced to be hypocritical.

But a state of the commune type, a soviet state, openly and
directly tells the people the *truth* by declaring that it is the dictatorship of the proletariat and the poorest peasantry, and by this very
truth it attracts tens and tens of millions of new citizens who are
oppressed in any one of the democratic republics, but whom the
soviets draw into political life, into democracy, into the governing
of the state.[8]

* In his "Kritik der Hegelschen Rechtsphilosophie" (MECA, part 1, vol.
1, pp. 460–461), Marx makes fun of Hegel's definition of the bureaucracy.
For one thing, Hegel had written that every citizen has the opportunity to
become a government official. This possibility, says Marx, is of a very
superficial nature. "Every Catholic has the opportunity of becoming a
priest (that is, to separate himself from the laymen and from the world).
But does this mean that the clergy is less of an otherworldly power facing
the Catholic? The fact that everyone is given an opportunity to acquire the
rights of *another* sphere proves only that *his own* sphere is not the reality of
this right . . .

"The identity which Hegel has construed between civil society and the
state is the identity of *two hostile armies* where every soldier has the
'opportunity' to become a member of the 'hostile' army through 'desertion';
and indeed Hegel thereby correctly describes the current empirical state of
affairs.

"The same applies to his treatment of 'examinations.' In a reasonable
state it ought to require an examination to become a cobbler rather than
an executive state official; for cobbling is a skill without which one can be
a good citizen, a social being, but the necessary 'state knowledge' is a
condition without which a man in a state would be living outside the state,
cut off from himself and from the air. The 'examination' is nothing but a
masonic formula, the legal recognition of citizenship, knowledge as a
privilege."

The affinity of these ideas with those expressed by Lenin in *The State
and Revolution* is very close.

This type of people's democracy was not merely postulated. The first months of Bolshevik rule were an attempt to put these anarcho-syndicalist principles into practice. In the establishment of the collegiate principle of responsibility, the Bolsheviks sought to create the political institutions of socialism. In the law of 14 November 1917, which established workers' control over industry, syndicalism was placed in the statute books of the new soviet state. At the Seventh Party Congress, in March 1918, Lenin broadened his demand for workers' control by asking for the "universalization of accounting and control over the entire production and distribution of products." [9] Significantly, however, he added that "this accounting and control shall at first be effected by the workers' organizations," and only "afterwards" by the "entire population *without exception*." [10] In theory his emphasis was still placed on eventual extension of universal control to the entire population, but in practice he was already stressing the fact that limitations had to be placed on optimistic prognoses.

At the same time, it should be noted that, during these earliest months of the regime, Lenin's boldness in decreeing socialism was accompanied by a curious reticence in real action. His actual program of economic reform was astonishingly mild. It amounted to the enactment of an eight-hour day for workers and the reorganization of the country's economy, modeled on the German war economy, though with workers' control. Lenin planned to introduce what he called "state capitalism," with nationalization held down to a minimum. As Kritsman put it,[11] the bourgeois revolution went full speed ahead to its logical conclusion, while the proletarian socialist revolution took only tentative steps. The Leninist regime started not only with a notable absence of terror and violence, but also without dealing capitalism any telling blows. Apart from wholesale legislation designed either as propaganda or as a step toward the socialist reorganization of production, effective measures of expropriation, nationalization, or socialization were resorted to only as resistance was encountered. The banks, for example, were left alone for almost two months and were seized only after they had refused to pay money to the new government. Foreign trade was not nationalized until April 23, 1918. The "class war in the village" — that is, the beginning of forcible seizures of grain — began only after the creation of the "committees of the poor" on June 11, 1918. Heavy industry and private railroads were nationalized as late as June 28 of the same year, and paragraphs 3 and 4 of the pertinent decree explicitly justified this measure as the only means of ensuring the continued operation of industry.* In short, the practical steps of converting Russia's economy to socialism were taken only under the pressure of civil war. Hence the label "War Communism." †

The political life of the country paralleled the economic. One important step, which indicated the socialist direction of the revolution, was the unceremonious dissolution of the Constituent Assembly on January 19, 1918. But for some months afterwards there was no violent terror. The nonsocialist press was not closed until the summer of the same year. The *Cheka*** began its reign of terror only after the beginning of the civil war and the attempted assassination of Lenin, and this terror is in marked contrast with the lenient treatment that White generals received immediately after the revolution.

It is interesting to speculate on the causes of this comparative inaction. The answer that Lenin and most of his followers might

* L. Kritsman, *Geroicheskii Period Velikoi Russkoi Revoliutsii* (Moscow, 1925), pp. 62–63, n. 46. Before this, expropriation of wealth chiefly took the form of official blackmail, consisting in forced tributes levied quite arbitrarily from private people of wealth. Nationalizations of individual enterprises were undertaken only as punitive measures. Paul Olberg, *Briefe aus Sowjet-Russland* (Stuttgart, 1919), p. 49, quotes the organ of the Supreme Soviet of the National Economy, *Narodnoe Khoziaistvo*, to the effect that up to March 1918, of twenty enterprises only one had been nationalized in the general social interest, the other nineteen for punitive reasons.

† The Russian term *voennyi kommunizm* is ambiguous. It can be translated simply as "war communism," in which case it implies that the measures for which the term stands were undertaken under the pressures of the civil and foreign war. But it has also been translated as "militant communism." In this case stress is laid on the militant idealism by which those wartime measures were rationalized, the implication being that the regime was sincere in its professed intention to introduce communism at once through militant radicalism.

** Abbreviation of *Chrezvychainaia Kommissiia* (Extraordinary Commission). The full name of this first political police organization serving the Soviet government was All-Russian Extraordinary Commission for the Struggle with Counterrevolution and Sabotage.

have given would be, first, that no "introduction" of socialism
had been intended,* and, second, that War Communism was
forced on the unwilling regime by the resistance of the Whites.
We can safely agree to the second reason; but, if we are correct
in taking the early decrees at their face value, the slowness with
which the Red Terror began must be explained by another
hypothesis: that Lenin, inebriated by the successful seizure and
the mass support his party had obtained, believed that communism was just around the corner and needed no help by
violent means. If we accept this theory, we can understand the
initial democratism of the new regime. Terror was considered
superfluous, since resistance came from only a negligible minority
of the population, and this resistance (given Lenin's premises)
would soon wither away. Hence it was not caution that delayed
the beginning of War Communism, with all its stringent measures
of discipline and control; it was not a case of the bourgeois
revolution running its full course while the proletarian or socialist
revolution was held back. On the contrary, the "bourgeois revolution" was allowed to run its full course just because the leaders
of the party believed that it would run directly and immediately
into socialism.†

* Lenin added the reservation that the struggle of power was still a
problem as long as foreign enemies threatened the new state ("On
Co-operation," Lenin, vol. 27, p. 396; translation in *Selected Works*, vol. 9,
p. 408). It is true that in April 1917 Lenin had warned the members of
his party's caucus at an all-Russian Conference of Soviets, "No 'introduction'
of socialism is our *immediate* task, but an immediate transition only to the
control by the Soviet of Workers' Deputies over the social production and
distribution of products" (vol. 20, p. 81; translation in *Collected Works*,
vol. 20, book 1, p. 101). But first of all, this was before the seizure
of power; and second, shortly before this seizure of power Lenin defined
socialism simply as "the continuation of capitalism under the workers'
control." With that definition in mind, it becomes apparent that he asked for
nothing else than the "introduction" of socialism as the immediate task, in
his April speech. For the definition of socialism as capitalism under workers'
control, see "Will the Bolsheviks Be Able to Maintain Themselves in
Power?" Lenin, vol. 21, pp. 256–264 (translation in *Selected Works*, vol. 6,
pp. 261–271).

† There are indications that most recent Soviet historiography is beginning
to distinguish between War Communism and a honeymoon period preceding
it, just as I am doing. Their aim is obviously to demonstrate that the
resistance of counterrevolutionary generals and foreign intervention forced
the ruthlessness of War Communism on a reluctant Lenin. While there is

This brings up the question of the sincerity of Lenin's early demands for universal control by the workers and for similar socialist measures. Lenin himself later asserted that he had never harbored such utopian dreams; he claimed that the decrees of late 1917 and early 1918 were instead propagandistic and programmatic, that they were designed to show the world what the long-range aims of the regime were, in order to serve as an inspiration to the revolutionary proletariat in other countries. William Henry Chamberlin, who accepts these arguments, adds the explanation that Lenin resorted to such propagandistic and programmatic legislation because he did not believe the regime would last; hence he wanted to put its achievements on paper, as a monument to another heroic revolutionary effort. Another explanation, implied by L. Kritsman in his book on the civil war, is that Lenin did not originally desire to decree workers' control and similar anarcho-syndicalist measures, but was forced to, in an effort to ride the waves of the spontaneous anarcho-syndicalism then rampant in the country. According to this explanation, the revolution had gone wild, and only by coming out in full support of all the *faits accomplis* could the Bolshevik government hope to tame its fury. This course of action would certainly have conformed to Lenin's traditional behavior pattern. It is most likely, however, that Lenin was neither so realistic as Chamberlin implies, nor so demagogic as the alternative theory portrays him. There are many indications that his starry-eyed legislation of the early months of his regime was fully sincere. Certainly he and his followers took these laws more seriously than he would admit later. The decrees did more than embody slogans. Some of Lenin's followers take them seriously still, just as they accept Lenin's dream of the "commune state." His book *The State and Revolution*, incongruous as it is with his realistic statements both before and after 1917, has nonetheless remained a widely known statement of intentions, against which the actual

undoubtedly a grain of truth in this, my own point is that the violence of the party's reaction to the emergency of the civil war is a result also of the utopian expectations with which the communists came to power. Had Lenin been less reckless and adventurous in his actions, less sanguine in his prognosis, there would have been neither the "honeymoon" nor the unspeakable horrors of War Communism.

achievements of the Soviet state can be measured. Needless to say, it is therefore a source of acute discomfort to party ideologists.[12]

It took only a few months of Soviet rule to convince Lenin that the communist ideal was not going to be realized immediately. With the gradual ebbing of hopes for a European revolution, not only was Leninist Russia forced to think of its own preservation as a national state; it also had to postpone the Good Society as far as domestic measures were concerned. The immediate causes for deserting socialist dreams were the exigencies of the civil war and the economic ruin following in its wake. The former required the abandonment of democratic ideals and the imposition in their stead of strict military discipline, not only on the population at large but also within the party itself, by means of the most ruthless terror. Workers' control, democratic centralism, and the people's state — all these ideals and institutions were scrapped in the grim fight for survival. The brief honeymoon of the October days gave way to the "heroic period" of the revolution, known as War Communism.

The distinction drawn here between the "honeymoon" period and the years of life-or-death struggle is not generally recognized by historians of the Russian revolution. The honeymoon, after all, was of so short a duration that it is easily forgotten or simply lumped together with the subsequent terror regime of War Communism. Moreover, it must be admitted that, throughout the period of civil war and terror, lip service was still paid to the ideals of communism, though probably less by Lenin than by some of his idealistic followers. Trotsky himself admitted years later that hopes for a speedy realization of socialism remained high for several years, based on the continuing expectation that the revolution would spread to western Europe.

Furthermore, the repressive measures devised to aid the regime during the civil war were defended by many communists as attempts to create immediately the communist or socialist society for which they had pledged their lives. Each new measure of nationalization and centralization, each new tightening of controls, was praised as the harbinger of true socialism. Lenin seized upon all manifestations of heroism and the spirit of sacrifices to show that the era of War Communism was witnessing the creation of the new, altruistic, class-conscious, socialistic proletarian.[13] As was his habit, he often mistook collaboration based on coercion for collaboration based on consent. The party, confident in the dawn of the socialist era, was drunk with a crusading spirit. As Kritsman put it:

the entire social order of the period was pervaded by a *spirit* of merciless *class exclusiveness.* . . . An exploiter, a member of one of the former ruling classes, a feudal gentleman or a capitalist was not only deprived of his former ruling position; he was put outside the pale of Soviet society, lived in hiding in its dark corners like a piece of scarcely tolerable dirt. The bourgeois had been turned into a despised and rejected creature — into a *pariah*, . . .[14]

At the same time, Lenin had to impose every step toward strengthening central control or perverting the ideals of democratic communism on his party against vigorous opposition from some of his own party comrades. These protests against the rigorous measures of War Communism were made in the name of radical democratic socialism, workers' control, soldiers' self-government, intraparty democracy, and other ideals taken primarily from Lenin's anarcho-syndicalist writings in *The State and Revolution.* His ideas of October 1917 thus served both to justify War Communism (by stirring expectations of the immediate coming of socialism) and to criticize it as violating the ideals of the Commune State. It appeared that Lenin's left-wing followers, who had been the most sanguine in their expectations, tended both to be more critical of War Communism and simultaneously to harbor greater illusions about its results. In contrast, the old-time Leninists, who had resisted Lenin in 1917, were less burdened with idealistic hopes and with squeamishness. Consequently, War Communism did not present them with such acute ideological problems.*

* Left-wing protests against the growing violation of communist ideals ranged from Lunacharsky's gesture of resigning his post as Commissar of Education (after hearing reports that historic parts of the Kremlin had been shelled and damaged during the struggle for the seizure of power in

In protesting against the perversion of democratic communism, the oppositionists within the party expressed the disappointment felt by broad sections of the population that had welcomed or assisted the Bolshevik seizure of power. Factionalism within the party thus expressed serious discontent in the population. In the end, Lenin took cognizance of this disaffected mood by changing his policy. But his first reaction was to suppress the troublesome factions within the party. At the Tenth Party Congress, in the spring of 1921, factionalism was branded as a breach of party discipline and a cause for expulsion. Thus there are a number of continuous strands linking the "honeymoon" with the period of War Communism, so that trying to separate them is of debatable value.

Finally, the difference between the two earliest phases is further obscured because the period that followed War Communism began with a decisive break in policy. Yet, in emphasizing the sharpness of the break between War Communism and the New Economic Policy, we tend to forget that they had features in common, which distinguished both of them from the brief honeymoon of late 1917 and early 1918. These two periods, and indeed the entire subsequent Soviet era, are in contrast to the anarcho-syndicalist dreams of those first few months, when the belief still prevailed that communism could be introduced by decrees.* Sharp as the break between War Communism and

---

Moscow) to large-scale opposition movements among party leaders and the mass following. Some of the major issues were the choice between revolutionary war and concluding a separate peace with Germany; the question concerning the role of trade-unions in a socialist state; the use of bourgeois "specialists" in important positions in the armed forces, the administration, and the economy; the re-establishment of officers' ranks and officers' command functions in the armed forces; the status of non-Russian nationalities within the Soviet state; and, finally, the right to dissent and opposition within the Communist Party itself. For an exhaustive account of these opposition movements and their fate, see Robert V. Daniels, *The Conscience of the Revolution* (Cambridge, Mass., 1961), in which the history of the oppositions is carried to the period of the First Five Year Plan.

* The ups and downs of this general retreat from revolutionary ideals is the theme that runs through almost every treatment of Soviet history, except official Soviet accounts. Among the more important works in this wealth of books are Franz Borkenau, *The Communist International* (London, 1938); David J. Dallin, *The Changing World of Soviet Russia*

th'e New Economic Policy may seem, it is nonetheless true that Soviet policies and Lenin's thinking show traces of the NEP from the earliest beginnings of War Communism. After the middle of 1918, Lenin again and again emphasized that the most urgent tasks of the Soviet regime were those of economic construction. He was impatient to get the civil war over with and to stifle all internal opposition, so as to get on with the job. The peace of Brest-Litovsk was welcomed as an all-too-short breather during which the regime might start building its socialist edifice. Every victory over White armies was similarly greeted, while every new threat from without or within produced irritation and exasperation, because it would again postpone the constructive tasks. "As soon as the war gives us an opportunity to relieve the center of gravity of the struggle with the bourgeoisie, of the struggle with Vrangel', with the Whiteguardists, we shall turn to economic policy." [15] This statement, typical of Lenin's attitude throughout the period of War Communism, shows his impatience with the continued struggle for power, which was considered only a prerequisite for the task of "building socialism."

War Communism can best be defined, therefore, as the period during which problems of power overshadowed all other problems of the regime, when all activities of the Leninist state were concentrated in a grim struggle for survival. Communist Russia was like a besieged fortress, and the party leaders behaved like commanders of one. A desperate effort was made to marshal all available resources. The last ounce of energy was squeezed out of every citizen. Legal niceties gave way to "revolutionary justice." Ruthlessness and naked terror were elevated to a principle of government. In Lenin's writings this situation led to a preoccupation with the concept of the proletarian dictatorship. He brutally emphasized the coercive, nay terroristic, features of his regime. Even during the "honeymoon," he had not under-

(New Haven, Conn., 1956); Barrington Moore, Jr., *Soviet Politics: The Dilemma of Power* (Cambridge, Mass., 1950); Arthur Rosenberg, *Geschichte des Bolschewismus* (Berlin, 1932); Nicholas S. Timasheff, *The Great Retreat* (New York, 1946); L. D. Trotsky, *The Revolution Betrayed* (New York, 1945); Hugh Seton-Watson, *From Lenin to Khrushchev* (New York, 1960); and Alfred G. Meyer, *Communism* (New York, 1960).

played them altogether. The communists, he wrote at that time, fully agree with the anarchists on the goal of abolishing the state, and this abolition may come very soon. Yet in the meantime they "do affirm that for the attainment of this goal a temporary utilization of the weapons, means, and devices of state power *against* the exploiters is necessary, as the temporary dictatorship of the oppressed class is necessary for the abolition of classes." [16] Again, he repeatedly demanded the complete destruction of the bourgeois state and the erection of a proletarian dictatorship. "Revolution must consist not of the new class commanding and governing with the help of the *old* state machine, but in the *smashing* of this machine, in their governing with the help of a *new* machine." [17] Still, we saw that he thought this new state machine would be a people's state of the commune type, a democratic dictatorship.

After the beginning of the civil war and the terror, when socialists in western Europe began to dissociate themselves sharply from the dictatorial methods of the Soviet regime, Lenin once again wrote a systematic treatise on the functions of the state in the revolution. He defined dictatorship therein, with great bluntness, as "power directly resting on coercion, not bound by any laws. The revolutionary dictatorship of the proletariat is power conquered and maintained by means of the coercion of the bourgeoisie by the proletariat, a power that is not bound by any laws." [18] No class — this is the traditional argument supporting the necessity for a proletarian dictatorship — has ever voluntarily relinquished its power over society; hence the bourgeoisie too will have to be forced out of power. "The Russian Whiteguardists are similar to their German and all other counterparts in that they can be neither convinced nor shamed, but only terrorized or crushed," Trotsky wrote at the same time; [19] and, in January 1918, Lenin told the soviet representatives that "not one question of class struggle has yet been solved in history by any other way than by coercion. Coercion, when it comes from the laboring, exploited masses, against the exploiters — why, we are in favor of such coercion." [20] "The abolition of classes," he wrote a year later, "is the work of long, difficult, stubborn *class struggle,* which even *after* the overthrow of the power of capital, *after* the destruction of the bourgeois state, *after* the erection of the dictatorship of the proletariat, does not disappear . . . but merely changes its forms and becomes still more violent in many respects." [21] For this reason, "the dictatorship of the proletariat is not the end of class struggle, but its continuation in new forms. The dictatorship of the proletariat *is* the class struggle of the proletariat after it has won a victory and taken political power in its own hands, against a defeated but not annihilated, not vanquished, bourgeoisie, which has not ceased to offer resistance, but has strengthened its resistance." [22]

Capitalism was not yet licked in Russia, according to Lenin's arguments. Individuals from the bourgeoisie still enjoyed advantages of wealth, education, and experience, in addition to the moral and material support they might still be receiving from abroad. Moreover, a large number of those exploited still retained the psychological heritage of capitalism. Thus another task for the dictatorship of the proletariat was to "awaken and educate the masses," so that they might be enabled to build socialism in the country of revolution;[23] and among the most important means to be used in this awakening process was the imposition of organization and discipline on the "advanced units of the working masses, their vanguard, their only leader — the proletariat." [24]

"Fellow workingmen!" Lenin had written a few days after the October Revolution, "Remember that *you yourselves* now govern the state. No one will help you if you yourselves do not unite and take the *whole business* of state in *your own* hands. *Your* soviets are from now on the organs of state authority; they are plenipotentiary, deciding organs." * But a few months after these sentences were written, the popular sovereignty that had swept

* From a proclamation to the population of Russia, upon the seizure of power (Lenin, vol. 22, p. 55). Similarly, in a document drafted for the First Comintern Congress, he wrote: "To destroy the power of the state is the aim all socialists have set themselves, among them, and heading them, Marx. Without the realization of this aim true democracy, that is, equality and liberty, are unattainable. The only practical step toward this aim, however, is creating the Soviet regime, or proletarian democracy, for it begins at once to prepare for the complete withering away of the state by drawing the mass organization of the working people into a lasting and unconditional participation in the administration of the state" (vol. 24, p. 14).

the Bolsheviks into power was already being destroyed. As early as 1918, sovietism was well on the road of turning into a democratic façade, concealing the leadership of the party behind the forms of local autonomy, popular initiative and control, the right of recall, and similar devices. Party control over soviet activities was exerted at first through the manipulation of all Bolshevik Party members within these popular institutions, in other words, by means of party discipline; later, means external to the soviet system were also used, the secret police, the Red Army, federal commissars, and mass organizations. On paper, the soviet system, in spite of the admitted and intentional inequalities of the workers' and peasants' franchise, was an institution of mass democracy. In practice, as Lenin was ready to acknowledge, it was but the form in which the party exerted its power over the masses.*

Established in the name of democracy, the Leninist state soon turned into a dictatorship of unprecedented ruthlessness. But civil war and terror were not ends in themselves. Our point has been that the very ruthlessness with which Lenin sought to secure his power indicates how impatient he was to get problems of security out of the way, how eager to tackle the job of "building socialism" and preparing the ground for communism.

SOCIALIST COMPETITION

The difference between socialism and communism plays an important role in the ideological justification of Soviet totalitarianism, and the predilection for pointing it out is usually ascribed to Stalin. But the distinction was first made by Lenin,

* For admissions of this by both Lenin and Zinov'ev, see the minutes of the Eighth Party Congress, held in March 1919 (*Protokoly VIII S"ezda RKP(b)*, Moscow, 1933), especially p. 60, where Lenin argues that even Soviet democracy can not but be an empty form in a backward country. See also Zinov'ev's speech, before the Committee on Organization (*ibid.*), especially p. 225, and his plenary speech, pp. 287–290, where he said: "All people who work should be organized in the Soviets within a short time. We must invite all working elements to [participate in] elections, *because that is the best way of gaining influence over them*" (p. 290; italics added). That these tendencies were not generally accepted by all party leaders is shown by Osinsky's speech before the same Committee on Organization, where he asked for a separation of powers between a legislative and an executive branch in the government, so as to combat the growing tendency toward centralization (p. 192).

in 1917,* when he hypothesized an interim stage between the seizure of power and the communist society, an interim stage that in 1917 was still a goal. Communism was formulated as the social relationship in an economy of abundance; socialism, as that form of society which alone could make the achievement of abundance possible. A new minimum program was thus evolved, the most important part of which was the task of economic construction. This indeed eventually became the *raison d'état* of the Leninist regime. With power more or less firmly in his hands, Lenin set out to build up an economy of abundance. "Communism," he wrote in a famous phrase, is nothing else but "Soviet rule plus the electrification of the entire country." [25] Soviet rule had been achieved; so that the erection of an industrial establishment of the most modern type ("electrification") was the major task facing the regime, apart from the job of making its power secure. Until this task was completed, all other aspects of socialism would have to be neglected; they were luxuries that only a satiated economy could afford. Economic needs would have to take precedence even over the demands of social justice. In Lenin's words, "the solution of this question [social justice] must be subordinated to the interests of production." †

In the honeymoon period, when Lenin saw communism just around the corner, he thought that economic tasks could be accomplished speedily and spontaneously. For, in the people's state, work would no longer be drudgery and wage slavery; instead, the masses would realize that they were working only for them-

---

* "The Tasks of the Proletariat in Our Revolution," Lenin, vol. 20, p. 132 (translation in *Collected Works*, vol. 20, book 1, p. 154). The two social orders were characterized by the familiar slogans of "From each according to his abilities — to each according to his work" (socialism) and "From each according to his abilities — to each according to his need" (communism).

† From a speech given on 15 March 1920 (Lenin, vol. 25, p. 80). The party platform written and adopted in 1919 stated this with similar clarity: "During the period in which the socialization of the means of production expropriated from the capitalists has already begun, the state power ceases to be a parasitic apparatus standing above the process of production; it begins to turn into an organization that directly fulfills the functions of directing the country's economy, and in that very measure the state budget becomes the budget of the entire national economy as a whole" (printed in *Protokoly VIII S"ezda RKP(b)*, pp. 397–398).

selves, not for the benefit of exploiters. Hence everyone would
co-operate in giving labor for the collective good to the best of
his abilities. In previous societies, people had to be made to
work, and, according to Lenin, every social system had had its
particular "incentives." Under feudalism it was the knout; under
capitalism it was hunger. Now, under the proletarian dictatorship, it would be the "free and conscious discipline of the workers themselves." [26] "Communism," he told the party, "if we take
the word in its strict meaning, is gratuitous work for the social
good, without consideration for individual differences . . ." [27]
And again,

Communist labor in the narrowest and strictest sense of the word
is unpaid labor for the good of society, labor rendered not for the
purpose of paying off a certain obligation, not in order to obtain
the right to certain products, nor in accordance with previously established and enacted norms, but voluntary labor, labor beyond norms,
labor which is being given without calculation of reward, without
conditions concerning reward, labor out of the habit of working for
the common good and motivated by a consciousness (which has
turned into habit) of the necessity of labor for the common good —
labor as a requirement of a healthy organism. [28]

In the early months of the honeymoon, Lenin thought he saw
this "free and conscious discipline" growing up fast. Soon, however, he noted that this enlightened incentive had not yet developed. We shall discuss later the explanation Lenin found for
this lag and the long-range remedy he proposed. At the time of
the civil war, however, he was not ready to accept slow-working,
long-range methods of changing human behavior. Socialism, he
insisted, could not wait; it would have to be built with the
human material that happened to be available to the regime.
Pending changes in men's habits, consciousness on a mass scale
should be replaced by ruling skill. In other words, consciousness
should be exercised by the party, and it would consist of the
ability to make the people do the work. We communists, Lenin
wrote, are but a drop in the bucket, and we alone cannot build
socialist or communist societies. We must build them with the
hands of the bourgeois and peasants. "The old utopian socialists
imagined that socialism could be built with different people, that

they would first of all create nice, clean, excellently educated people, and, out of them, would construct socialism." To wait that long would mean giving up the effort altogether. "We have bourgeois specialists — and there is nothing else. . . . Socialism must win out, and we socialists and communists must prove in fact that we are able to construct socialism out of these bricks, out of this material; that we are able to construct a socialist society out of proletarians who enjoy culture only in an insignificant amount, and out of bourgeois specialists. If you are not going to construct a communist society out of this material, then you are empty phrase-makers and windbags." [29]

The problem of incentive during the stage between capitalism and communism was thus far from solved. In an effort to create new incentives, Lenin as early as 1917 demanded that the proletarian state should organize competition. Competition by plan, which meant a rational allocation and use of labor forces, became his catchword to characterize the system of incentives by which he proposed to enlist the masses' co-operation in building communism. The overthrow of capitalism would not do away with competition, then. But, claimed Lenin, organized competition would be different from competition under capitalism. In fact he used different words for the two things. Competition under capitalism was designated by the word konkurentsiia, whereas socialist competition was labeled sorevnovanie, which in Soviet texts is translated "emulation." Lenin claimed virtues for the latter that competition under capitalism did not have. Konkurentsiia, he argued, is a misdirected and thwarted sort of cutthroat competition; sorevnovanie is competition "in its non-bestial, in its human forms." [30] (Still, it was a method of forcing unwilling workers to give labor to the state, and the very necessity of making the workers work was a blow to proletarian aspirations as well as to previous socialist theory.) Lenin emphasized the need for hard work and sacrifice. The country is poor, he argued, and all demands for social benefits, shorter working hours, or higher wages are therefore meaningless.[31] The Russian worker would have to learn how to work, and Lenin proposed to teach him this socialist virtue. He proposed to teach him by applying the most hated development of capitalism, the Taylor system of scientific management, which had been one of the pet bugaboos of the socialist movement. As Lenin put it;

> The Russian worker is inefficient in comparison with the workers of advanced nations. He could not be otherwise under the regime of tsarism and the harshness of what was left of serf laws. To learn how to work: that is the task which the Soviet regime will put before the people, with all that it implies. The highest development of capitalism in labor efficiency — the Taylor system — like all other progressive features of capitalism, incorporates both the subtle bestiality of bourgeois exploitation and a number of the richest scientific achievements in the job of analyzing mechanical motion during work, elimination of superfluous and awkward motions, . . .[32]

All the progressive features of the Taylor system were to be adopted.

It presently became an important task of the dictatorship of the proletariat to supplement the incentives of "organized competition" with more coercive means. The beginning of this trend can be traced to what Lenin called the "conquest" of the trade-union movement by the party and the Soviet state.[33] The unions became agencies of the government.

This imposition of coercive methods on the workers went against all socialist tradition, and it was fiercely resisted by the workers as well as by many prominent party members. Lenin denounced their arguments as bourgeois sentimentality. The demand for higher pay and shorter hours, he wrote, was an important slogan in the struggle against capitalism. But, once the revolution had given power to the party of the proletariat, all continued resistance to excessive work must be exposed as one of the evil heritages of capitalism. He told his followers to "fight against the old habit of looking at the measure of labor and the means of production from the point of view of a man who is under coercion." They should stop worrying about "how to liberate themselves from the excessive weight, how to wrest but a little bit of a concession from the bourgeoisie." [34] In other words, once the worker is being oppressed by a workers' regime, he should forget that he is being oppressed, because it is his own representatives who drive him to work.

That socialism did not necessarily imply immediate equalization of wages had been made clear by him even before the October Revolution.* He had emphasized, furthermore, that a socialist economy meant a planned economy. Planning, however, required management, and management, wrote Lenin, required granting authority to individuals.

All large-scale machine industry — the very material, productive source and fundament of socialism — demands absolute, strictest unity of will, to direct the co-ordinated work of hundreds, thousands, and tens of thousands of people. Technically, economically, as well as historically, this necessity is obvious and has always been recognized as a condition of socialism by all those who think about it. But how can the strictest unity of will be guaranteed? By the subordination of the will of thousands to the will of one.†

* See Lenin's speech to party leaders shortly after his return to Russia in 1917 (Lenin, vol. 20, p. 80; translation in *Collected Works*, vol. 20, book 1, pp. 93–100). The Ninth Party Congress, which sat in March and April of 1920, spelled this out in a lengthy resolution, as follows:

"V. Labor competition—Every social system (slave, feudal, capitalist) has its methods and ways of coercing and educating labor in the interests of the exploiting upper classes.

"Before the soviet system in all it comprises looms the task of developing its own methods of influencing — with the purpose of raising the intensity and expediency of labor — the foundation of the socialized economy in the interest of the entire people.

"Together with the influence over the working masses by agitation of ideas and the repressions directed against known loafers, parasites, and wreckers, the mightiest force for raising the productivity of labor is *competition*.

"In capitalist society competition had the character of being cut-throat [literally: *sorevnovanie* had the character of *konkurentsiia*] and led to the exploitation of man by man. In a society where the means of production have been nationalized, competition in labor, no longer destroying solidarity, should only raise the general sum of labor's products.

"Competition between factories, regions, shops, workrooms, and individual workers should become a subject for careful organization and attentive study on the part of trade-unions and economic agencies.

"The bonus system should become one of the most powerful means of stimulating competition. The system of food supply should be adjusted to it: so long as the Soviet republic has not enough foodstuffs, the industrious and conscientious worker should be provided for far better than the one who does not care . . ." (printed in Lenin, vol. 25, pp. 550–551).

† "Urgent tasks facing the Soviet regime," Lenin, vol. 22, p. 462 (translation in *Selected Works*, vol. 7, p. 342). For an attempt by Lenin to demonstrate that individual managerial authority was compatible with the principles of mass democracy, see his first draft to the same article (vol. 22, pp. 419–421).

In claiming to represent the working class, the party, exercising its dictatorship over Russia, proclaimed its enmity to all groups whose presumed interests conflicted with those of the proletariat as a whole.* Ironically enough, the dictatorship of the proletariat applied this principle to the proletariat itself. In supporting Lenin and the October Revolution, the Russian workers had surely not bargained for the sweatshop socialism Lenin sought to impose on them. The dictatorship of the proletariat turned into a dictatorship over the proletariat, because, in Lenin's words, the working class "had not got rid of the deficiencies and weaknesses of capitalist society. In fighting for socialism, it is simultaneously fighting against its own deficiencies." [35] This meant in fact that the party was fighting the deficiencies of the workers. The Leninist state was therefore a dictatorship of the proletariat, for the proletariat, but not by the proletariat,† or, as Otto Bauer phrased it, a "dictatorship of the idea of the proletariat." [36] The Soviet state assumed, in Leninist theory, that virtue and that rationality which for Hegel had been embodied in the Prussian state: The wheel of Marxism had come full circle. Both Marx and Lenin thought of revolution as a political act, the seizure of control over society by the urban working class. For both of them, however, the political act would make sense only in combination with the substructural economic change of society from capitalism to socialism. The difference between them is that Marx supposed that the fundamental economic revolution would have to precede the political revolution, whereas Lenin,

---

* This was established as a principle in the first constitution of the RSFSR, of 10 July 1918, where Article 23 reads as follows: "Guided by the interests of the working class as a whole, the RSFSR deprives individual persons and individual groups of rights which they enjoy to the detriment of the interests of the socialist revolution" (English translation of this constitution in James H. Meisel and Edward S. Kozera, *Materials for the Study of the Soviet System*, ed. 2, Ann Arbor, Mich., 1953, pp. 79–91).

† At the Eighth Party Congress Lenin said this openly: "so far, we have not achieved the state where the working masses could participate in government — except on paper; there is still the cultural level, which you will never render subject to legislation. This low cultural level has the effect of making the soviets, which according to their program are organs of government *by the working people*, actually into organs of government *for the working people*, by the advanced elements of the proletariat, but not by the working masses" (Lenin, vol. 24, p. 145).

after seizing political power, became aware that the economic revolution was yet to come. To carry it out was the task he allotted to the dictatorship of the proletariat.

STRATEGIC RETREAT AND STOCK-TAKING

The New Economic Policy in one sense broke with and in another sense continued the policies of War Communism. It was introduced in the early months of 1921, at a time when one of the aims of War Communism had been realized and another had been revealed as unrealistic. What had been achieved was the political supremacy of the Leninist regime in Russia. The civil war had been won, against all odds. The forces of intervention had been expelled, and oppositions cowed. For the first time the regime could tackle constructive tasks with relative immunity from military problems. The failure which had become apparent was the impossibility of going on with the terroristic regime of War Communism and with the attempts to maintain communist principles of class exclusiveness. The civil war had exhausted the country. Industrial production was at an all-time low. The workers had largely dispersed into the villages to keep from starving. The peasantry was in open rebellion against the system of grain seizures, which had been imposed as a military measure in order to feed the Red Army and the urban population. In mute but effective resistance, the peasants had resorted to curtailing agricultural production to their own household needs. Never had the government been less popular. Even the naval fortress of Kronstadt, vanguard and hero of the October Revolution, was in revolt against the terror and the bureaucracy of the Bolshevik state. Paradoxically, the period of War Communism had both consolidated the regime and brought it close to economic and political collapse.* The "incentives" of terror and organized com-

* At the Eleventh Party Congress, in 1922, Lenin said that the regime was living on the political credit given it by the peasantry, and warned that this credit was not inexhaustible. Continuing with this metaphor, we might say that the abandonment of War Communism was Lenin's admission that he had overdrawn his account. Moreover, the problem of how to refrain from overdrawing this account is one of the most serious recurrent problems of Soviet domestic policy. It has continued to be a particularly burning issue since the inauguration of the five-year plans.

petition had not proven efficient; instead, they had alienated the entire population.

The NEP was an attempt to provide better incentives. Its principal features were the abolition of the requisitions system in favor of a fixed tax in kind, and the re-establishment of a legal market, which gave the peasantry an incentive to resume full production. To back this up, the currency had to be stabilized. In order to give the peasants an opportunity to buy goods with their money, a number of other measures were taken: a certain amount of private enterprise in trade and in some industries was revived, and foreign capital was invited to make investments in Soviet Russia on a concessions basis. Although Lenin never stated them, we can detect great similarities between the social and political structure of the NEP and his own ideas about the revolutionary democratic dictatorship of the proletariat and peasantry. Private enterprise in agriculture and small production, the expropriation of the squires and the capitalists, political leadership in the hands of the "proletariat" (that is, the party) — these features characterizing the NEP had been part of the "American capitalism" that was Lenin's minimum objective between 1906 and 1917.

The realization that the party had failed in "telescoping" the bourgeois and the proletarian revolution, had failed in letting the minimum program "grow over" into a communist society, was, of course, very painful. Lenin and his followers spoke of the NEP as a strategic retreat, and felt extremely awkward about making it. Yet initially there seem to have been no important Bolshevik leaders who objected to the new measures. The horrors of War Communism and the dread of the Kronstadt Rebellion, symbol of the waning of all popular support for the regime, were too fresh in their memories.* At the same time, every communist had

* N. N. Volski, in an unpublished memoir work deposited at the Columbia University Archive on Russian and East-European History and Culture, argues rather convincingly that Lenin shortly before his death had become convinced that the NEP was to be maintained as a pattern of social organization for a long period; that he was supported in this favorable attitude toward the NEP by very few of his followers; and that, in fact, the overwhelming majority of party members, leaders as well as rank and file, were hostile to it and impatiently pressed for a return to a more "socialist" course

to ask himself, "Where do we go from here?" This question was soon to become the burning issue that would literally tear the party to pieces, but the schism occurred after Lenin's death, and we cannot deal with it here.

Lenin himself had but vague ideas about the future development of Soviet Russia. In general, he appeared confident in the gradual but inevitable growth of socialism. The regime seemed politically secure as long as the peasantry remained satisfied with the new dispensation, and as long as the "commanding heights" of the national economy remained in the hands of the workers' state. The continued existence of private enterprise in such a state was disturbing, but here too Lenin breathed confidence, arguing that private enterprise was bound to wither away because it was doomed to defeat in competition with the socialized sector of the economy. More and more peasants, he believed, would be won over to socialist principles of co-operation and collective management because the living example of socialist enterprises, with their greater efficiency and productivity, would be constantly before their eyes. Co-operative practices would increasingly become the pattern of Russian life. Lenin's articles on this score breathe a good deal of sanguine optimism: the troubled days were over and socialism would be constructed peacefully and gradually.* In this sense, the idea of *pererastanie* lived on in a rather mild form.

If anything worried him, it was the problem of obtaining an efficient public administration. Russia had been notorious for the corruptness and inefficiency of its bureaucracy. Not long after the October Revolution, similar conditions arose in the administration of the Soviet state, where people unfamiliar with administrative problems suddenly found themselves either running a vast

of action. In his political report to the Eleventh Party Congress, in March 1922, Lenin sharply attacked such critics, accusing them of sowing panic during a strategic retreat.

* See particularly "On Co-operation," Lenin, vol. 27, pp. 391–397 (translation in *Selected Works,* vol. 9, pp. 402–409). As to the international situation, we should keep in mind that Lenin did not live to see the end of the turbulent aftermath of World War I, which to him looked very much like a revolutionary situation. For a further discussion of the international ramifications, see Chapter 10.

governmental apparatus or creating new organs of government out of nothing.* Lenin seems to have believed at first that consciousness was the sole qualification necessary to an administrator. Since, according to Lenin's definition, consciousness was the exclusive possession of party members, the conclusion was very simple: administrative problems would be licked most readily by putting trusted communists into responsible positions. To be sure, not being sufficiently numerous to fill all administrative posts, Lenin's party comrades had to rely on the assistance of bourgeois specialists and other nonparty elements. But the faith prevailed that an administrative apparatus both efficient and reliable could nonetheless be assured as long as communists retained supervision and control over such elements. The result was far from encouraging: Soviet Russia's administration in the first years of the regime was nothing short of chaotic. One of the several reasons for this was undoubtedly the fact that the skills and qualifications of a professional revolutionary are by no means identical with the skills and qualifications of a government administrator. Indeed, they may exclude each other. Could the party's leader be expected to accept such reasoning?

Lenin had a simple explanation for the ensuing bureaucratic mess. To him it was a painful consequence of Russia's backwardness, particularly the backwardness of the common man: his lack of education, of political consciousness, of experience in industry, of the spit and polish of life in the modern city. He blamed this on the absence of self-discipline, even among the working class. Here we have his rationalization for "organizing competition" and for measures of outright coercion. The boorishness of Russian masses, in his eyes, was the major obstacle on the road to socialism. "The problem is how to unite the victorious proletarian revolution with bourgeois culture, with bourgeois science and technology, which has up to now been the property of the few — let me repeat it; this is a difficult task." [37] Capitalism was lingering in the minds of the workers, even though it had been eliminated from the political scene. "When we threw off capi-

---

* For an early eyewitness account of the unspeakable conditions in Soviet bureaucratic agencies, and an attempted explanation, see Paul Olberg, *Briefe aus Sowjet-Russland* (Stuttgart, 1919), pp. 39–51, n. 12.

talist institutions we found that there was still one other form by which capitalism is being maintained — and that is the force of habit. The more decisively we threw off all the institutions upholding capitalism, the more clearly the other force came out which had supported capitalism — the force of habit. An institution can, with luck, be shattered at one blow, but a habit can never be, not with any sort of luck." [38] In time, Lenin became brutally frank in comparing backward Russia with the West. In his political report to the Eleventh Party Congress, in March 1922, he defined the task of the NEP: catching up with the West. "Learning from capitalism" was one of the catchwords of this important speech.* Summing up this argument in one of his last articles, Lenin declared that an entire cultural revolution was required to lick this problem.

Properly speaking, *"only"* one thing remains for us to do, to make our population so "civilized" that it understands all the advantages of individual participation in co-operation, and that it arranges for such participation. *"Only"* that. No other brainstorms are required for us now in order to go over to socialism. But in order to effect this, *"only"* an entire revolution is necessary, an entire era of cultural development for the whole mass of the people.†

Not only the mass of the people, however, would have to acquire "culture" by learning from capitalism. No, he castigated even the "vanguard of the proletariat," including the most highly placed party leaders, for their dearth of culture, claiming they had been unable to adjust themselves to the postrevolutionary

* Lenin, vol. 27, pp. 225–259. This admitted turn to capitalism for guidance is reminiscent of the slogans advanced two decades before by such Legal Marxists as Struve and Tugan-Baranovsky. The difference is that Lenin proposed to study capitalist methods and achievements only after the party had deprived the bourgeoisie of power and seized the "commanding heights" of economic control.

† "On Co-operation," Lenin, vol. 27, p. 393 (translation in *Selected Works,* vol. 9, pp. 404–405). Concerning the great length of time the cultural revolution would require, see a speech Lenin made in 1921 at a congress of political propagandists (vol. 27, pp. 51–52). For a discussion of the use of the word "culture" in Leninism, see Alfred G. Meyer, "The Use of the Term Culture in the Soviet Union," in A. L. Kroeber and Clyde Kluckhohn, *Culture: a Critical Review of Concepts and Definitions of Culture,* Papers of the Peabody Museum, vol. 47 (Cambridge, Mass., 1952).

era and were therefore responsible for the bureaucratic mess that
worried him so. He spoke of *oblomovism** in Soviet bureaucracy, asserting that it could be explained in part by the fact that
the administrative and industrial apparatus was staffed by professional revolutionaries. No one doubted their loyalty, but instead of learning how to manage the economy, they were holding
discussion meetings. "Our worst internal enemy is the communist
sitting in a responsible . . . Soviet job who enjoys universal
respect as a conscientious man, but who had not learned how to
fight against red tape, does not know how to fight, and is even
covering it up." [39] Speaking before the Fourth Comintern Congress, in November 1922, he admitted that the old state apparatus, which ought to have been smashed, had instead been taken
over, and might yet win out over the communists even while
they thought they were at its helm.† In a sweeping indictment,

---

* *Oblomovism* — the behavior of Oblomov, pathetic hero of Goncharov's
novel of the same name, who prefers to contemplate and discuss the universe, including his own predicament, instead of taking an active part in
solving his problems and participating in life.

† "Five Years of the Russian Revolution and the Perspectives of World
Revolution," Lenin, vol. 27, p. 352 (translation in *Selected Works*, vol. 10,
p. 330). The Trotsky archives at the Harvard University Library contain
a series of notes written by Lenin in December 1922, from which the following is quoted: "That which we call our apparatus is still completely
alien to us; it represents a bourgeois, tsarist mechanism." Lenin went on
to say that it was staffed mainly by bourgeois specialists and other remnants of the old order. The deficiencies of bureaucracy were thus to be
explained by the lack of culture among the personnel. Once the apparatus
was cleansed of its bourgeois elements, Lenin would no longer find fault
with it. This is clearly implied in the same notes, where he referred to the
"diplomatic apparatus" of the regime as "exceptional in the body of our
state apparatus. We have admitted to it not one man in any way influential
from the old tsarist apparatus. In it, all of the apparatus which is the least
bit authoritative is composed of communists. For this reason this apparatus
has already won (I may say this boldly) the name of a tested communist
apparatus, incomparably purified, at an immeasurably higher level than the
old bourgeois and petty bourgeois apparatus which we are compelled to
get along with in the other commissariats."

These notes were first published in 1924 in the Menshevik *émigré* journal
Sotsialisticheskii Vestnik (Berlin). Since the completion of this manuscript,
they have also, at last, been published in the Soviet Union, both in the
party's theoretical journal and in a separate pamphlet, which also contains
Lenin's so-called "testament" and one other document — *Pis'mo k s"ezdu*
(Moscow, 1956).

One of the bitterest disappointments for Lenin was to see that the very

he told his party comrades at the Eleventh Congress that they were not fit to govern the country:

It is *kulturnost'* * which those communists who are in the leading positions are lacking. Let us take Moscow, with its 4700 responsible communists, and that weighty bureaucratic machine — who is running it? I greatly doubt whether one can say that communists are running that heavy thing. To tell the truth, it is not they who are running it; it runs them. Something has happened here that is similar to what they used to tell us about history in our childhood. This is what they taught us: Sometimes it happens that one people conquers another people, and then the people who conquered are the conquerors, and the conquered ones are the defeated. That is very simple, and everyone can understand it. But what happens with the culture of these peoples? Here matters are not so simple. If the people who did the conquering are more cultured than the defeated people, then the former will impose their culture on the latter, but if it is the other way around, then what happens is that the defeated will impose their culture on the conquerer. Has not something similiar happened in the capital of the RSFSR; is it not true here that 4700 communists (almost an entire division, and all of them the very elite) turn out to have been subjugated by an alien culture? Indeed, we might even get the impression here that the defeated have a high culture. Nothing of the sort! Their culture is miserable and insignificant, and yet it is greater than ours. However pitiful, however miserable, it is nevertheless greater than that of our responsible communist functionaires, because they do not have sufficient skill in governing.[40]

Thus Lenin blamed the "bourgeois specialists," the backwardness of the masses, and the ineptness of his own followers for the inefficiencies and abuses of the Soviet and party bureaucracy, but he never thought of criticizing himself or his principles. Whatever the deficiencies of the apparatus, the organizational ideas

---

commissariat which had been created for the purpose of combating red tape, corruption, and other ills of bureaucratism, the Workers' and Peasants' Inspection headed by Stalin, turned out to be the worst of them all. See his articles entitled "How We Should Reorganize the Workers' and Peasants' Inspection" (vol. 27, pp. 402–405; translation in *Selected Works*, vol. 9, pp. 382–386) and "Better Less but Better" (vol. 27, pp. 406–418; *Selected Works*, vol. 9, pp. 387–401).

* *Kulturnost'* means the quality of being cultured. As used by Lenin and subsequent Soviet writers, this means the ability to get along in or cope with the things constituting modern industrial society. Lack of this quality would be found in a hick, a boor, or a bumpkin.

which had given rise to it were never blamed. It was the weak-
lings and class enemies within the apparatus who were corrupt-
ing it — Lenin had faith in his own leadership to the end of his
life.*

* Trotsky in his autobiography hints that toward the end of his life Lenin
contemplated forming a coalition with him for the purpose of fighting
against the apparatus (*Mein Leben,* Berlin, 1930, pp. 465–466).

Chapter 10

Socialism in One Country

The business of construction is entirely dependent on how fast the revolution will be victorious in the most important countries of Europe. Only after such a victory can we seriously take up the business of construction.

LENIN

A complete, final victory of world proportions is impossible in Russia alone; it is possible only when the proletariat is victorious in all advanced countries or perhaps in several of the largest advanced countries. Only then will we be able to say with full conviction that the cause of the proletariat has won, that our first aim — the overthrow of capitalism — has been attained.

But it has been realized here in one country, and has confronted us with a second task. Since the Soviet regime has been made a reality, and the bourgeoisie has been overthrown in one country, the second task is a struggle of world proportions, on a different plane: the struggle of the proletarian state in the midst of capitalist states.

LENIN

BREST-LITOVSK

In his victory address on the day of the Japanese surrender, in September 1945, Joseph Stalin exulted over the fact that finally, after forty years, the shameful Russian defeat at the hands of the Japanese had been avenged and the lost territories recuperated. For those who are familiar with the Leninist policy of revolutionary defeatism, and who know the fervency with which all revolutionaries in Russia wished the defeat of the tsarist armies in 1905, this appears to be such an about-face that it requires explanation. The purpose of this chapter is to show how Soviet national patriotism developed even during Lenin's lifetime, despite all slogans of proletarian internationalism and revolutionary defeatism.

In order to trace this development it is, perhaps, best to go back to the Treaty of Brest-Litovsk, because the controversy that arose among Lenin's followers just before its conclusion provides the keynote for the emergence of Soviet patriotism. The situation at the time when this treaty was signed was about as follows: the October Revolution was an accomplished fact. Russia was ruled by a government of Bolsheviks, together with some Left Socialist Revolutionaries. The Russian armies had dissolved into almost nothing; the Bolsheviks, at least before their seizure of power, had encouraged this dissolution. Russia's boundaries were virtually open to any foreign invader. The country's economy was utterly disrupted as a consequence of four years of war and one year of revolution. The population was tired of the war. Politically, the regime was still in the honeymoon period. Drunk with success, the Bolshevik leaders did not trouble to push reforms by any very drastic means, for the reasons discussed in the preceding chapter. Nor did the regime have a foreign policy, if by one we mean an attempt to regulate the relationship between sovereign states. Soviet Russia had no intention of regulating its relations with the outside world, because Lenin and his followers were convinced that the sovereign states of Europe were about to collapse. The only policy of the Foreign Commissariat (significantly headed by the leading strategist of the revolution, Trotsky) consisted of attempts to hasten the collapse, and the only means by which Russia at that time could implement this policy were propagandistic means, such as the publication of the famous secret treaties and other diplomatic documents designed to embarrass the bourgeois governments of the world, and the sweeping peace offers made to all the countries at war. This foreign policy designed to end all need for foreign policy was still being pursued when, in late December 1917, the German armies, taking advantage of the revolutionary disturbances in Russia, began an all-out offensive to end the war on their eastern front. The German advance posed the first real foreign-policy problem to the Leninist regime: the Bolshevik government was faced with the necessity of deciding how it would seek to shape its relations with the bourgeois world.

Lenin's previous pronouncements were clear on what should be done: submission to Germany was out of the question; hence Russia should fight once again. Since her armed forces were dispersed, however, fighting would make sense only if she could find allies. On finding allies, Lenin's wartime writings are specific. He had expected that, if Russia were invaded, the workers of the world would rise, and, together with the revolutionary regime in Russia, turn the international war into a revolutionary war. In the light of his pronouncements, it is significant that the Central Committee of the party, with Lenin's concurrence, decided to resist the Germans. But instead of counting on an international revolution, they voted in favor of requesting aid from the Western Allies, who were still at war with Germany. Apparently the party leaders thought it wiser to do this than to bank their hopes exclusively on the German proletariat.

Help from the Allies was not forthcoming. The Germans continued to advance, and General Hofmann's peace conditions were staggering. He asked for a settlement that would have deprived Russia of her richest agricultural and industrial areas and made her virtually a tributary power of the German *Reich*. During the month of January 1918, three different plans were discussed in the Central Committee. One was symbolized by Trotsky's slogan, "Neither peace nor war." What Trotsky proposed was that Russia declare unilaterally that the Soviet state had no quarrels with Germany and was therefore demobilizing its armed forces and proposing to convert swords to ploughshares. This, Trotsky thought, would have a contagious effect on the armies of the imperialist nations. They too would lay down their arms, or, even better, turn them against their capitalist oppressors. Against Lenin's objections, the Central Committee voted to try this plan. As it turned out, Trotsky's calculations were false; the German soldiers did not revolt, and their generals

lost patience at the Russian commissar's procrastination and demanded capitulation and a peace treaty in traditional forms.

The second policy proposed in the Central Committee was
based on Lenin's prerevolutionary idea of transforming the war
into a world revolution. As we know, Lenin had always denied
the possibility of achieving socialism in Russia alone.* Should
the world revolution not come off, however, even then the alternative could only be revolutionary war on the part of the Russian
proletarian dictatorship. Thus he had written shortly before the
October revolution:

if the least likely case should occur, that the capitalists reject the
peace terms of the Russian workers' government, defying the will of
their peoples, then the revolution in Europe will come a hundred
times nearer, and the army of our workers and peasants will elect
for themselves not hated but respected leaders and commanders; they
will become convinced of the justice of the war after peace has been
offered, after the secret treaties have been torn up, the union with the
landlords and the bourgeoisie has been severed, and all the land been
given to the peasants. Only then will the war turn into a just war
for Russia; it is only such a war that the workers and peasants will

* Statements to this effect abound in Lenin's writings. As early as 1905
he emphasized that socialism could be realized in Russia only through an
all-European proletarian revolution (Lenin, vol. 8, p. 426; translated in
Selected Works, vol. 3, pp. 134–135). He reiterated this shortly before returning to Russia in March 1917, in his farewell letter to the Swiss workers,
stating flatly that "the Russian proletariat can not by its own power alone
carry the socialist revolution to a victorious conclusion" (vol. 20, p. 69;
Collected Works, vol. 20, book 1, p. 87). For similar statements in his
subsequent works, see his speech at the Seventh Party Congress, March
1918 (vol. 22, p. 319; Selected Works, vol. 7, p. 291); report at the
Moscow Provincial Conference of Factory Committees, 23 June 1918 (vol.
23, p. 146); speech at the First Congress of Councils of National Economy,
26 May 1918 (vol. 23, p. 42; Selected Works, vol. 7, p. 391); speech at
the plenary session of the Party Executive Committee, 29 June 1918 (vol.
23, p. 157); report of the Soviet Executive Committee to the Seventh
Soviet Congress, 5 December 1919 (vol. 24, p. 591); speech at a celebration of the anniversary of the revolution in Moscow, 6 November 1920
(vol. 25, p. 474); and speech at a meeting of Moscow party cell secretaries,
26 November 1920 (vol. 25, p. 512). One reason why this profusion of
evidence should be cited is the subsequent development of the theory of
"socialism in one country," which contradicts these statements. Still, although Stalin based this theory on one lonely quotation torn out of context, we shall see in the present chapter that, to a certain extent, Lenin
himself was the father of the theory of "socialism in one country."

wage, not under the lash, but voluntarily, and such a war will bring still nearer the inevitable workers' revolution in the advanced countries.*

In other words, should the capitalist governments be more intransigent than expected, and should the workers of Europe fail in their mission of forcing their governments to make peace, there was still the working class of Russia, which would take up the crusade for socialism by invading Europe and in this fashion unleashing the world revolution.

Now, all of a sudden, Lenin proposed a third plan. To the dismay of most of his comrades, he asserted that revolutionary war would be a hopeless venture which would jeopardize the Bolshevik regime, and he advocated acceptance of the German terms at once, however harsh they were and however blatantly they violated hallowed party traditions and slogans. Even after the failure of Trotsky's plan, Lenin had to bully the party leaders into accepting this proposal. We will summarize here the arguments he used, since they are still the basis of Soviet foreign policy today.

Lenin had to defend his proposal of surrender to Germany against those who argued that any treaty concluded with an imperialist nation would taint the proletarian regime with the stain of opportunism in the eyes of its supporters at home and abroad. He did so by arguing that revolutionary war would also necessitate making deals with imperialist powers. Economically and militarily, the Soviet state was not prepared to do any further fighting, hence waging war against Germany would make Soviet Russia dependent on the Western powers from whose domination she had just liberated herself by revolution. In addition, Lenin pleaded that a renewal of military activities, even in the name of the revolution, would be political suicide for the regime, for the masses were not prepared to do any more fighting and would therefore be estranged from it. Finally, Lenin resur-

* Lenin, vol. 21, p. 140. Even after the conclusion of the Brest-Litovsk peace treaty, Lenin confirmed this: "Our press has always talked about the necessity of preparing for revolutionary war in case of the victory of socialism in one country and the preservation of capitalism in the neighboring countries. That is beyond debate" (from a polemic against the Left Communists, entitled "About Revolutionary Rethoric," Lenin, vol. 22, p. 261).

rected the bogus of an all-imperialist bloc, by warning that if Russia declared revolutionary war, Germany and the Allies might make peace with each other and unite in a joint war against the revolutionary regime.

To most of his opponents, these arguments were beside the point. They maintained that they were under no illusions that Russia by herself could win a revolutionary war. But they did not therefore propose to enlist the aid of the Western powers. Instead, they reasserted their faith in the European proletariat, which would come to the aid of the country of the revolution. Indeed, the heroic gesture of declaring revolutionary war against the most overwhelming odds would inspire the proletariat of the West. This would be able to save the revolution, whereas the existence of an impoverished and dependent Soviet Russia could only compromise it.

In his rebuttal, Lenin argued that what his opponents called a certainty (referring to imminent revolutionary upheavals in western Europe) was in reality nothing more than the faith of fools. Immediate outbreak of the revolutionary chain reaction in Europe, he said, was highly doubtful at best. He did not doubt that it would in the end take place. "All our hopes for the *eventual* victory of socialism are based on this conviction and on this scientific foreknowledge." But the exact moment of these events could not be predicted; hence they should not be made the basis for policy decisions. In general, he argued, an accurate appraisal of the world situation was impossible at the moment, so that the party should not make any plans that were based on events or probable events in Europe. Instead, "the state of affairs concerning the revolution *in Russia* must be made the basis for all determinations of the international tasks of the Soviet regime, for the international situation in this fourth year of the war has become so complicated that the probable moment of the outbreak of a revolution . . . can not at all be taken into consideration." [1] In this manner, Lenin despaired of "scientific socialism" as an adequate tool for analyzing the current moment and pronounced himself in favor of "muddling along" on the basis of admittedly inadequate data.

In advocating that the Soviet state surrender to Germany unconditionally, he wished to sacrifice territory and national prestige for the purpose of gaining time. This was one of the keynotes of his arguments. The question that we have to ask in analyzing it is this: gaining time for what? In Lenin's answer to this question lies the gist of the controversy between him and the majority of the Central Committee. The opposition maintained that the choice was between world revolution, aided by revolutionary war, and world-wide defeat of the revolution. Russia, they argued, should continue to lead the world proletariat in revolutionary activism, otherwise the revolution would be smothered not only in Europe but even in Russia. Lenin claimed that the spread of the world revolution could not be prevented, even though its precise timetable could not be ascertained. Meanwhile, however, revolutionary war waged by a weak and shaky communist regime in Russia would be a childish venture, leading to the loss of everything gained so far.

The conflict between Lenin and his opponents, then, was over the most expedient way of carrying on the proletarian world revolution. Throughout they spoke in terms of proletarian internationalism. Throughout they maintained that they had the interests of the world revolution at heart, not the interests of the Russian state or the Soviet regime. It was thus not a fight of Russian patriots against antinationalists, even though Lenin tried to drag that issue into the fight, by accusing his opponents of patriotism (a term of contempt) for their unwillingness to sign a shameful and onerous peace treaty.* This was certainly a "smear," because the oppositionists were even less concerned over *Russian* national interests than was Lenin himself. What was actually at stake in this controversy was the existence of the new Soviet state. The advocates of revolutionary war, probably quite consciously, were prepared to risk the existence of that state for the sake of promoting the chain reaction of world-wide revolutions, which Leninist theory had made the central condition for the success of the Russian revolution. Moreover, conditioned by this Leninist theory, they saw absolutely no meaning in the existence of the Soviet state unless the chain reaction took

* The revolt of the Left Socialist Revolutionaries in June 1918 was to some extent an act of protest against the shame and burdens of the treaty.

place. The existence of the Soviet state in the midst of hostile capitalist states in western Europe would, they argued, compromise the cause of the Marxist movement and therefore be harmful to the over-all development of the world revolution. Trotsky, too, appears to have believed at that time that the Soviet state was not worth saving if the revolution did not develop on a world-wide basis. By the policy summarized in his slogan "Neither peace nor war," he may have tried to minimize the risk of losing Russia, but he did not really shrink from facing it. Lenin, however, suddenly distrustful of the proletariat in the Western countries, and basing his policy on a more realistic appraisal of the world-wide revolutionary situation, thought that under the present circumstances the continued existence of the Bolshevik state, the first great achievement of the proletarian world revolution, would be a major guarantee that this revolution would go on to its victorious conclusion. Thus, in preserving itself at all costs,* the Soviet state would be acting in the spirit of proletarian internationalism, according to which the revolution should not voluntarily yield any of its gains.[2]

The Soviet state, according to Lenin, should seek to preserve its existence in a hostile world by investing, as it were, in proletarian revolutions abroad. But in addition to this it should also pit one imperialist power against another: it should play the old game of supporting a balance of power.[3] The pursuance of this policy is not influenced by whether one power is more "reac-

---

* One item on the list of principles to be sacrificed was Lenin's adamant espousal of national self-determination, for, clearly, signing away territories and peoples to Germany, without consulting the peoples affected, was a violation of this principle. In defending this, Lenin wrote: "Not one Marxist will be able to deny, without breaking with the foundations of Marxism and of socialism in general, that the interests of socialism stand higher than the interests of the right of nations to self-determination. Our socialist republic has done everything it could — and is continuing to do so — to realize the rights to self-determination of Finland, the Ukraine, and so on. But when the concrete state of affairs has become so involved that the existence of the socialist republic is exposed to danger at a given moment on account of the violation of some nations' right to self-determination (such as Poland, Lithuania, or Kurland), then, of course, the *interests of preserving the socialist republic stand higher*" (from his "Theses" advocating the conclusion of a peace with Germany, Lenin, vol. 22, pp. 198–199).

tionary" than another; even the most democratic of bourgeois regimes is still bourgeois. This old argument, that one type of capitalism is as bad as another, served as additional ammunition for Lenin, in his campaign for accepting the conclusion of a peace treaty with Germany (considered more reactionary than England, France, and the United States). Whether Russia made peace with Germany or continued to war against her, wrote Lenin,

we do not completely break out of all entanglements with one or the other bloc of imperialists; and it is obvious that we cannot fully break out of them so long as we have not overthrown world imperialism. The correct conclusion to be drawn is that, from the moment of the victory of a socialist government in one country, we have to decide questions not from the point of view of whether we prefer this or that [brand of] imperialism, but exclusively from the point of view of the best conditions for the development and strengthening of the socialist revolution which has already started.[4]

Is this not opportunism? No, said Lenin, it is only expediency.* The situation of the Soviet government, he repeated several times, was like that of a man caught in a holdup: in such a case it is quite proper to give money to the robber, even though one does not customarily support such a person financially. Similarly, in signing away territory to the German imperialists, the Soviet government would not be giving its approval to the German regime or the German social structure; it would merely be submitting to blackmail in order to save its very existence.

Finally, Lenin argued that the policy he advocated did not mean that he had given up all hopes of seeing the revolution spread throughout the world. On the contrary, he continued to profess his belief in the theory of the spark — only now he tempered it by the injection of a time factor. Between the Russian revolution and the world-wide chain reaction there would be an interim, brief indeed, but nevertheless a precarious pause during

* According to Webster, opportunism and expediency are virtually synonymous. But in Leninist vocabulary, the former is a bad word, the latter a good one. This is but one of many such word pairs in the Leninist language. Others are nationalism-patriotism, competition-emulation, and deception-propaganda.

which the Russian revolution would have a chance to catch its breath. Signing the peace treaty would guarantee Soviet Russia this interim; that is what Lenin meant when he said he was sacrificing territory for time. "Our present tactics should not be based on the principle of supporting any imperialist bloc offering advantages to us, but on the principle of protecting the socialist revolution and giving it a chance to gain strength; and if we can not strengthen it, then we should simply hold on to the gains we have made in one country until other countries join the camp of the revolution." [5]

THEORETICAL CONSEQUENCES

"To count on a European revolution is obligatory for a Marxist if a revolutionary situation is at hand." When Lenin hurled these words against Kautsky in 1918, he was summing up all the fighting optimism with which he had embarked on the revolutionary work in Russia. But even before he wrote them, he had already lost faith in an immediate European revolution, though he still seemed to think that, basically, a revolutionary situation was at hand in Europe. The practical result of this disappointment was the conclusion of the Treaty of Brest-Litovsk. Ever since then, opponents of Lenin have had an easy time blaming him for not reappraising the situation *before* seizing power in October 1917, and accusing him of irresponsibility and adventurism. The heat with which Lenin repudiated such accusations indicates the sharpness of their sting. As late as the end of the civil war, he claimed defensively that his theory of the spark had proven correct, even though in a modified manner. He based this claim on the fact that an overwhelmingly stronger imperialist world had not been able to crush the revolution in Russia. For this he gave credit to the European proletariat, who had given the imperialists so much trouble at home that they could not pursue their interventionist policy with sufficient vigor. In December 1919, he proclaimed:

When we said from the very beginning that we staked our hopes on the world-wide revolution, they laughed at that and declared a hundred times (as they are still declaring now) that it was impossible.

But for two years now we have been receiving exact material for verification. If we were to speak of this hope as one for a quick, immediate uprising in Europe, we would have to admit that this has not taken place. But it is an undeniable historical fact . . . that this hope has been profoundly gratified in its fundamentals, and that it has from the very beginning taken the ground from under the feet of the armed intervention of the Entente.[6]

Although an immediate uprising of the European proletariat was thus no longer expected, the injection of a previously neglected waiting period did not weigh heavily at first. Lenin continued to think in terms of a relatively short interim — a few weeks, perhaps, a few months, or at most a year or two. The remaining year of world war and its aftermath continued to give him reasons to expect the chain reaction to set in very soon. Each event that seemed to bear out his expectations was greeted with triumphant enthusiasm, possibly born of secret ominous premonitions. Thus, on the eve of the German revolution of November 1918, Lenin cried out:

A whole group of countries is seized with the flame of the workers' revolution. In this respect our efforts and the sacrifices that we have made have been justified. They have turned out to be *not an adventure,* as claimed by the slander of our enemy, but a necessary transition to the international revolution, through which a country must pass which has been placed in a position of leadership in spite of its undeveloped and backward state.[7]

But each seemingly propitious event was followed by a setback, and each setback was a greater disappointment. One such disappointment was the failure of the Red Army at the gates of Warsaw. The offensive in Poland and the setting of Warsaw as the objective of this offensive had been intended as a last desperate gamble to break Soviet Russia's isolation from Europe, and to bring about another revolutionary situation in the West. Its failure affected Lenin more deeply, perhaps, than any of the others. With every new setback, the theory of the spark suffered an additional blow. For this reason it gradually turned into a different theory altogether. The new theory was that of the transitional period, during which the Soviet state must preserve itself as the home of the revolution,* a revolution that would take a very long time to spread. Lenin no longer talked about a single great upheaval throughout the whole world; instead, he spoke of an era of world wars and revolutions, in which the capitalist order would be replaced by socialism. During this era, the Soviet state would still represent the most important achievement of the revolution, and its leaders would have the duty of preserving it. In Lenin's eyes, the new situation was not so good as he had expected, but not so bad as it might have been, either. This is what he told the Moscow regional party conference in November 1920:

When three years ago we raised the question concerning the tasks and conditions of victory of the proletarian revolution in Russia, we always said specifically that this victory could not be a safe one if it were not supported by a proletarian revolution in the West, that a correct appraisal of our revolution were possible only from an international point of view. In order to attain a safe victory, we must attain the victory of the proletarian revolution in all or at least in several of the principal capitalist countries; and, after three years of fiercely stubborn war, we see in what respect our predictions have not come true, and in what respect they have come true. They have not come true in that there has not been a rapid and simple solution of this question. Of course, none of us expected that such an unequal war as Russia's war against all the capitalist powers of the world could last for three years. We see that neither one nor the other side, neither the Soviet Russian republic nor the entire remaining capitalist world, attained either victory or defeat; and at the same time we see that if our predictions have not been fulfilled simply, rapidly, and directly, they have been fulfilled inasmuch as they gave us the main thing; for the main thing was to safeguard the existence of the proletarian regime and the Soviet republic, even in case the socialist revolution in the entire world were to be delayed. And in this respect it must be said that the international position of the republic has now developed so as to give the best and the most exact confirmation of all our calculations and our entire policy.[8]

* The Russian term is *ochag revoliutsii*. In literal translation this means the "hearth of the revolution." Like the German word *Herd*, the Russian *ochag* denotes not only the domestic fireside and, figuratively, the home itself; it is also used to signify the starting point and center of a conflagration. Hence *ochag revoliutsii* rings far more dramatically and dynamically than the translation "home of the revolution."

He summed up these developments by claiming that, even without winning the international victory (which should still be considered the only *real* victory of the Russian revolution), the Soviet state was now in a position "in which we can exist side by side with the capitalist powers who are now forced to enter into trade relations with us. In the process of this struggle, we have won for ourselves the right to independent existence." [9]

The theory of the transitional period, the era of world wars and revolutions, leads directly to the development of Soviet nationalism (or "patriotism," to use the official Soviet word) and a Soviet *raison d'état*. In a previous chapter we discussed Lenin's ambivalence toward the phenomenon of nationalism: nationalism was desirable as a force of destruction, but undesirable as a principle of organization. It was undesirable both because sovereignty was an outmoded principle in a world united by modern technology and also because national states were the typical form of organization of capitalist society. Now, however, his attitude became even more ambivalent: nationalism and patriotism and the defense of the fatherland were not, after all, objectionable in themselves, but only as bourgeois phenomena. When they are given a "proletarian content" they become desirable and just: "If the class of exploiters wages war with the aim of fortifying its rule as a class, then it is a criminal war, and rallying to the defense of the homeland in *that kind* of war is infamy and a betrayal of socialism. If the war is waged by the proletariat after it has defeated the bourgeoisie in its own country, waged in the interests of fortifying and developing socialism, then the war is lawful and holy." * Similarly, bourgeois wars create revolutionary situations, because, being unpopular with the masses of the

---

* "On 'Leftist' Childishness and the Petty Bourgeois Attitude," Lenin, vol. 22, p. 510 (translation in *Selected Works*, vol. 7, p. 357). For another example of a war which Lenin called just, see his letter to the American workers, in which he writes: "The history of modern civilized America opens with one of those great, really liberating, really revolutionary wars of which there have been so few. . . . It was a war of the American people against the English bandit who had oppressed America and was keeping her in colonial servitude" (Lenin, vol. 23, p. 176; *A Letter to American Workers*, New York, 1934, p. 9).

population, they lead to discontent and unrest. But once a revolutionary regime had been established, foreign wars actually serve to strengthen the regime domestically: "The past two years show us . . . a strengthening of the Soviet regime under the heavy blows of foreign invasion, which had as its aim to smash quickly the home of the revolution, to smash the republic of workers and peasants who have dared declare war against international imperialism. But, instead of smashing Russia's workers and peasants, they have only hardened them." [10] Indeed, in the very first years of the Russian revolution, the world heard the first tones of a new militarism, from the very same men who had promised that the proletarian people's state would do away with militarism: "In the creation of an army, the class society has become accustomed to see the supreme test of an economic and political structure. By the strength or weakness of the army it judges the strength or weakness of an economy and a state. The Soviet regime has, under fire, created a mighty armed force . . ." [11]

Lenin became very careful in differentiating between two different types of loyalty to one's country: one was patriotism; the other, chauvinism. Patriotism was good, and chauvinism was bad. Chauvinism, the bourgeois antithesis of democratic patriotism, he defined as the readiness to defend one's country "even when its activities are directed toward the enslavement of foreign countries." [12] Along with this, we should consider some of his numerous eulogies of Soviet patriotism: "We are for the defense of the fatherland, but that patriotic war toward which we are going is a war for a socialist fatherland, for socialism as a fatherland, for the Soviet republic as a unit of the world army of socialism." [13] Perhaps, the following statement is the most concise: "Whoever shows flippant attitude toward the defense of a country in which the proletariat has already won, is breaking his ties with international socialism." [14] At least we see clearly that Lenin identified the interests of the proletarian world revolution with the interests of the Soviet Russian state. To be sure, he was modest enough about the achievements of the Russian proletariat: "We represent only one unit, which went a bit further than other units in the workers' army, not because it is better than the others, but because the stupid policies of our bourgeoisie allowed the working class of Russia to shake its yoke off their shoulders faster." [15] But the cause of this Russian proletariat is still identified with the cause of world socialism: "Now, when we fight for the socialist order in Russia we are fighting for the socialism of the entire world." [16]

The implications were drawn most clearly in the manifesto of the Second Congress of the Communist International, which says that "the fight for Soviet Russia has merged with the struggle against world capitalism. The Soviet Russian question has become the acid test for all organizations of the working class," and concludes by stating that "the Communist International has declared the cause of Soviet Russia to be its own cause." * These implications were inherent in Lenin's arguments in favor of concluding the Treaty of Brest-Litovsk. The gist of this argument was the question: what things are expendable in the fight for the success of the world revolution, and what things are not expendable? Lenin's opponents were ready to sacrifice the existence of the Soviet state for the sake of maintaining socialist principles and proletarian orthodoxy.† Lenin, on the other hand,

---

* *II Kongress Kommunisticheskogo Internatsionala, stenograficheskii otchet* (Second Comintern Congress, Stenographic Report; Petrograd, 1921), p. 647. Similarly, Lenin himself said at the Baku Congress, in November 1919: "Due to a number of circumstances — among others, Russia's backwardness, her vast spatial extension, and the fact that she serves as frontier between Europe and Asia, between West and East — it has been up to us to take upon ourselves the entire weight (in which we see a great honor) of being the advance commando of the world war against imperialism. Hence the entire course of the events facing us heralds an even wider and more stubborn fight with international imperialism, and will inevitably be bound up with the struggle of the Soviet republic against the forces of united imperialism: Germany, France, England, and America" (Lenin, vol. 24, p. 542).

† At the same time, the opposition warned against the consequences of creating a Soviet national interest. In April 1918 they came out with a pamphlet of "Theses," of which no. 12 reads, as follows: "The course outlined above, taken as a whole, and the tendencies to adopt this course, are, we think, dangerous in the extreme to the cause of the Russian and the international proletariat. This course will emphasize the separation — begun by the Peace of Brest — of the 'Great-Russian' Soviet republic from the

thought that maintenance of the revolutionary regime in Russia was imperative. Its continued existence, he argued, was indispensable for the progress of humanity. Principles could be violated; constructive tasks even in Russia might have to be postponed. What mattered was that the party preserve its stronghold in at least one country. Once this stronghold was secure, the worldwide revolution might run its course, rapidly or slowly, as the dialectics of history would determine. The base would be in firm hands, and nothing else was of equal importance. "When we shall, in the fullest measure, have realized the dictatorship of the proletariat in our own country, the greatest unification of its forces through the vanguard, through its advanced party, *then we can wait for the world revolution.*" [17]

---

all-Russian and the international revolutionary movement, locking it into the framework of a national government, with a transitional economic and a petty bourgeois political order.

"In foreign politics . . . this course will subordinate the Soviet republic to imperialist ties, breaking its ties with the revolutionary proletariat of all countries. It will weaken even more the international revolutionary sigificance of the Soviet regime and the Russian revolution" (printed in Lenin, vol. 22, pp. 568–569).

PART FOUR

The New Image of Capitalist Society

The Theory of Imperialism

Leninism is Marxism in the age of imperialism.

STALIN

The immediately preceding chapters were devoted to Lenin's revolutionary strategy, his minimum program and the changes it underwent whenever his estimate of the situation was amended. Strategy, we saw, was formulated in very close co-ordination with his analysis of the current moment, which we will term "theory"; and practical programs were kept in step with changes in theory. But the relation of theory to strategy was not nearly so one-sided, not such a cause-and-effect relationship, as this pattern might suggest. A change in theory was not always the "cause" of changes in strategy. For one thing, theory sometimes originated as a rationalization of strategies previously adopted. In that case the cause-and-effect relationship was reversed. In addition, the pattern is complicated by the fact that we have to distinguish between various levels of both theory and strategy, various levels of abstractness and concreteness, various ranges of applicability in time and in space. Even if we assumed that it were sufficient to distinguish between only two ranges of strategy (long-range and short-range, maximum and minimum programs) and only two levels of abstractness in theory, that would give us four different variables in a fairly complicated interrelationship. It would be idle to try to formulate laws to describe this interrelationship more exactly. Instead, if we wish to learn more about the relationship between these variables, we ought to trace the actual, historical, cause-and-effect patterns between long-range strategy, short-range strategy, concrete analysis of the current moment, and abstract theory, in Leninism.

One could argue, though with a good many reservations, that abstract theory dominated Lenin's thoughts before the year 1905. He accepted without question the Marxist scheme of historical development and the underlying image of capitalist society and defended them hotly against narodnik and revisionist attacks; they formed the theoretical framework in which concrete analysis, as well as long-range and short-range strategy, was adjusted. Lenin's analysis of Russian society around 1900 obviously fitted into the Marxist scheme. He claimed that capitalism had become the prevailing mode of production in Russia, even though the peculiarities of her political and social system were "hiding" this "truth" from view, and were rendering her capitalism a perverted one. Lenin realized that the camouflage was very effective, so effective indeed that it almost seemed to make an application of Marxism to Russia senseless.

What, may I ask, is the sense of explaining to the workers the form of value, the nature of the bourgeois order, and the revolutionary role of the proletariat, if here in Russia the exploitation of the working people is generally and universally explained not at all by the bourgeois organization of the social economy, but, for example, by the lack of land, by the redemption payments, or by the tyranny of the administration? What sense lies in explaining to the workers the theory of class warfare if that theory can not explain even their relations to the factory owner (our capitalism being artificially planted by the government), not to mention the masses of "the people" who do not belong to the class of factory workers which has formed? [1]

But, instead of scrapping Marxism as unsuitable to the Russian environment, Lenin's strategy in those early years was clearly an attempt to make Russia fit the Marxist scheme, which was axiomatic to him. If you want Marxism to be of any use in explaining Russian conditions (so Lenin seemed to say), then you must strive to make Russian conditions explain themselves in Marxist fashion, for all to see. This was the meaning of his early minimum program, with its stress on the destruction of the *ancien régime* by the bourgeois revolution, its aim of Westernizing Russia and making her into an acceptable member of the European society of nations.

Lenin's attitude toward established Marxist theories and programs of action was thus flexible. What he meant by regarding Marxism not as a dogma, but as a guide to action, was, of course, that it was to be a guide to thinking, to examining social situations, and to analyzing current moments. Marxism was not a rigid doctrine of the nature of the modern world, the trends inherent in it, and the patterns of development that all societies were to follow. Lenin considered it rather a set of concepts comprising the tools of analysis, a method of looking at the contemporary world, which took the form of crucial questions to be asked in viewing any situation. What is the mode of production prevailing in the society under investigation? Who controls the means of production? What is the nature of the class conflicts raging in the society? What are the major ideologies by which the exploited are kept in their state of ignorance and the exploiters deceive themselves about the inevitability of their own downfall? What are the political institutions through which the ruling classes formulate and enforce their policies of control and management? These are some of the questions that a Marxist would ask, if he were mindful of Marxist theories concerning the functioning of all human societies. Similarly, in formulating a program for action, one should use Marxism as a guide, not a dogma. Strategy was to be formulated, not by blindly imitating what Marx and Engels had advocated in different situations, but only by following their method of deriving programs from the problem of the moment. Again, what characterized Lenin is the readiness with which he improvised new courses of action, the cavalier fashion with which he overrode well-established Marxist traditions, even though to many of his comrades those traditions were integral parts of Marxist theory. In this sense, Allen Whiting is correct when he describes Lenin's attitude as being "If Marxist theory demands a certain course of action not in line with my own program, so much the worse for theory." [2]

Lenin's strategy, therefore, evolved in the direction of adjusting the minimum goal to conditions peculiar to Russia. But, unless Russian conditions could be explained in Marxist terms, the very recognition of them might threaten to undermine faith in the Marxist scheme. Indeed, the fact that a backward nation like Russia could even exist begged for explanation in Marxist terms. Any attempt to fit such a nation into the Marxist scheme would lead to changes in that scheme itself. And we shall see in the present chapter that the Leninist theory of imperialism, which does incorporate an explanation of backward societies, differs in many important details from the original Marxian image of capitalism.

Other factors also pressed for the development of some such theory. For one thing, any detached observation of the world around the time of the First World War would have revealed many important flaws in the original Marxist prognosis. Furthermore, Leninism is characterized by a constant and extreme radicalism, quite apart from Russia's actual situation. As a Marxist, Lenin could not but feel obliged to justify this radicalism theoretically, on the basis of class analysis. We have seen that Lenin found his justification in arguments that combined a continual analysis of the Russian political and social scene with the theory according to which the Russian revolution would serve as the spark to kindle the world conflagration, thus linking the effort of the Marxist movement in backward nations to the proletarian struggle in the capitalist world. But both his domestic observations and the spark theory necessitated, in the final analysis, a new theory of capitalist society.

Marxism can be defined as a science of revolution.* Like any other science, it comprises both theory and application. The application of Marxism consists of the program, strategy, and tactics of the revolution; it is to these that all the preceding chapters have been devoted. The theory of Marxism explains why the revolution is inevitable. According to it, the nature of capitalism makes the proletarian revolution both morally justifiable and objectively inevitable: justifiable, because capitalism is seen as an evil form of civilization, which dehumanizes man by making

---

* It should be self-evident that, by calling Marxism a science, we do not make any judgment on its adequacy as a science.

him into a piece of equipment, and which cripples his intelligence and perverts his emotional life; inevitable, because capitalism is rent by inherent contradictions that will surely tear it asunder. These contradictions are, basically, economic; they follow from such alleged laws as the growing accumulation of capital and the parallel decline in the rate of profit. In sociological terms, capitalism is seen on the way to its doom because it creates the very social forces that will destroy it. Competition between individuals who own the means of production will constantly narrow the social basis of capitalism, by eliminating an ever increasing number of men from the ruling class and converting them into dispossessed proletarians. The trend toward monopoly and the trend toward proletarization are thus part of the same development.

To Marx the proletariat constituted the living embodiment of all the evils and all the promises of capitalism. Capitalism, in the words of Lenin, is "commodity production on the highest stage of its development, when labor power itself turns into a commodity." [3] And socialist consciousness is the self-consciousness of objectified man, of man as a commodity.* For, according to Marx, the extreme character of man's dehumanization under capitalism leads its victims to an increasingly clearer understanding of the realities of capitalism. In addition, the proletariat is educated for revolution by the ruling classes themselves. It is also unburdened by material goods. No vested interests blind it against a radical recognition of the ills of capitalism and their causes. Hence the proletariat is capable of the heroism of desperation. Unaffected by loyalties, ideologies, human ties, or religion, the proletariat alone can be internationally minded, atheistic, and scientific. Finally, it is considered to be the only class working productively. It is the exclusive creator of values. In the eyes of Marx, it was therefore the logical successor to the obsolete ruling class.

By the end of the nineteenth century, Marxist theorists began to realize that something was decidedly wrong with this descrip-

* For an exposition of the Marxist image of the proletariat see Alfred G. Meyer, *Marxism: The Unity of Theory and Practice* (Cambridge, Mass., 1954), esp. ch. 4.

tion of capitalism and its trends. Some of the features in the picture were entirely unrealistic. Others had disappeared instead of intensifying. New ones that were not part of the Marxian image of capitalism at all had been added. In short, the entire face of modern industrial society was decidedly different from the Marxist description. Most important, two generations after the *Communist Manifesto* was published, capitalism had not produced a proletarian revolution, at least not one in a typically capitalist society. History had not, as at least some Marxists thought it would, "taken care of itself." The forces of production created by capitalism had not proved strong enough to break the fetters. The proletariat had not by and large shown itself sufficiently class conscious to seize power from the bourgeoisie; and where power had been seized, the proletariat did not seem to know what to do with it. In the backward countries, where the working class was more radical than elsewhere, it was outnumbered many times by the peasantry: wherever the proletariat was moderately conscious, the economic base of society was too weak to allow for a socialist transformation. Furthermore, national feeling and the old, traditional divisions of the world were still far stronger than the Marxists would have liked to admit. Thus, instead of breaking up over its "insoluble" contradictions, capitalism had developed into another "final" stage: the age of imperialism.[4]

For a Marxist, the age of imperialism would never have come about had things gone according to Marx's prognosis. Its arrival has been a bitter disappointment, and has necessitated serious rethinking of all the axioms and laws of the Marxist science of revolution. What went wrong? What opportunities were missed? Why had not capitalism led directly to a world-wide proletarian revolution? These were the questions it became the business of all Marxists to answer. The theory of imperialism is an attempt to explain the stubborn fact that the revolution had not yet taken place in the most highly developed capitalist countries.[*]

[*] None of the basic ideas making up the theory of imperialism were original with Lenin. Instead, he adopted them from the Liberal English critic of imperialism, Hobson, and from such Marxist writers as Hilferding, Luxemburg, and Bukharin, without, however, giving them full credit for their contributions. Although in the academic world this would be a serious

Reduced to the simplest terms, this explanation runs as follows: instead of having developed its internal contradictions and tensions to a point where a revolutionary break must occur, capitalism has found a way out of these contradictions that were previously deemed insoluble. The way out is expansion into the whole world in search of cheap raw materials, ready markets for commodities and for excess capital, and, most important, cheap labor which could be exploited in unprecedented measure. This expansion of capitalism is called imperialism.* By embarking on it, capitalism has for the time being staved off the revolution and its own downfall. The reasons for this become clear as we examine the specific features which Lenin attributes to imperialism and to its consequences.†

breach of etiquette, it was more customary in the revolutionary movement, where there was a continuous active interchange of ideas, and where new ideas were proposed not for the sake of coming nearer to truth or of gaining academic prestige, but mainly for the purpose of convincing all comrades of the usefulness of certain strategies. Hence a young man like Bukharin probably felt pleased if Lenin, the "old man" of the movement, plagiarized his ideas.

* In his "Imperialism as the Highest Stage of Capitalism" (Lenin, vol. 19, pp. 143ff; translation in *Collected Works*, vol. 19, pp. 161ff), Lenin argued that one ought not to talk of imperialism as a "policy," because the use of this term would imply that imperialism was something modern capitalism could either take or leave. Though certain non-Leninist critics of imperialism may have wished to convey this idea, Lenin maintained that imperialism is not a policy that can be adopted or abandoned at will, but an inevitability for rotting and moribund capitalism. At the same time he himself used the phrase "policy of imperialism" thoughtlessly (*ibid.*, p. 159; translation, p. 178).

† In describing Lenin's theory of imperialism, we are not judging its correctness or adequacy. We can not, however, forego noticing the inadequacy of some of the criticism which has been leveled against it. I have in mind those critics who give the word "imperialism" a broader meaning than that given it by Lenin and then prove that imperialism can not be explained in Leninist terms. Schumpeter, for instance, identifies all phases of colonial expansion with imperialism and then shows easily that this imperialism was not caused by excessive capital accumulation and falling profits (*Capitalism, Socialism and Democracy*, New York, 1942, p. 53). Similarly, Kautsky and others defined imperialism as a foreign policy striving toward the annexation of foreign territories. Lenin correctly pointed out that imperialism is nothing but a word that can be defined in any way a writer pleases ("A Caricature of Marxism," vol. 19, p. 207; *Collected Works*, vol. 19, p. 229). He admitted that Rome, too, was "imperialistic," but argued that this statement merely obscured the issue. What he meant to do was to describe actual social processes as he saw them, and these

At first glance it appears that imperialism is nothing but vast intensification of the features of capitalism sketched above. Lenin himself emphasized this point: "A characteristic trait of capitalism in general," he wrote, "is the separation of the ownership of capital from the application of capital to production, the separation of money capital from industrial or productive capital, the separation of the *rentier* (who lives only on income from money capital) from the entrepreneur. . . . Imperialism is the highest stage of capitalism, where this separation takes on tremendous dimensions."[5] This intensification of the features of capitalism is traced by him through various additional aspects, for instance, the narrowing of the social basis of capitalism. Imperialism, according to Lenin, means the growth of tendencies toward monopoly until monopoly virtually takes the place of free competition. Monopoly becomes the economic essence of imperialism;* the terms "monopoly capitalism" and "imperialism are considered synonymous and are used interchangeably. Parallel with this growth of monopoly, the proletarization of the middle classes and the commercialization of all life reach their completion. Everyone has become a small cog in the huge machinery of monopoly capitalism; everyone has to sell himself. A minute number of monopolists now exploit virtually the entire society.†
This is the Leninist image of modern imperialism.

---

processes he named "imperialism." In order to disprove him it would be wrong to show that "imperialism" is in reality something else. What would have to be done would be to prove that the social processes he described either did not take place or were described inadequately by him. See also "Imperialism as the Highest Stage of Capitalism," vol. 19, pp. 137 (*Collected Works*, vol. 19, p. 155).

* "A Caricature of Marxism," Lenin, vol. 19, p. 207 (translation in *Collected Works*, vol. 19, p. 229). Lenin distinguished the following epochs in the growth of modern imperialism: (1) the 1860's and 1870's, which saw the maximal development of free competition and the weak beginnings of monopoly; (2) the half generation after 1873, during which wholesale cartelization took place, although some major industries were still escaping the trend; (3) the years after 1900, when cartels became the accepted form of monopoly capitalism ("Imperialism as the Highest Stage of Capitalism," vol. 19, p. 86; *Collected Works*, vol. 19, p. 98).

† Against the familiar contention that the joint-stock corporation has brought a considerable element of economic democracy into monopoly capitalism, Lenin held that, on the contrary, the scattering of stock among relatively disinterested small investors enables small cliques of big investors

But if this is realistic, why does not a revolution occur in which the exploiters are expropriated by the expropriated nation? Why do not the masses of the population throw out that small group of oppressors? The reason is that the intensification of this feature of capitalist society has not entailed a corresponding intensification of the strains and stresses that Marxists call the "contradictions of capitalism." On the contrary, the trend toward monopoly has lessened some of these strains. For one thing, monopoly capitalism, according to Lenin, reduces the so-called "anarchy of production," that state of affairs where the individual entrepreneur was hopelessly lost in the maze of the market economy. The growth of monopoly means that a small, oligarchical group of monopolists is in control of the major industrial establishment. They have been forced to get together, in an attempt to save their rule and to organize their productive apparatus more rationally. In part, this attempt to organize production under monopoly capitalism is the unwanted and unforeseen result of the growing importance of large banks. In the days of free competition, Lenin wrote, the stock exchange served as the indispensable regulator of competitive capitalism. In monopoly capitalism, banks fulfill a similar role, and the importance of the stock market declines proportionally.[6]

In addition, the monopolists themselves were waking up to the necessity of bringing order into anarchy, Lenin held, and, by cartelization and fusion agreements, they were partially doing so. Finally, monopoly capitalism, shaking on its narrow social basis, is forced to seek protection under the strong arm of the state. But the state, always ready to become an end in itself, in turn takes command over the processes of production and inaugurates the final measures toward the organization and integration of the economy. Through forced arbitration and forced cartelization, it integrates conflicting monopolistic powers even against their will and seeks to remove the last traces of the old anarchy of production. Monopoly capitalism leads to state

to enforce their domination over corporations, even with far less than 51 per cent control of all shares ("Imperialism as the Highest Stage of Capitalism," vol. 19, pp. 108–109; translation in *Collected Works,* vol. 19, pp. 122–123).

capitalism, and state capitalism is no longer anarchic. Lenin credited the First World War with speeding up the process of converting monopoly capitalism into state capitalism and producing what Bukharin called "organized capitalism." Wrote Lenin:

As early as 1891, Engels said that capitalism should not be identified with planlessness a priori. That is old stuff by now. Where there are trusts there is no more planlessness. Particularly in the twentieth century, the development of capitalism has progressed with giant steps, and the war has done what twenty-five years did not do. The nationalization of industry progressed not only in Germany, but also in England. From monopoly in general they have gone over to state monopoly. The objective state of affairs shows that the war has accelerated the development of capitalism, and it progressed from capitalism to imperialism, from monopoly to nationalization.*

Politically, monopoly and state capitalism are so firmly entrenched by virtue of their control of the means of production that they can easily afford to extend the blessings of democracy, at least formally — civil rights, freedom of the press, the franchise, and so forth. By the same token, democracy in the opinion of Lenin had lost the last trace of meaning and value. It had become mere formality and hypocrisy. The extension of formal liberties was only the political aspect (and there are other aspects, for instance, the ideological) of the economic benefits by which monopoly and state capitalism ensured the loyalty of the masses. In brief, the Leninist theory of imperialism

---

* Lenin, vol. 20, p. 249 (translation in *Collected Works,* vol. 20, book 1, p. 286). Surprisingly, Lenin drew optimistic conclusions from this analysis. All this, he continued, "has advanced the socialist revolution and has created the objective conditions for it. Thus the socialist revolution is being furthered by the course of the war."

In general, he thought of imperialism as the most advanced and progressive phase of capitalism — as capitalism which has closely approached socialism, so that only the expropriation of the monopolists remained to be done. He maintained that monopoly capitalism, by socializing, organizing, and rationalizing all aspects of production except property relations, also leads to technical progress. Capitalism "in its imperialist stage leads close to the most universal socialization of production; it drags, as it were, the capitalists against their will and conscience into some sort of new social order, the transition from full freedom of competition to full socialization" ("Imperialism as the Highest Stage of Capitalism," vol. 19, p. 89; *Collected Works,* vol. 19, p. 101).

maintains that the extortion of super-profits from their world dependencies enables the monopolists to use part of these super-profits to bribe the proletarized masses, or at least their influential higher layers, into acquiescence. Imperialism is thus seen as the only way by which the proletarian movement can be neutralized or robbed of its most dangerous sting.* For, with the help of super-profits, the bourgeoisie succeeds in averting the increase in the misery of the masses that Marx had considered inevitable. The super-profits are distributed in such a manner that everyone in the imperialist society benefits from them — the proletarians themselves thus turn into exploiters! "The Roman proletarian lived at the expense of society. The world of today lives at the expense of the modern proletarian. . . . Imperialism is changing this a bit. The privileged layer of the proletariat in the imperialist countries lives partly at the expense of hundred of millions of uncivilized peoples." †

This means that the proletarization of the masses, indeed, affects their *status* in relation to the monopolists, but does not lower their absolute standard of living, as Marx had predicted it would. Lenin claimed, moreover, that the bourgeoisie had often succeeded in obscuring the differences in economic status by means of formal concessions in all fields, not only

* With great relish Lenin quoted the warning of Cecil Rhodes, "If you do not want civil war, you must become imperialists" ("Imperialism as the Highest Stage of Capitalism," vol. 19, p. 134; translation in *Collected Works*, vol. 19, p. 175).

† "Imperialism and the Schism of Socialism," Lenin, vol. 19, p. 302 (translation in *Collected Works*, vol. 19, pp. 338). These and similar considerations allowed Lenin to describe capitalism in highly moralistic terms as a form of parasitism. The parasitic figure of the rentier has become so generalized, he wrote (leaning heavily on data furnished by Hobson), that entire nations are now on the verge of turning into rentier nations. In this connection he also pointed to the fact that imperialism means the export not of commodities but of capital to underdeveloped areas. And "the export of capital is parasitism raised to the second power." Imperialism could therefore be defined as "rotting capitalism" (vol. 19, pp. 301–302, and ch. 8 of "Imperialism as the Highest Stage of Capitalism," vol. 19; *Collected Works*, vol. 19, pp. 169–177). For some non-Leninist ideas somewhat similar, see Riesman's concept of the "age of consumption," as developed in his *The Lonely Crowd* (New Haven, Conn., 1950). Riesman speaks about this as a phase in our culture, while Lenin speaks about parasitism as a phase in the rule of a certain class.

political and economic, but also social and ideological. In turn, the proletariat, he claimed, had accepted the bourgeois way of life; or, as he contemptuously put it, the proletariat had turned "respectable." [7] Consequently, the inevitable "proletarization" of the middle classes in the age of imperialism actually "looks like" what we like to call the growth of the "new middle class," that is, the great white-collar army of salaried employees and experts of all sorts. In Lenin's eyes, this new middle class is the proletariat in a very transparent disguise.[8]

Another thing that corrupts the class consciousness and the international class solidarity of the workers is the fierce struggle between the imperialist nations. This divisiveness grows because sections of the proletariat acquire a vested interest in imperialism, from which they derive substantial benefits. The political parties and the trade-union movements of the workers therefore turn from their old revolutionary goals to a struggle for obtaining a maximal share in the benefits of imperialism. From revolutionary aspirations to trade-union consciousness, and from the latter to what Lenin called "social-chauvinism" — that is the way the workers' movement became the left wing of the bourgeoisie.[9] All the classes in an imperialist society, however bitterly they fight over the distribution of the spoils, are now united in a posi- tive — today we should say, bipartisan — attitude toward im- perialism and its policies. The classes have declared "civic peace." Class war has ceased. The International has broken up.

At that point the chances for revolution seem to have disap- peared, and some Marxists, even some of Lenin's own followers, tended to think so.* Leninism, however, is that school of

---

* Bukharin's theory of organized capitalism carried this implication. Bukharin's thoughts are marked by a rather pronounced pessimism. Lean- ing more toward anarchism than did Lenin, Bukharin in his writings deals more with liberty and the lack of it. He was therefore the first to discuss the political consequences of imperialism in terms which seem like a pre- view of the fascist state or Harold Lasswell's "garrison state" (Nikolai Bukharin, "K teorii imperialisticheskogo gosudarstva," in *Revoliutsiia Prava*, vol. 50, 1925). At the time of the controversy over Brest-Litovsk and in the early period of War Communism, Bukharin's pessimism made him a leader of the left-wing opposition, which wanted to break out of Russia's difficulties by a renewal of radical revolutionary activity on a world-wide scale. Later, during the 1920's, his fear of dictatorship led him to espouse

Marxism in the age of imperialism which did not let this conclusion remain the final word. Instead of resigning themselves to
the failure of the original Marxian prognosis, or even taking
pleasure in the changed prospects, the Leninists are in continual
search for forces not recognized by Marx as revolutionary,
forces that will carry on the fight for the socialist revolution in
lieu of the Western proletariat. In that sense, Leninism is the
last refuge of that optimism which characterized the doctrine
of Marx, and thus it maintains the spirit of the *Communist
Manifesto*. And yet, there is at times a note of desperation in
Leninism that betrays an inner uncertainty, a profound pessimism, an unconscious or half-conscious doubt in the actuality
of further chances for the proletarian revolution. Since it is
hardly ever conscious, this pessimism is never made explicit;
hence we have difficulty in demonstrating its existence.[10] One
indication is the very fanaticism of the faith that the Leninist
professes in the inevitable success of his final aims. Psychologically, this fanatical conviction is a means of compensating for
his inner uncertainty and silencing his secret doubts. It is like
whistling in the dark — and perhaps as blind as a man in the
dark.*

According to Lenin, of course, this faith in ultimate success is
by no means blind. In fact, not only is the theory of imperialism
an explanation of why the revolution has not yet taken place; it
is also an attempt to justify this faith by proving that the
revolution will, nonetheless, occur. The Leninist theory of imperialism asserts, just as Marx's theory of capitalism asserted,
that capitalism cannot function without leading to crises and

---

moderation and an almost Fabian gradualism. Tito's attempts at experi-
menting with democratic communism have quite a Bukharinist hue.

* This loudly proclaimed faith in the inevitability of the revolution is
matched by a crusader-like activism logically opposed to it. Functionally
and causally, however, they are related: functionally, because both the
faith and the activism help to silence the pessimistic doubts on which Leninism rests; causally, because these doubts are their psychological source.
Further, the pessimistic tendencies of Leninist thought help to explain its
bent toward totalitarianism. Leninism is Marxism beset with many inner
doubts — a distrust of history, of the masses, even of the conscious leadership. This leads to the preoccupation with manipulation, organization, and
coercion.

revolutionary situations. Both theories rest their optimism on the demonstration that there are forces within capitalist or imperialist society that are not bound by vested interests or other fetters of consciousness and will therefore be conscious enough to lead mankind toward a better future. The inevitable doom of imperialism and the existence of revolutionary forces are the kernel of Lenin's theory.

Marx had considered the insoluble contradictions of capitalism the guarantee of the proletarian revolution. But these contradictions were not insoluble at all; they had seemed so partly because Marx thought in narrow western European terms. Once it became apparent that the whole world was open for the large-scale expansion of capitalism, the Marxian prognosis collapsed. But — and this is where Lenin begins his analysis — as soon as the entire globe becomes a single capitalist-imperialist society, all the old "contradictions" reappear. They are the same forces that Marx had analyzed in capitalist society, but, transferred to a global scale, they appear in different guise. Imperialism, as Lenin saw it, consists of the "classical" features of capitalism transformed on an international level.*

One of the contradictions of capitalism, according to Marxism, had been the fact that collective industrial production was run by owners of private property. Lenin argued that this "contradiction," transferred to a global level, lives on as the continued existence of sovereign nations and large international monopolies that dominate world economy, which begs to be integrated and to be freed from the anarchy resulting from conflicting sovereignties. Thus competition with all its undesirable results continues, the different imperialist nations partially assuming the role formerly played by capitalists. Nations, not individual entrepreneurs, compete for survival and for monopoly positions. "The preponderance of finance capital over all other forms of capital highlights the ruling position of the rentier and the finance

* Lenin insisted that in the era of imperialism any sensible analysis of the situation should be made on a global scale. "From the point of view of Marxism it is stupid to stop at [examining] the position of just one country when speaking about imperialism, at a time when the capitalist countries are so closely tied to each other" (Lenin, vol. 22, p. 248; translation in *Collected Works*, vol. 20, book 1, pp. 280–281).

oligarchy, as well as the emergence of a few states with financial
'power' from among the others," [11] Lenin wrote; and he devoted
an entire chapter in his book on imperialism to a discussion of
the fact that the world had finally been divided among a few
big powers, first under colonialism, and later by the subtler
method of acquiring satellites among the lesser powers.[12]

Having accepted much of this analysis as an adequate description of contemporary society and its trends, Karl Kautsky made
the prognosis that these tendencies would lead to a continual
decrease in the number of great powers, until the world would
finally be organized in one great "ultraimperialist" bloc. With this
development, the danger of war between nations would finally
disappear. Lenin, after blasting Kautsky for obscuring existing
contradictions by positing an imaginary future harmony (a very
reactionary thing to do), sought to refute him by maintaining
that the uneven development of imperialism in the various
capitalist nations would inevitably result in a mortal struggle
between the major imperialist blocs.[13] Those very nations which
are late-comers to imperialism would, he claimed, develop their
imperialism faster than the leading nations, in an effort to catch
up. Hence a sharp disproportion would emerge between the
development of the national forces of production and the
accumulation of surplus capital on the one hand, and the division
of colonies, satellites, and spheres of influence on the other. This
disproportion, he concluded, could be corrected only by war
between the imperialist nations. For, "once the power pattern has
changed, what can resolve the contradictions, under capitalism,
except force?" [14]

These observations are connected with the hypothesis by
which Lenin sought to explain why imperialism could not for long
save capitalism from its inherent contradictions, why imperialism
is moribund capitalism. This hypothesis is the economic heart of
Lenin's theory of imperialism. Briefly stated: the contradictions
of imperialism are caused by the fact that imperialism entails the
export not of commodities but of capital to backward areas; in
fact, it might be defined satisfactorily as the export of capital.
To illustrate this, Lenin sketched the history of modern imperialism in the following manner. England, he wrote, was the

world's workshop at the beginning of the nineteenth century; she enjoyed a virtual monopoly of world trade and industrial production. But gradually the Continental countries and the United States began to catch up with her. The speed of this process increased until, in the second half of the century, there was an unprecedented development of industrial production in these once backward countries. Tremendous amounts of surplus capital were accumulated in the European countries and in North America. According to the laws of capitalism, this steadily accumulating capital could not be used for the purpose of raising domestic standards of living, for that would relieve the misery of the proletariat and correspondingly reduce the rate of profit. Much greater profits could be earned by this surplus capital if it were invested in underdeveloped countries, where capital was scarce, wages were low, and where both land and raw materials were cheaper than at home. Consequently, European capitalists began to exploit these areas by exporting surplus capital to them.[15] But, as the entire globe was engulfed by European capitalism, it became increasingly difficult to dispose of surplus capital. Hence the incessant struggle for *Lebensraum* among the imperialist nations. Moreover, while the export of capital relieved the contradictions within the exporting imperialist nation, at least for a while, the contradictions of capitalism in general were being spread all over the world, even into countries that had not been affected by them before. "The export of capital influences the development of capitalism in those countries to which it is directed: it speeds it up considerably. If, therefore, this export can to a certain degree lead to some delay in the development of the exporting countries, it occurs only at the price of extending and deepening the further development of capitalism in the entire world." [16] Moreover, in the measures in which capital exports build up the capitalist mode of production in the hitherto backward areas, the profitability of capital export diminishes. The need to expand production, which Lenin believed to be inherent in the nature of capitalism, and the possibilities of disposing of the product profitably come into increasing disharmony. According to Lenin, there is no way out of this impasse except the abolition of private property and, with it, of the need for profits as the indispensable precondition of production itself.[17]

The age of imperialism, then, is one in which all the international solidarities characterizing the nineteenth century had broken down. The collapse of the Second International has its counterpart in the simultaneous collapse of the bourgeois international.* The economic result of this breakdown is the replacement of relatively free world trade by modern economic nationalism, protectionism, neomercantilism, and similar practices, while the political consequence is war, or a number of wars, between the imperialist nations for the division and redivision of the world. Thus competition, which is, according to Marxism, the cause of the anarchy of capitalist production, lives on in international affairs. National economies may be integrated, self-sufficient, and rationalized; yet, from the point of view of the world community, the clash of sovereign imperialist nations is nothing else but the old competitive struggle between capitalists in a new form.

Exploitation, too, appears on a global scale and in different guise, according to the theory of imperialism. For, even while the proletariat in the imperialist nations may get a share of the super-profits reaped by the system, and may temporarily become part of the imperialist class, certain groups remain in the modern world that are being exploited as openly and as miserably as the working class in mid–nineteenth century England. These groups, according to Lenin's theory, are the backward nations. They fulfill the same role in relation to the exploiter nations that the proletariat did in relation to the capitalists; and they are similarly affected by this relationship. Just as capitalism had educated the working class for revolt, in the Marxist view, imperialism is now seen as educating the backward nations for revolt against it. The backward nations are turning into bearers

* See Lenin's report on Soviet foreign policy made on 14 May 1918, in Lenin, vol. 23, p. 405. But he made a similar observation as early as 1895 in a draft party platform (vol. 1, p. 436; translation in *Selected Works*, vol. 1, p. 482). According to Zinov'ev, the collapse of the Second International reflected the collapse of the bourgeois order itself (*II Kongress Kommunisticheskogo Internatsionala* (Second Comintern Congress), Petrograd, 1921, p. 11).

of proletarian "class" consciousness; the class struggle itself is being shifted to an international plane. Nations become its protagonists.

So far, we have sketched the Leninist theory of imperialism in bold strokes. Although we were able to document the major outlines of the image of modern imperialism by quotations from Lenin's works, the reader should be aware that many of the assertions made were by no means exclusive with him. On the contrary, he was slower in appropriating some of the major ideas of the theory than were many of his comrades. He was demonstrably loath to abandon traditional Marxist schemes for the new theories, and he failed to give his ideas on imperialism the clear and systematic form in which we present them here.

In stressing Lenin's reluctance to tamper with Marxist doctrines, we seem to contradict statements made at the beginning of this chapter. This contradiction will have to be explained. The curious fact about Lenin is that he combined at once the doctrinaire rigidity of an orthodox Marxist and the flexibility of a pragmatic tinkerer endowed with amazing political horse sense. We have seen that the theoretical schemes of Marxist doctrine dominated his political strategy for a number of years, but that Marxism subsequently emerged as a "guide to action." Lenin became a strategist who scorned the doctrinaire orthodoxy of some of his comrades, and was ever ready to tell them that "living life" was stronger than the abstractions of Marxist armchair philosophers. In crucial moments he flung theory aside, saying that the pulsating course of actual events defied classification and analysis. He used theory, if at all, to rationalize his novel courses of action, though it is highly significant that he felt keenly the need for rationalization. The pattern that emerged was one of constant changes in strategy, accompanied or followed by a continual search for a new theoretical framework to support his unorthodox actions.

At this juncture, however, Lenin would come into conflict with himself. Flexible as he was as a strategist, he was unwilling to tamper with the broad theories of history bequeathed him by Marx, far more unwilling certainly than a Trotsky or a Luxemburg. Hence he was severely handicapped in working out his rationalizations on a more abstract level. This conflict had two consequences. First, he became impatient with theory, and particularly with those comrades who used it in arguments against him; and this impatience with theory became one of the traditions of the party, to be carried to surprising lengths by his eventual successor. Second, the conflict prevented Lenin, as we have noted already, from becoming fully conscious of the implications inherent in the theoretical changes he did bring himself to make, so that he did not work out his theory of imperialism systematically. Instead, the thoughts presented coherently here came to be mixed in with his previously held notions, often without being explained or put into their places. For instance, Lenin in 1912 began to speak of exploiter nations and exploited nations. In October 1917 he acknowledged that there was a trend toward the development of one-class societies, a trend toward the division of the world into almost purely imperialist and almost purely proletarian nations, which would have made a "proletarian" revolution likely only in backward, "proletarian" nations.[18] Yet as late as the spring of that same year he had been maintaining that the revolution would occur in highly developed industrial countries, that any turn of events which ran counter to this logic of economic determinism would be accidental and unimportant, that the Russian revolution should therefore be regarded as an accident of history.* All the naïve astonishment with which he viewed the still unbelievable *fait accompli* was expressed some weeks later, at the party's April Conference, where he said, "Marx said that France would start and Germany would finish the job. And now, what do you know? — the Russian proletariat has achieved more than anyone else!" [19] Quite typically, his first theoretical readjustment to make the theory fit the facts took the form of a dogmatic statement: "Comrade Rykov says that socialism must come forth from other countries with a more developed industry. But that is not so. We cannot tell who will start and who will finish. [Rykov's statement] is not Marxism but a parody on Marxism." [20]

---

* "Farewell Letter to the Swiss Workers," Lenin, vol. 22, p. 68 (translation in *Collected Works*, vol. 20, book 1, p. 86). He emphasized this point again in 1918, at the Seventh Party Congress, when he wanted to dramatize the difficulties facing the Soviet regime (vol. 21, pp. 316ff).

Some time later he stated more definitely (in retrospect!) where the revolution would begin: "For anyone who has really put his mind to studying the economic preconditions of the socialist revolution in Russia, it cannot but be clear that in Europe it is immeasurably harder to start the revolution, while with us it is immeasurably easier to start, though it will be more difficult here than there to continue the revolution." [21] For the first time he spoke of Russia's backwardness as a factor in bringing about the revolution. "We see today a different configuration of the forces of international socialism. We should say that the movement starts more easily in those countries not belonging to the group of exploiter countries, which have the possibility of grabbing more easily and are able to bribe the upper strata of their workers." [22]

Yet, not only was Lenin slow in adopting these ideas, he also remained skeptical about the scope of their application. Unwilling to give up the notion that the really effective proletarian revolution should and would originate in the advanced Western countries, he engaged in a vehement polemic against Rosa Luxemburg's theory of imperialism, which was another attempt to show the global difficulties that would lead to the final collapse of modern capitalism.* Nor did he agree with Bukharin's theory of organized capitalism, according to which imperialism removed all features of the anarchy of production within the imperialist nation. Although he admitted that imperialism had contributed considerably toward the removal of some features of that anarchy, he held that new ones had been added in their stead, so that the contradictions *within* the imperialist nations remained at least as important as the revolt of the backward nations. In the first place, he claimed, there was sharp competition among the monopolies for division of the world, a competition that was national as well as international in scope.† In addition, he

---

* Rosa Luxemburg, *The Accumulation of Capital* (London, 1951). It is typical of Lenin as a thinker that his main criticism of Luxemburg's theory was based on practical considerations. He felt that a theory which virtually predicted the collapse of world imperialism as certain might give the proletariat and its leaders an excuse to let their revolutionary activism flag.

† Lenin devoted an entire chapter (chapter 5) in his main work on imperialism to a description of how the world was being divided up among

claimed that "the monopoly which grows up in *some* branches
of industry intensifics and sharpens the chaotic character of
capitalist production as a whole," because it results in a greater
discrepancy in the development of industry and agriculture.
Moreover, the privileged position of heavy industry, he wrote,
increases the planless chaos in other industries, and technological
advance remains chaotic and uncontrolled.[23] Finally, the struggle
between big and little capitalists, characteristic of preimperialist
capitalism, repeats itself in the period of imperialism as the
struggle between monopoly capitalists and banks.*

According to Lenin's further speculations, the wars for the
distribution and redistribution of spheres of influence, colonies,
and satellites would tax both the victors and the vanquished,
and this situation would intensify domestic tensions within the
imperialist nations. In desperation, the bourgeoisie would then be
forced to scrap bourgeois democracy, because the ultimate failure
of imperialism to bribe the masses had become apparent to the
broadest sections of the population. In a desperate effort to
maintain its rule, monopoly capitalism would have to abolish
democracy and to rely frankly on coercing the dissatisfied. Reaction and the abolition of democracy, Lenin wrote in a sweeping
statement, are the political superstructure of monopoly capitalism.† When they occurred, the hypocrisies of formal democracy

---

national and international monopolies. This complicates the analysis of imperialism as international competition between sovereign imperialist nations,
without, however, making it invalid.

* "Imperialism as the Highest Stage of Capitalism," Lenin, vol. 19, p. 105
(translation in *Collected Works*, vol. 19, p. 119). In this struggle, he wrote,
the capitalists often yearn for the good old days of free enterprise and free
competition. This yearning for a return to rugged individualism, he continued, was the form petty bourgeois mentality took in the age of imperialism (*ibid.*, p. 90; translation, p. 102).

† "A Caricature of Marxism," Lenin, vol. 19, p. 207 (translation in *Collected Works*, vol. 19, p. 229). In his *The 18th Brumire of Louis Bona-
parte*, wrote Lenin, Marx maintained that "the state machine is a bureau-
cratic-military machine in the majority of capitalist states"; and he added
the comment that now, in 1917, this should be said about *all* capitalist
states (*Leninskii Sbornik*, Moscow, 1924–1938, vol. 14, p. 223). An early
comment by Lenin on the mob violence, scapegoatism, and gangster methods typical of modern fascism is contained in his article "On the Black
Hundred" (Lenin, vol. 14, pp. 137–168), written in 1909. Another, much
weaker point is his reference to the strict wartime curbs on civil rights

would be revealed openly, for the continued exploitation of the domestic proletariat by monopoly capitalism could not remain obscured. But this development would mean a renewal of the revolutionary spirit among the working classes of the Western industrial nations, and thus the inevitability of socialism would be re-established.

---

enacted even in the most liberal democracies, such as England. Before the war, he said, England could afford a maximum of political liberty because there was no revolutionary movement. If now it has to apply tsarist measures of repression, that can mean only that the revolutionary movement is growing (Lenin, vol. 20, p. 249; *Collected Works*, vol. 20, book 1, p. 282).

Chapter 12

The Dialectics of Backwardness

And, behold, there are last which shall be first, and there are first which shall be last.

LUKE 13:30

If a certain level of culture is required for the creation of socialism (though no one can say what that certain "level of culture" should be), why can we not start out from the conquest, by revolutionary means, of the preconditions for that certain level, and only then, on the basis of the worker-peasant regime, and the soviet order, move further to catch up with the other nations?

LENIN

The theory of imperialism as we have presented it gives a certain unity and completeness to Leninist thought that it did not have before the First World War. We shall discuss this function of the theory later. But first let us take up two ideas implied by the theory of imperialism, ideas of a more theoretical, or abstract, nature. They are attempts to explain the new features of capitalist society that the theory of imperialism describes. They deal with the nature of social development in general, and with the broad theory of the proletarian revolution. In presenting them as an integral part of Leninism, we have to add a note of caution. The ideas presented in this chapter were not articulated by Lenin, at least not in systematic form. Nor have other communist theoreticians developed them as clearly and cohesively as we present them here, although Trotsky,

Bukharin, and others, took important steps in this direction. They are implied, however, in the thoughts of Lenin and his friends about imperialism; they can be abstracted from the more concrete observations with which he satisfied himself. Moreover, they have definitely become part of the Leninist ideological heritage. Vaguely, half-consciously, unsystematically, the ideas we shall discuss here are accepted, perhaps as commonplace, by communist theoreticians, even though they might, for political reasons of the moment, disavow them. Somehow, the rigid and forbidding terminology used by contemporary Leninists expresses the thoughts we shall now discuss. Somehow, this is the image they have of social and political developments in the twentieth century.

This chapter deals with two hypotheses by which Leninists have come to explain the new contradictions of capitalism in the age of imperialism. One of these hypotheses is the doctrine of the uneven development of capitalism, to which reference has been made already. At first glance, this is nothing else than the trite observation that some nations have made greater and speedier advances than others in the development of their industrial establishment. It seems to be but a negative statement, another acknowledgment that things have not gone according to the universally valid pattern, or "laws," established by Marx. The fact that Marx himself was aware of the high degree of abstractness characterizing his theory, and that he warned his readers to expect to encounter modifications in every concrete instance, did not prevent his followers, not only among the Leninists, from taking his scheme too literally. The "modifications," therefore, had to be discovered gradually, and these discoveries led to revisions of Marxist thought.* The abstract

---

* Perhaps the flexibility of Marx has been overstated. His reservations, indeed, were expressed: "in theory it is the custom to assume that the laws of capitalist production evolve in their pure form. In reality, however, there is but an approximation. Still, this approximation is so much greater to the extent that the capitalist mode of production is normally developed, and to the extent that its adulteration with remains of former economic conditions is outgrown" (Karl Marx, *Capital*, Chicago, 1919, vol. 3, p. 206). Precisely this, however, is not the case in so-called backward areas, so that hypotheses like those discussed in the present chapter become necessary.

schemes had been belied by what Lenin called "living life," and the doctrine of uneven development is a theoretical acknowledgment of this.

To a certain extent, it is a face-saving device; at least it originated in the necessity to save theoretical face. Actually, it does not really save face to acknowledge that "capitalism develops unevenly," and we should not trouble to discuss it if it did not contain certain new insights. The concept of uneven development is not only an admission of theoretical inadequacy, but also a positive attempt to find new and better "laws" of historical development. The doctrine that, gropingly and very vaguely, arises from Lenin's theory of imperialism is such an attempt, and I propose to call it the doctrine of the "dialectics of backwardness." In brief, Leninism asserts that backwardness is a crucial causal factor of change, and with this theorem it resurrects and buttresses the old Marxian contention that revolution is inevitable.

In the abstract, the dialectics of backwardness is but a rephrasing of an old principle of Marxism: that the exploited are the carriers of progressive consciousness, the Chosen People who form the mass basis of progressive social and political movements. Concretely, the Leninists apply this to the world of nations in the twentieth century, and arrive at some surprising conclusions. For one thing, this doctrine gives Russia a central place in the history of human progress and thus continues a Russian nationalist tradition going back to Peter Chaadaev and other writers of the early nineteenth century. In addition, it succeeds in linking two broad social movements of our time that have often been thought unlinkable, nay poles apart: nationalism and Marxist socialism. (Incidentally, the fact that many of the Russian Slavophiles and Westernizers of the nineteenth century were both nationalists and socialists is another indication of the traits Lenin had in common with them.) Nationalism is linked with socialism in that the dialectics of backwardness serves as a Marxist explanation and interpretation of the phenomenon of modern nationalism, which is thus fitted into historical materialism for the first time. Hence, in practice, national movements among backward peoples are assigned a conspicuous role in the revolution, which is still called "proletarian" even though it has come to assume a very different character.

Let us see how modern nationalism is explained in Marxist terms. The Marxist regards history as the development of higher and higher modes of production, one rising out of the other. According to the Leninist version, the development lacks uniformity when looked at on a world-wide scale; it proceeds at markedly different speeds in different areas. As a matter of fact, the highest mode of production developed so far, capitalism, developed mainly in the comparatively narrow area of western Europe, and only toward the end of the nineteenth century began to engulf the rest of the world. The process of spreading capitalism all over the world was, we saw, called imperialism.

To the nations thus drawn into the orbit of Western civilization for the first time, imperialism poses a profound problem: whatever their past history, their past culture, their established way of life, they are compelled to adjust to the imperialist world. The West is trying to force its way of life onto foreign cultures, and this threat is their major contemporary problem. And a threat it is, because capitalism, or the capitalist nations, technologically superior to all others, menaces the very existence of these cultures and threatens to swallow up the entire world. Even if no attempt is made to take political possession of backward areas, even if there is no danger of extinction to a given backward nation as a political unit, the rising tide of imperialism is nevertheless a menace, so that "political imperialism" is but a marginal issue. Imperialism does not mean merely the seizure of colonies; that is only a by-product. The essence of imperialism, to the Leninist, is the export of capital, and therefore of capital-*ism*, a policy which is not only exploiting the labor of backward nations by the most modern methods, but also corroding their entire pattern of culture, class structure, and way of life.

By developing capitalism in backward nations, however, the West is showing these nations a way out of the danger of being swallowed up. For, if a backward nation wishes to maintain its national integrity, it will have to rival the strength of the dominant nations, and it can do so by adopting the features that give the ruling societies their strength. For a Marxist, this prospective solution can mean only an admonition to the backward nations to develop capitalism for themselves, or more broadly, to adopt the leading nations' superior mode of production. Industrial civilization, which is encroaching on traditional nonindustrial ways of life, promises to help other nations emancipate themselves from Western rule.

These thoughts are not peculiar to Leninism. Many people who have contributed to the theory or the tradition of modern nationalism have seen things similarly.* One might adduce Alexander Hamilton and Friedrich List, who sought to "copy" the industrial establishment that England had pioneered, or the European cameralists, who were eager to promote in their own realms those trades, crafts, and manufactures which had contributed to the wealth of their stronger neighbors. One of the most dramatic examples is the Russian tsar Peter the Great, whose entire life was devoted to a feverish attempt to copy the mercantilist-absolutist pattern of political economy he had studied in western Europe. Peter became the hero of the so-called "westernizers" in Russia, that school of thought which regarded Russia as a member, albeit a backward one, of the European family of nations, and saw Russia's historic mission or "destiny" as catching up with the West in political, social, and economic developments.

All Russian Marxists were squarely in this westernizing tradi-

---

* Marx, too, spoke of uneven development in a number of side remarks. Thus, in his letter to Annenkov of 28 December 1846, he wrote, "One can say that up to the year 1825 . . . the demands of consumption in general increased more rapidly than production, and the development of machinery was a necessary consequence of the need of the market. Since 1825, the invention and application of machinery has been simply the result of the war between workers and employers. And this is only true of England. As for the European nations, they were driven to adopt machinery owing to English competition both in their home markets and on the world market. Finally in North America the introduction of machinery was due both to competition with other countries and to lack of hands, that is, to the disproportion between the population of North America and its industrial needs" (printed in Karl Marx, *The Poverty of Philosophy*, Chicago, 1910, p. 156).

tion, but significant differences developed between them over
the question of implementing a program of westernization. Their
different answers to the question of how Russia could catch up
with the West illuminate the schism between Leninism and
Menshevism. The moderates, upholding Marxian ideas about the
development of capitalism, maintained that backward nations like
Russia would have to follow Europe by recapitulating the entire
course of development outlined by Marx. They compared early
twentieth-century Russia with late eighteenth-century France,
and said that Russia's next goal would be a Russian 1789. Only
then would the time come for further tasks. We have seen that
these ideas were held not only by the Mensheviks but also by
Lenin, in his early years, before the schism in the party had
developed. The widening of the gap between himself and the
moderates was a gradual process, in which the tendency of the
moderates was to paint a relatively optimistic picture of
Russia's westernization, while Lenin more and more stressed her
backwardness. The practical corollary of this optimism on the
part of the Mensheviks was their disapproval of violent revolutionary activity, since it could only disturb the inevitable progress
of Russia in the direction of capitalism, westernization, and
democracy. Even today some scholars claim that, had Russia not
fallen into the hands of revolutionary adventurers, she would
now be a respectable member of the family of democratic
nations, and they denounce the October Revolution as a needless
and harmful interruption in Russia's gradual and inevitable ad-
justment to the West.[1]

Lenin went in the opposite direction. His growing appraisal
of Russia as a backward nation was coupled with increasing
radicalism. His alliance with the propertyless masses in active
pursuit of the "bourgeois revolution" was an intermediary step
in a line of development that led him from the demand for a
Russian 1789 to the very active promotion of an immediate
proletarian revolution. For he gradually came to the conclusion
that a "1789" would not suffice to solve Russia's problems in the
modern age. "If our revolution were to stop here, it would go
into history no less than the revolution of 1793. But they will say

to us: That was in the eighteenth century. For the eighteenth century that was sufficient, but for the twentieth it is too little." *

Now, if a "1789" is not sufficient in the twentieth century, it follows that Russia cannot possibly cope with her problems in this century merely by copying the pattern of development characterizing the history of the West. What she must copy is the West's achievements. Russia, China, India, and all other backward countries that wish to preserve their national integrity must imitate the modern industrial way of life of Western imperialism.†

But, in copying Western industrialism, the backward areas, in Lenin's opinion, should avoid duplicating the superstructure of Western capitalist property relations. These capitalist relations of production are considered outmoded; hence it is not necessary to

---

* Lenin, vol. 22, p. 490. This was directed against Kautsky, who had expressed his satisfaction that the February Revolution had been the last bourgeois revolution, predicted that it would transform Russia into something like a Jeffersonian democracy, and appeared satisfied with this trend of development (Karl Kautsky, *Die Diktatur des Proletariats*, Vienna, 1918, p. 50). Lenin countered this by writing that in the twentieth century such a "new democracy" could only be the basis for building up a modern industrial society, if indeed Russia hoped to survive as an independent nation ("Urgent Tasks of the Soviet Regime," vol. 22, pp. 443–444; translation in *Selected Works*, vol. 7, pp. 318–319). Trotsky's thoughts on permanent revolution are exactly the same (*Permanentnaia Revoliutsiia*, Berlin, 1930, pp. 58–59).

† "We need Europe for another few decades," Peter the Great is reported to have said, "but then we shall have to turn our back to her." Thus he saw in westernization a means of revolting against the West. Similarly, Lenin saw himself as a Russian national liberator. At the celebration of *Pravda's* tenth anniversary he spoke of Russia's national awakening in the October Revolution (*Sobranie Sochinenii*, Moscow, 1920–1923, vol. 18, book 2, pp. 73ff), and, after the conclusion of the Treaty of Brest-Litovsk, he wrote that this setback would only increase "our will to liberation, our endeavor to rise anew out of servitude to independence; our unbending decision to achieve at all cost that *Rus'* may no longer be miserable and powerless, that she may become mighty and rich in the full sense of the word. *Rus'* will become thus, if she will throw off all despondency and all phrases, if she will grit her teeth and gather all her strength, if she will strain every nerve, tighten every muscle, if she will understand that salvation is possible *only* through that international revolution on which we have embarked . . ." ("The Main Task of Our Days," vol. 22, pp. 376–377). Note the use of the traditionalist, romantic name *Rus'* for Russia; it rings strangely in the mouth of a social democrat.

adopt them together with industrialism. Capitalism is not even considered essential to the industrial way of life at present. In the West, to be sure, modern industry was built by capitalism; hence, in the "normal" Marxian scheme of development, capitalism was a precondition for the development of modern industry. But today it is no more than a relic of the tortuous history of the West, which in the virgin soil of the "a-historical" backward countries can be skipped.

We have here an entirely new theory of development, which, let us emphasize again, is never expressed as clearly and unequivocally as we express it here, but which most Leninists nonetheless accept tacitly. According to this theory, two types of society exist within the capitalist world, those societies which are advanced in the development of the modern industrial apparatus, and those which are not. The former type will tend to be interested in preserving the *status quo*, because it benefits from its advanced development and from the backwardness of the others. It will therefore develop ideologies in which the present state of affairs is idealized and justified. The latter type of society tends to be revisionist or rebellious in fact and in thought. Chafing under the domination of the advanced nations, it will strive to attain the achievements of the leading societies and to improve on them.* The high level of economic achievements in one type of society is therefore matched by a high degree of political consciousness in the other, and these two features are mutually exclusive. Efficiency in production and radical political ideas develop in inverse proportion, not in direct proportion as Marxism had held. The revolution is bred not in countries where capitalism is highly developed, but in countries where it is in its infancy.†

Even though this theory is considerably out of tune with

* Stalin's so-called "law of industrialization" is but a pompous and formalized expression of this. It means that catching up with the industrial West is an absolute necessity for the Soviet state and a task which takes precedence over all others. Long before Stalin formulated this law, his left-wing critics said the same thing in calling for a policy of "primitive socialist accumulation."

† Again, there are strong affinities between these Leninist ideas and the thought of the Slavophiles, who preceded Lenin by two generations.

original Marxist theories about historic development,* it can be reconciled with other aspects of Marxism, particularly with the Marxist sociology of knowledge, which strongly implies (though it does not prove) that the underdog is always readier and better equipped to criticize and transcend evil and outdated features of the ruling group. Lenin's theory identifies the underdog in imperialist society with the working classes in backward and semicolonial nations; more broadly, and with some reservations, in Leninism backward nations as such become the underdogs of imperialism, who will build new and better societies. Backwardness can turn into a blessing. As one American social scientist put it:

> What Lenin teaches . . . is a division of labor in promoting a world-wide proletarian revolution among the differently developed countries. The more advanced countries present the model of development on the basis of which the young backward countries have kept abreast in their development, but to be one of them is not a privilege. When they arrive at the doors of socialism they find themselves unable to enter. . . . While the economic and social structure is ripe for the revolution, the political form is already too rigid to permit revolution. History might have run into a blind alley, if it were not for the greater mobility of the younger countries.[2]

* It is not so completely out of tune with Marx's thought as one might think. Marx too had ideas about a dialectic of backwardness. Together with Engels he wrote (in a book Lenin never read):

"It is understood that big industry does not attain equal levels of development in every locality of a country. This does not, however, retard the class movement of the proletariat, because the proletarians begotten by big industry assume leadership over this movement and carry the entire mass with them [here Marx and Engels express Lenin's principle of proletarian leadership over the petty bourgeois masses] and because the workers who are excluded from big industry are placed by this big industry into an even more miserable condition of life than the workers of big industry itself [a very curious departure from stereotyped conceptions of the theory of maturity!]. Furthermore, the countries in which big industry has developed have an impact on the *plus ou moins* nonindustrial countries, *in the measure in which world traffic has dragged them into the universal struggle of competition*" ("Die deutsche Ideologie," in *MEGA*, part 1, vol. 5, p. 50 — italics added).

See also their remark concerning the secret of North America's rapid development. They attribute this to the fact that the virgin soil of the New World was settled by progressive people with an advanced social organization, who had left Europe because it was too reactionary for them (*ibid.*, pp. 62–63).

In short, Lenin believed that the last would be the first, and the first would be last, not because it *ought* to be so on moral grounds, but because of compelling trends inherent in contemporary history,* which are summarized in the hypothesis of uneven development.

The second hypothesis designed to explain the contradiction of imperialism is closely related to it. It is the theory of combined development, which, together with the theory of uneven development, constitutes what we have chosen to call the dialectics of backwardness.

It has been stated already that Lenin sharply opposed those theorists who concluded that the struggle between classes had turned entirely into a struggle between nations. He thought that backward nations had indeed become carriers of proletarian class consciousness, but still he insisted that class war continued to rage within each type of nation, advanced as well as backward. It might subside for a while or even become atrophied in the exploiter nations, but, sooner or later, when the failure of imperialism becomes obvious to the masses, it would flare up with renewed vitality. Nor were the backward nations internally unified, and previous passages in which we spoke about the reaction of "backward nations" against Western imperialism should not be interpreted as implying such. To Lenin and to most of his followers, the backward nations appeared to be shaken by a class struggle even more violent than anything taking place in a normal bourgeois society. For in backward societies not only did the proletariat struggle against the bourgeoisie, but the bourgeoisie itself was still fighting against autocracy, feudal privilege, or other relics of precapitalist conditions. According to the theory of combined development, two class struggles went on at the same time; two revolutions had to be fought simultaneously.

To express this in more general terms: all backward societies, Lenin held, combine features characteristic of different stages of development. Social phenomena, institutions, modes of life,

* Lenin clearly implied that he saw in the dialectic of backwardness a working hypothesis for a general theory of historical development. See "Backward Europe and Progressive Asia," Lenin, vol. 16, pp. 395–396.

ideologies, classes, technological features, belonging to different periods of the development of capitalism in the West, are tele-scoped into one period in the backward nations.* Here too, our first reaction might be that, like the theory of uneven develop-ment, this hypothesis is nothing else than an admission of failure, testifying to the impossibility of applying the Marxist scheme of development to backward societies. They do not fit Marxist theory, and Marxist theory does not fit them. They show that Marx and Engels deceived themselves when they blandly generalized from the history of England or, at best, of western Europe, and then applied their generalizations to the whole world, at least by implication. Yet in actuality the theory of combined development is a positive attempt to formulate new and better generalizations, and it concerns itself with the domestic aspects of the law of uneven development. For the coincidence of "noncontemporaneous" features within backward societies is but a reflection of the world-wide coexistence of non-contemporaneous societies, which Leninism calls "uneven de-velopment."

According to Leninist theory, such a telescoping of non-contemporaneous features occurs when a backward society is drawn into the orbit of an advanced civilization. It is this en-croachment of capitalism on peasant economies which, to Lenin, explains why both the most modern types of industrial capitalism and the most primitive agricultural methods could exist in Russia — to give only one example.†

* The hypothesis of combined development is developed most clearly by Trotsky, who used the term "telescoping." But Lenin obviously thought in similar terms. See, for instance, "The Second Duma and the Second Wave of the Revolution," Lenin, vol. 10, p. 369.

† "If we compare the precapitalist era in Russia with the capitalist era, . . . we have to recognize that the development of the national economy under capitalism is extremely rapid. But if we compare that rapidity of development with the rapidity which would have been possible, given the modern level of technology and culture in general, then the actual de-velopment of capitalism in Russia must in fact be considered slow. And it could not help being slow, for in no capitalist country have institutions irrec-oncilable with capitalism survived in such abundance, institutions which retard the country's development and immeasurably worsen the position of the producers who 'suffer as much from capitalism as from the insufficient development of capitalism,' to quote the phrase of Marx" ("The Develop-

Furthermore, "combined development" could take place only in those backward societies which have already been affected by imperialism, so that the term "backwardness" when used in connection with the theory of imperialism is restricted to those societies which are already on the margin of Western civilization, and excludes those unaffected by it. Even the consciousness of backwardness is awakened only among those nations which have come into contact with the West, for poverty is recognized only in comparison with the wealth of others.* In the modern world, a consciousness of poverty in underdeveloped nations turns into indignation when the inhabitants witness the havoc wrought by so-called "overproduction," that *crise pléthorique* which Marx and his followers considered an inevitable consequence of capitalist commodity production.†

To the revolutionary strategist, combined development opens up exciting new perspectives for action. For it makes possible unique combinations of social forces; it creates class relations of new and ever shifting character, which have to be examined anew in each backward country, and for every current moment. It is by means of these unique constellations of the class struggle that Lenin could justify his conception that backward nations might carry on and take over noncontemporaneous Western developments. Moreover, all of Lenin's pragmatism, all his readiness to try methods previously scored by the Marxist movement, all his contempt of the Menshevik preoccupation with accepted

---

ment of Capitalism in Russia," Lenin, vol. 3, p. 469; translation in *Selected Works*, vol. 1, p. 385).

* Marx gives the example of the house which becomes too small for its owner and thus no longer satisfies his wants when the houses around it begin to grow larger. "Our wants and satisfactions originate in society; we therefore measure them against society; we do not measure them against the objects of their satisfaction. Because their nature is societal, their nature is relative" ("Lohnarbeit und Kapital," in *MEGA*, part 1, vol. 6, p. 487).

† This is what Marx and Engels wrote, two generations before Lenin's thoughts on imperialism: "In our conception, all collisions in history have their origin in the contradiction between the forces of production and the form of traffic. By the way, it is not necessary that this contradiction, in order to lead to collisions in a given country, come to a point in this country itself. The competition with industrially more developed countries, which is caused by the ever spreading international intercourse, is sufficient to cause a similar contradiction even in countries with less developed industry" ("Die deutsche Ideologie," p. 63).

means and traditions of the workers' movement — all these typical features of Leninist strategy and his operational code found theoretical justification in the theory of combined development. His elitism and his shifting attitude toward the various classes, his attitude toward national movements, his demand for the transformation of international wars into civil wars, every one of these formulas and devices, which arose as *ad hoc* changes in Marxist orthodoxy and could at first be justified only by the needs of the moment and the peculiarities of the Russian conditions, now appeared to be normal and perfectly orthodox. They could be justified by the law of combined development, which converts the experience of western Europe, hitherto considered the standard pattern of development, into nothing but a unique, perhaps even a marginal, case.

Specifically, it becomes clear in the light of this hypothesis why the leaders of a revolutionary party in a backward country could adopt and develop the most radical ideology that had originated in an advanced society, why, in short, backward nations could become carriers of "proletarian class consciousness." Clearly, the popularity of Marxism in underdeveloped areas appears paradoxical when we realize the conditions which gave rise to this movement, and the premises on which it is based. Marxism is a product of the industrial age, and all its ideas about society arise from an acceptance of the machine as the most basic fact of modern life. At the same time, it is radically critical of the social institutions and relationships of the industrial age. Transformed into the theory of imperialism, this ambivalence toward industrial capitalism turns into an ambivalence toward the West, and this mixture of hostility and admiration develops naturally among politically conscious men in underdeveloped areas. In espousing Leninism, such men can advocate a program of westernization without abandoning their hatred and fear of the West. Their very advocacy of westernization is a proclamation of rebellion; just because they are afraid of the West they must westernize, so as to be able to proclaim their independence.

Ambivalence toward the West is one of the most important elements of modern nationalism, and by expressing it Leninism exerts a tremendous attraction on national leaders in backward areas. Modern national consciousness is produced by the same Western civilization against which it is directed: Western capitalism, in expanding on a global scale, not only creates, educates, and equips the proletariat, as Marx had held, but also creates, educates, and equips the underdeveloped nations, which then rise against their creator. Finally, ambivalence toward the West can be seen simply as an expression of the fact that during the process of being sucked into modern industrial civilization, the underdeveloped nations are both part of the West and not part of it, both within the stream of European history and outside of it. Their revolutions, from the Russian Revolution on, are both Western and anti-Western, proletarian and colonial. "World imperialism," said Lenin, "must fall when the revolutionary onslought of the exploited and oppressed workers within each country . . . unites with the revolutionary onslought of hundreds of millions of men who up to now have been standing outside of history, have been considered only as its objects." [3]

Here nationalism has merged with socialism, and an entire new theory of revolution has emerged. The slogans coined by Marx are no longer adequate to the new strategy, and the best-known Marxist slogan, "Proletarians of all countries, unite," was amended by the Second Congress of the Communist International, at Lenin's suggestion, to read, "Proletarians of all countries, and oppressed nations, unite." Said Lenin, in proposing this new slogan, "Of course, from the point of view of the *Communist Manifesto*, this is wrong. But the *Communist Manifesto* was written under completely different conditions; and from the point of view of the present political situation, this is correct." [4] For in Lenin's opinion the class struggle had merged with the struggle between nations. Moreover, even what is left of the class struggle is viewed differently by Leninists, and the attitude of Lenin toward the working class is therefore quite different from that of Marx, and particularly from that of the moderate Marxian socialists. The latter, following in the footsteps of Marx, identified Marxism with the working-class movement and held that labor's efforts against exploitation, no matter how imperfect and naïve they might be from the point of view of revolution-making, should be supported without fail; for, without labor, there would be no Marxist movement. Leninism, however, drifted toward the separation of socialism and the workers' movement. Its point of departure is not the conditions of the working class, but the conditions of society as a whole, which are unfailingly viewed critically. The Leninist endeavors to detect within society forces of disintegration and construction, and give them consciousness and organization, no matter what the forces are.

An entirely new conception about the preconditions for a "proletarian" (this word must now be written in quotation marks) revolution emerges. The old ideas about the maturity of social and economic conditions make no more sense when applied to individual countries. A high level of industrialization no longer leads directly to internal revolution, nor does the existence of a numerically strong working class. Instead, these factors are now seen to lead to revolution somewhere else. Revolution in the leading imperialist countries will come only as they decline. In addition, the revolution itself will have aims that were not outlined in the original Marxist theories. Marx had discussed two possible reactions of the exploited to the economic instruments of exploitation. They could either attempt to destroy these instruments, as the Luddites and the Silesian weavers attempted to smash the machines that had destroyed their preindustrial way of life; or they could endeavor to seize them, to appropriate the means of production and utilize them for the benefit of society as a whole. In the opinion of Marx, the latter was to be the aim of the working class and the purpose of its revolution, which, in turn, would lead to the abolition of all features of alienation, the smashing of the superstructure, and the flourishing of liberty. But with the new Leninist theory, the aim of the "proletarian" revolution is not to destroy capitalist industry nor to seize it but to create adequate means of production in those areas of the world which lacked them. Its aim is economic construction for the sake of national emancipation, and this could be accomplished only through the use of political, ideological, in short, "superstructural," means. In western Europe, industrialism developed organically and spontaneously. Having grown up there, it becomes a political goal for every nation in which it has not developed naturally, all ideas about "economic determinism" notwithstanding.* Here all the supposed laws of Marxist historical materialism are overthrown. Political action determines economic development; consciousness is stronger than social relations. Causes turn into effects, and effects into causes.

Leninism thus developed into a theory of state, and the tasks Lenin attributed to the state were similar to those which capitalism had carried out in previous centuries. In Marxist terminology, this task was "accumulation." In praising the Taylor system, in "organizing competition," and in admonishing the party to "learn from the capitalists," Lenin expressed the need for building up a modern industry on the European model, for accomplishing that "primitive accumulation" which was later demanded by Stalin's left-wing critics. Anyone who has read the pertinent chapter in the third volume of Marx's *Das Capital* will recall the horror with which the term "primitive accumulation" is fraught. And, in using it, the left-wing economists wished bluntly and frankly to point out that backward countries catch up with the West only by imposing the same terrible sacrifices on their populations that capitalism imposed on its victims in the early decades of the industrial revolution. Stalin and his spokesmen never admitted the necessity for such sacrifices, but they imposed them nonetheless, and every Leninist is secretly convinced that they are absolutely necessary if the goal of their revolution is to be reached. The industrialization of backward areas, once they have revolted against the West, must be bought at the expense of their peoples' welfare.

In addition, the modernization and westernization of these

* Compare the following comment: "The conception of class suffices to explain the internal development of a civilization from stage to stage, or at any rate that of the particular civilization with which we are practically concerned in the world today; but it does not suffice to explain the action of one civilization upon another. It does not follow that for the explanation of other civilizations, or of the impact of one civilization upon another, we have to go outside the economic field. For a distinction needs to be drawn between the theory that economic forces are the final determinants of social change and the secondary theory that these economic forces are in all cases necessarily personified by economic classes" (G. D. H. Cole, *What Marx Really Meant*, New York, 1934, pp. 38–39).

areas necessitates that cultural revolution which Lenin demanded after 1918, and this remaking of men from peasants into workers is even more painful, perhaps, than are the material sacrifices imposed by the Leninist state. In the attempt to carry out the cultural revolution, the Leninist state accomplishes the double task of first cutting the individual loose from his primary ties, in order to destroy the old established institutions and groups into which he has been born, and then constructing a new network of organizations and associations, entirely dependent on the state and on the party that is sovereign in it. This double process of atomization and organization is an essential feature of totalitarian states; and it has become apparent that Soviet totalitarianism is an integral part of the Leninist theory of revolution.

Finally, the revolution acquires duration in time. Marx, thinking of the revolution as an act of expropriation, could conceive it as a momentary event, which would with one stroke lead mankind from the realm of exploitation and alienation into the realm of freedom. With Lenin, the revolution turns into an era of undetermined length, in which the breakdown of capitalism is a long process of disintegration, and the proletarian dictatorship, a painful period of construction and transformation, during which "socialism" remains confined to a single country or a group of countries within a hostile imperialist world.

Chapter 13

Leninism after Lenin

*The "idea" has always made a fool of itself insofar as it differed
from the "interest." On the other hand, it is easy to understand that
every mass-generated "interest" making itself felt in history, when it
first enters the world stage, in the "idea" or "imagination" far
transcends its real limits and confuses itself with the human interest
altogether. This illusion forms what Fourier calls the tone of each
individual historical period.*

MARX AND ENGELS

The word "Leninism" was used for the first time in the
struggle for succession after Lenin's death in January 1924. Rivals
for power tried to assume the mantle of orthodoxy which he had
worn, and coined the term "Leninism" to describe their own
interpretations of his political heritage. This struggle, which
shook the Soviet state and the communist movement for over a
decade, has often been described as a fight for power among
ambitious leaders. Undoubtedly it was one, but many writers
forget or neglect the fact that it was also a conflict of differing
policies, strategies, programs, estimates of the situation, and
broad conceptions of the nature of the modern world. In fact, in
the course of the theoretical disputes that flared up in connection
with the struggle for power — now rationalizing it, now feeding
it additional issues — the entire theoretical heritage of Lenin
was subjected to scrutiny. In approaching any political problem,
Lenin's successors inevitably asked themselves and each other
what Lenin himself would have done to solve it. In justifying

their every decision, those in power always turned to decisions made by Lenin, often under entirely different circumstances, only to find themselves confronted by other decisions he had made that pointed in the opposite direction. In the attempt to give all conceivable enterprises of the Soviet state a theoretical foundation based on Lenin's writ, conflicting philosophies were propounded. For this reason, the very meaning of "Leninism" had to be established, once the term had come into use, and defining it turned out to be an exceedingly difficult undertaking. The outcome of the struggle for power did impose a specific interpretation of Leninism on the communist movement, at least for a while. Significantly, the very manner in which the theoretical conflict was "resolved" was quite in keeping with certain traditions of Leninism, but the same could be said for the repudiation of this resolution.

Leninism is a school within the Marxist movement that has manifested a degree of radicalism and unceasing activism matched only by that of Marx and Engels themselves. Lenin's activity, however, seems much more dramatic and effective than that of the movement's founders, partly because of his great successes. But the successes can be explained in part by the fact that he applied the theories of his teachers under more propitious circumstances, and that he did not hesitate to change them. Lenin's political life began in the early 1890's, a period that was an important turning point in European history. In Germany, it was the end of the Bismarckian era in domestic and foreign policy, marked by events such as the repeal of the antisocialist laws in Prussia and the abandonment of the German-Russian "reinsurance" treaty. This in turn was part of a general shift in the European diplomatic scene, as the forces that were to generate World War I aligned themselves. The era of the combustion engine, of electricity, of monopolies, and of imperialism was dawning. Throughout the Western world, a rapid rise in the standard of living was accompanied by far-reaching changes in the social and economic structure. Russia herself was deeply affected by this transformation: feverish industrialization made cities and factories mushroom, created an urban proletariat, and introduced the ups and downs of the business cycle. Coupled with the results of an unusually hard famine in 1891, these changes helped stimulate the Revolution of 1905, which gave Russia her first taste of constitutional government and produced fully organized political parties, which agitated for a renewal of revolutionary activity.

Lenin engaged in revolution-making armed with theoretical equipment which differed from that used by Marx and Engels in the revolution of 1848. At that time, Marx and Engels had only begun to develop their theory of "scientific socialism." What they had thought out and written was primarily the philosophical foundation of their theory. They had not yet gathered much practical experience. It was the Revolution of 1848 that put Marxism on its feet, as it were, by forcing its founders to draw concrete, practical tenets from their unexpected defeat. By 1890, the practical lessons had been learned — as a matter of fact, some had already been forgotten. Still, the Marxist movement had established itself firmly within the European political scene and had gathered mass support in some of the Continental countries. It was within this movement that Lenin grew. Reading the classics of Marxism and living in the well-developed organizational network of the social democratic movement determined his political personality.

We have seen that Marxism as adopted by Lenin was colored by an unstated but nonetheless persistent pessimism, perhaps even desperation, a feeling of doubt about the historical process in which Marx and Engels had expressed unbounded confidence. The rise of such doubt is easily explained by a number of factors: the changing nature of the working-class movement; changes in social structure and economic conditions; and, not the least, Lenin's own Russian environment, which fitted into the Marxist scheme of analysis only after a good deal of stretching and amending. The decided note of pessimism pervading Leninism is the seed from which his entire operational code grew: the spirit of manipulation, the belief in organization, the preoccupation with strategy and tactics, the willingness to apply any means, the flexibility as well as the ruthlessness displayed in Lenin's attempt to bring about the revolution by trial and error. Pessimism is also related to that most characteristically Leninist trait, the stress laid on consciousness as the history-making force par excellence, by which the pre-eminence of the party is rationalized.

Leninism applies the operational code and the pre-eminence of the party specifically to Russia, and, by analogy, to all other countries that lag behind in their technological development. It is a merger of Marxism and earlier Russian thought, because it grew up on the soil of Russian conditions and acquired many traditions familiar to the student of previous revolutionary movements in that country. But the specifically Russian experience acquired world-wide significance. Whether correctly or not, Lenin and his followers attempted to abstract generalizations from this Russian experience that would be valid for revolutionary strategy and communist policy in all parts of the world. In some measure, this extension in scope was achieved with the help of the theory of imperialism, which is a wholesale reassessment of contemporary world problems and a thorough revision of Marxist theory. As we have seen, it not only provides an explanation of why some of Marx's prognoses have miscarried, but also resurrects the belief in the inevitability of the proletarian revolution, although this revolution will be carried out with a different strategy and will have different aims and consequences from the one Marx and Engels had in mind.

Every student of Leninism might, perhaps, agree that this is an adequate summary of its most essential traits. It is not difficult to see, however, why sharp controversies could nevertheless arise over a "correct" definition of Leninism. For, as soon as an attempt is made to fill in these very general outlines with more concrete policies and traditions, unresolved contradictions appear that are inherent in Leninism. A cursory survey of Lenin's writings will reveal a number of such inconsistencies, all of which have plagued his interpreters. For example, the so-called "operational code" is a handbook of tactical advice, which tells the Leninist little or nothing about precisely which measures to employ in any given circumstance. Far from being a foolproof guide to action, the code is hence a continual source of dispute, because it invariably offers multiple and contradictory suggestions. The reason for this confusion is that the code makes sense only after other steps have been taken, such as the thorough assessment of the current moment, the estimate of long-range trends, the determination of long-range objectives, and the relation to them of the minimum aims.

In making his assessment of a situation and in outlining his goals, Lenin was almost always more radical than other Russian Marxists. He felt surer of the impending doom of the capitalist system, and he wanted to drive developments further on the road toward the proletarian revolution than did his more moderate comrades. As well as being more radical, Leninism is also more pessimistic; Lenin showed less faith in the intelligence and good will of anyone else than did other Marxists. Finally, Leninism is "hard" Marxism: Lenin tended to be far less squeamish about the means he employed than were other Marxists. But again, these traits that distinguish Leninism from other, "soft" schools within the Russian Marxist camp do not lend themselves to precise definition.* We can recognize them only as tendencies; we can say only that Lenin was a good deal *more* radical, pessimistic, and hard than the Mensheviks. But the proportions of these and other elements varied from time to time, so that there are in reality several Lenins. The Lenin who wrote *The State and Revolution* combined the acme of radicalism with comparative softness and optimism, whereas the Lenin who shortly afterwards wrote *Left-Wing Infantilism* had become pessimistic and hard, and had shed a good deal of his most extreme radicalism. There are the Lenin who believed in democracy and the one who instituted centralism; the internationalist and the Soviet patriot; the political realist and the man who thundered against oppor-

---

* For a good discussion of "hard" and "soft" labels see Bertram D. Wolfe, *Three Who Made A Revolution* (New York, 1948), pp. 155–158. It has become fashionable vaguely to identify the "soft" trend with the Western liberal heritage and to explain the "hard" trend as a Russian or Asiatic tradition or even to identify it with the romantic nationalist school of the Slavophiles. But this oversimplification neglects too many authoritarian traditions in Western civilization itself; and Slavophile thought can be traced directly to Herder, Hegel, Rousseau, Burke, and other men whose writings are integral parts of the Western heritage. Some of the complexities of tracing continuities in social thought are discussed briefly in Alfred G. Meyer, "Russian Utopians and Soviet Ideologists," *World Politics*, vol. 9, no. 1 (October 1956), pp. 118–128.

tunism; the gradualist of the article "On Co-operation" and the advocate of permanent revolution or *pererastanie*.

Very often, conflicts in Lenin's views and policies can be explained as responses to a changing concrete situation, and differences can be reconciled within a longer-range view. But matters are not always so easy. The various Lenins were not always separated in time; they could coexist. He often pursued different, nay conflicting goals, simultaneously, justifying all of them theoretically. A good example of this is the early policy of the Soviet regime in Asia, which, while not wholly Lenin's own policy, was pursued during his lifetime and probably based on his ideas. It included such divergent activities as alliances with Chinese war lords and Near Eastern princes, support of Dr. Sun's revolutionary movement in Canton, encouragement and support given to local communist movements, the establishment of communist regimes on foreign soil by force of armed intervention, and old-fashioned expansion for the sake of strategic or economic advantages. Moreover, theoretical support given any one of these policies meant the necessity of finding theoretical grounds for condemning all the other moves. Needless to say, Lenin always found such grounds. Subsequent theoreticians have been able to distill a number of conflicting versions of "Leninism" from his writings, his pronouncements, his political decisions, and his very manner of decision-making, and each has been justified in calling his version "Leninism."

The reason for this ambiguity of Leninism as a guide to action lies in that ambivalent attitude toward everything which we have seen to be an underlying psychological and theoretical trait of the Leninist. It extends to capitalism and all it entails, to democracy and reform, to the bourgeois revolution and all the forces supposed to be engaged therein. This ambivalence extends even to the working class, and, as we have seen, to Marxist theory itself. Its consequence is the inner conviction that any method may lead to success, and that everything is suspect and expendable.

Further, some of Lenin's followers were attracted to him chiefly by his comparative radicalism, which they often combined with "softness" in regard to the means employed, while others followed him primarily because of his "hard" approach to political decision-making. If we probe specific issues or attitudes on various broad problems, we find that, behind the general acceptance of Lenin's leadership by all party members, there lurked a multitude of disagreements. In the history of Leninism, certain leading figures stand out as relatively consistent adherents of definite positions. But, depending in part on the balance of conflicting forces within the party, a man consistent on one matter could be inconsistent on other problems over long periods. Thus Trotsky, who after 1923 must be reckoned a member of the radical, "left-wing" faction, was ruthlessly authoritarian in the early years of the revolution. But, in the mid-twenties, after he had recognized that power had slipped out of his hands, he became, however reluctantly, an advocate of intraparty democracy. Bukharin, on the other hand, seems to have been attracted to Leninism chiefly on account of its radical criticism of contemporary society, a society in which he discerned the most perturbing antiliberal tendencies. Bukharin was foremost an antitotalitarian figure, a collectivist liberal, almost an anarchist. These beliefs placed him among Lenin's devoted followers during most of World War I and the entire revolutionary year 1917, made him a spokesman of extreme left-wing criticism during the period of War Communism, and converted him to a belief in gradualism, a striving for democracy, in a sense even a conservative bent, during the middle and late 1920's. Yet these democratic leanings, this "softness" did not prevent him from playing the role of a ruthless machine politician in the fight against the left-wing oppositionists of the 1920's.

The fact that the party usually changed its "line" whenever Lenin changed his mind has contributed to the conception of his position as a "center" one between "right" and "left" deviations. Lenin escaped the labels of "right" and "left" because his position usually became the official position, and the party, by definition, is always right. But this overlooks the fact that the party itself changed when Lenin changed his mind: it frequently meant that he had attracted a new following and was surrounding himself with an entirely different entourage, while breaking with the followers he had had before. Many of Lenin's most crucial decisions were made against the advice of his closest associates. They inevitably spelled severe crisis for the party, as his former friends turned into political enemies.

Numerous examples could be given for this. We might mention Lenin's isolation in the spring of 1907, when he decided that the party should not boycott the elections to the Second State Duma; or the wholesale resistance by faithful Bolshevik organizers to his efforts between 1908 and 1912 to emphasize and perpetuate the break between Bolsheviks and Mensheviks, and to sabotage all efforts at reconciliation. Again, Lenin's radical program of April 1917, especially his refusal to work for a coalition of all socialist parties, was opposed not only by Zinov'ev and Kamenev, but by the vast majority of precisely those party organizers and leaders who had been loyal to Lenin during the hard years preceding the First World War. They stuck to the slogans worked out by Lenin between 1905 and 1914, and turned into oppositionists when Lenin declared those slogans obsolete. Against their stiff resistance, Lenin during 1917 turned more and more radical, until by the time of the seizure of power he sounded virtually like an anarcho-syndicalist. He visualized the entire world aflame in revolutionary upheaval; he talked about promoting revolutionary war in case the flames were slow in spreading; and when, in his enthusiasm, he insisted that the party seize power immediately, a sizable majority of its leaders was reluctant even to listen to him. His frantic letters from his Finnish hideout to the underground headquarters in Petrograd were pigeonholed without debate.

Meanwhile, his party had been swelled by a host of former opponents who came to join him during the war, particularly in the summer of 1917. These Mensheviks and pseudo-Mensheviks were attracted to his party by the boldness of his vision and the radicalism of his slogans — though we might say they were attracted to it because he had taken over their own slogans. Were they the better Leninists? Was Lenin deviating from his own doctrine? The absurdity of these questions demonstrates the impossibility of defining Leninism.

A few months later, at the time of the Brest-Litovsk negotiations, Lenin again battled against a majority of dissenters. But this time he was the advocate of caution and "realism," denouncing those in favor of revolution as petty bourgeois idealists. And suddenly the "strike-breakers" Zinov'ev and Kamenev were again among his closest entourage, while the enthusiasm he had so painfully and laboriously fanned among his friends of October 1917 was labeled "ultra-left oppositionism," a childhood disease. Thus a true "Leninist" can be defined with no greater assurance than can the doctrine itself.*

Once this difficulty is realized, a question frequently asked, and one with which we must deal in this work, finds an answer, although perhaps not a very satisfactory one. This is the question of the relationship between Leninism and Stalinism. In taking it up, we should, first of all, beware of glib generalizations concerning the latter. Just as Leninism cannot be defined without a good deal of vagueness and overgeneralization, so Stalinism defies satisfactory definition, because the Stalin of 1925 was very different in his outlook on long-range and short-range problems from the Stalin of 1935, the only common denominator being his well-known ruthlessness in applying the "operational code" to the management of party affairs. We have seen, however, that Leninism is far more than the operational code, and that this code contains a great deal of ambiguity. Stalin's opponents, who came to stress the democratic aspects of the party's traditions, could base their arguments on the Leninist writ, just as Stalin's successors, in repudiating one-man rule and in stressing collectivist practices, are no less Leninist than was Stalin. Even Tito, in repudiating a great many Soviet practices and policies, could do so on the basis of hallowed Leninist traditions.

Still, Stalinism can and must be defined as a pattern of thought and action that flows directly from Leninism. Stalin's way of looking at the contemporary world, his professed aims, the decisions he made at variance with one another, his conceptions of the tasks facing the communist state — these and many specific

---

* The ambiguous nature of Leninism and its relation to the heterogeneous character of Lenin's associates is one of the major themes in the pioneer work on the communist party oppositions by Robert V. Daniels, *The Conscience of the Revolution.*

traits are entirely Leninist. It is true that by upbringing, social origin, and temper, by the experiences that molded his life and by the kinds of friends he cultivated, Lenin was markedly different from Stalin. He would surely have avoided some of Stalin's mistakes and doubtless committed others; he would have acted differently, if only because his survival would have brought about entirely different problems. Yet the kinds of decisions made by Stalin and the manner in which they were made and executed were prepared by Lenin. In his stress on the primacy of the party and the power struggle, his preoccupation with problems of economic construction and cultural transformation, his readiness to manipulate men and institutions, his faith in organization, and his ruthlessness in implementing policies — in all these traits Stalin has trod in Lenin's footsteps. And yet, we must repeat again, the many non-Stalinist or anti-Stalinist interpretations are derived from the same Leninism which gave birth to Stalinism.

We might similarly examine the question whether Leninism is inherently totalitarian, although an affirmative answer has become generally accepted. Lenin's aims were indeed sweeping, and perhaps utopian. Possibly they could be realized only through totalitarian means. Recent writings by religious political philosophers have stressed this aspect, in calling Leninism a secular religion, and have pointed out that such religions inevitably lead to totalitarianism. They argue that the very desire to establish paradise on earth is sinful and presumptious, a pre-emption of God's own program. Due to the state of sin into which Adam's disobedience plunged mankind, it is also impossible to realize utopia in this world, and the attempt can not but lead to totalitarianism. This *hybris* of wishing to create an earthly Eden leads to the ruthlessness that characterizes Leninism, to the deliberate stress Lenin laid on the utilization of any means because the end sanctified them and because any abstention from using them would only perpetuate the terror and misery of the existing system. Whether this ruthlessness has anything to do with the religious nature of Leninism or not, it certainly does lead to totalitarian practices. We have already observed that the "dialectics of backwardness" leads to a conception of the proletarian revolution in which an era of totalitarianism forms an integral part, an era that is bound to last until backwardness has been overcome.

In pointing out this totalitarian trend, we should nonetheless remain aware that these consequences of radicalism, ruthlessness, and manipulation often go against a Leninist's grain. For one thing, Leninist writings, which are treated with veneration in the communist world, have managed to keep democratic traditions, if not alive, then at least in print, readily available to all; and even the use of totalitarian means is always justified or rationalized by the Leninist policy-makers. The Leninist feels compelled to apologize for his totalitarianism or to explain it away, something that Hitler, for example, never considered necessary. We can understand this dualism if we consider the motivation underlying communist totalitarianism, as contrasted with the motivation of what we call "fascism" for lack of another word. The Leninist is driven to his ruthless revolutionary activism by moral revulsion against social conditions that he feels are unjust and intolerable, or by an aesthetic revulsion against the sordidness of proletarian life. In the case of the Leninist who comes from upper classes and enjoys the pleasures and comforts of wealth, his motive may be a feeling of guilt, through the awareness of inequalities, misery, and hopelessness. Lenin, as well as many other Russian Marxists, also felt a very strong emotional attachment to the workingman, a mixture of respect, confidence, and brotherly love that is in strange contrast to the suspicion and impatience he showed toward the workers in political matters. All these motives are basically antitotalitarian, and it does seem that Lenin and many of his followers had at times to give themselves a push in order to be ruthless and totalitarian, just as Lenin had to make a deliberate effort to kill his own emotions. All this does not make Leninism any less totalitarian, but it does provide the vista of an alternative, which acquires a faint tinge of realism by the fact that there have always been Leninists who did keep democratic traditions alive, who fought for them and died for them. Future attempts to revive these traditions in practice will depend on favorable circumstances, in addition to good will. But if they are ever successful, the attempts will be made in the name of Leninism.

At the same time, it is well recognized today that the traditions of democracy, liberalism, individualism, and the liberties associated therewith have little meaning precisely in those areas and among those classes where Leninism exerts its strongest appeal. This appeal has a number of roots. For one thing, Leninism is a theory concerning the nature of the modern world, and it represents a major contribution to contemporary social science, whatever the adequacy and realism of its doctrines and hypotheses. It does so because it attempts to analyze a number of phenomena of which most other theories take less account, particularly the life situation of the working class and the problems of underdeveloped areas. In concentrating on these aspects, Leninism has become the doctrine to which those people have become accustomed to turn who wish to obtain an explanation of the conditions of the underprivileged. They find that not only does Leninism have answers for them, but these answers also are phrased with deceptive simplicity and lucidity and accompanied by assurances that they are the last word in social science. It is easy for Western academicians to scoff at the outmoded economic concepts with which Leninism continues to operate, or to ridicule the assurance with which Leninism reduces world-shaking problems to the continued reign of private property. Spokesmen of the European working class and socially conscious intellectuals in underdeveloped areas have come to rely on these and other Leninist ideas to such an extent that in discussing the problems of these classes and people, even the non-Leninist can hardly avoid talking in Leninist terms.

Furthermore, Leninism speaks as the voice of "progress," a word that has a magical effect, particularly among the underprivileged. Only the satiated tend to be blasé about it. The Leninist promise that his victory will lead to the establishment of paradise on earth exerts a tremendous appeal on men who have been brought up with lofty ideals. It promises the new Eden as the result of vigorous revolutionary action, in which many a bewildered seeker finds meaning for an otherwise futile existence.

Leninism, with its self-assured conviction of having found the only valid key to an understanding of the world, provides a rock of faith and a means of self-orientation for many of those who feel that the modern world is out of joint. It combines this with moral overtones of righteousness, which give to its adherents the comfort of belonging to the chosen vanguard of mankind and makes them see the outsider as a pitiable and contemptible unbeliever, doomed by his stubborn resistance to the voice of truth and justice. Leninism is a doctrine of salvation and damnation, which to its followers does fulfill many of the functions of religion, and its religious appeal may be intensified by the prospect of martyrdom for those who confess it.

These attractions are balanced by a number of features apt eventually to repel those who tend to be drawn to Leninism. For one thing, the seeming simplicity of its image of reality dissolves when the seeker investigates the concrete analysis of the current moment or of specific local conditions. Readiness to engage in revolutionary action does not make it easy to decide exactly how to act in a fluid, dynamic world, or to adjust without inner conflicts to sudden and radical shifts in the party line. The ambivalence characterizing Leninism is difficult to maintain, because it can take a man to the brink of neurosis and insanity, or compel him to take refuge in a simpler and more one-sided view. Similarly, the moral indignation that leads many to espouse Leninism may not be easily reconciled with the moral relativism of the operational code, which makes everything the party does, every means it employs, right by definition, be it the Taylor system, a peace treaty of annexation, militarism, the police state, or concentration camps. The rebel against society who joins the revolutionary movement may also find it difficult to submit to the military discipline imposed upon him by the Leninist hierarchy; he will strain against the bit over the inefficiencies and heartaches of democratic centralism; and he will be shocked to realize that he has joined, not only a collectivist brotherhood of devoted revolutionaries but also a strife-torn organization, racked with fear of its own members, with mutual suspicion of the comrade's motives, and with continual bitter struggle over policies, strug-

gles which from a purely theoretical standpoint can not be resolved satisfactorily.

All political action demands choice, which is based on a system
of values. Given the ambivalence of Leninism, judgment becomes purely pragmatic, because every possible course of action
forces the Leninist to make compromises with reality, to violate
some principle of Marxist orthodoxy. Hence he does not ask what
would be the just way of action or what course would call for the
least onerous moral compromise; he is interested solely in acting
in the most expedient fashion possible. How can the revolution
be furthered most effectively? What benefits, advantages, conquests have to be sacrificed; which should be saved, and at what
cost? We have seen, in the struggle over the Peace of Brest-
Litovsk, what painful decisions were required. The course actually taken at that time turned out to be a foundation for the later
Stalinist doctrine of "socialism in one country," and for the conduct of Soviet foreign policy. And still, in a deeper sense, the
issue was never settled, and comes up again and again; for
theory does not and can not tell the Leninist which of many
possible courses of action will be most expedient. The answer to
this eternal question is given by political horse sense, experience,
and pure Machiavellianism.

Even as Lenin, whenever he suddenly changed his strategy,
would point out to his protesting comrades that Marxism was "no
dogma, but a guide to action," so his successors have said the
same about Leninism. Our attempt has been to show that, in the
latter case, the slogan does not apply. Indeed, as we have pointed
out, Leninism does provide some guidance to the bewildered in
orienting themselves; it does establish broad goals and an elaborate set of rules for attaining them, which are based on certain
broad generalizations about the nature of the world and the
nature of politics. But, in discussing these and other "guides for
action," we also probed into their unresolved ambiguities. Lenin
himself, in calling Marxism a guide to action, implied that it was
an entirely clear-cut guide, that, given true consciousness, the
correct policy would always emerge. This belief was based on the
Marxist assumption that the proletariat was forced by historical

circumstances to recognize in full the nature of reality. The
ideology of the working class spelled the end of all false ideologies. Hitherto all knowledge had been class knowledge, and
therefore false, but by the proletariat true knowledge would be
gained. And, since Lenin regarded the conscious vanguard as the
representative of the working class, this vanguard, the party,
could regard its own views as scientific, so that Lenin's insistence
on partisanship in social science was not originally meant as an
exhortation to distort reality. On the contrary, only the partisan
views of the communist elite represented the truth.

If we were to assume that Marx's view of historical development was a correct description of the course that all nations
would take by necessity, then this "true consciousness" would indeed be an infallible guide to action. We have seen, however,
that Marxism was transformed into a strategy designed to help
the movement fight not one but two revolutions, in alliance with
a great variety of nonproletarian forces. With this change,
Marxist-Leninist actions became a matter of choice between
many alternatives. Theory is silent on how best to choose. Yet
Lenin firmly maintained that there was such a thing as a correct
solution to every problem of strategy, if only Marxist principles
were applied faithfully and carefully. This confidence in Marxism, correctly interpreted, not only served to justify his dogmatic
self-assertion in leading his faction; it also helped to obscure the
ambiguities inherent in his doctrines and slogans, and therefore
it also prevented him and many of his followers from thinking
some crucial problems of Leninism through to their logical conclusion. In this sense, Lenin's conception of Marxism as an un-
failing guide to action was a serious pitfall, perhaps the greatest
of all the fallacies to which he succumbed. For it helped to make
Leninism both rigid and blind, despite the unprecedented flexibility with which he continually changed Marxian doctrines. And
this is the way Leninism presents itself to us, combining percep-
tion with blindness, doctrinaire rigidity with opportunistic adapt-
ability; it is simple yet infinitely complex, forthright in its principle, and utterly elusive in application.

To this fallacy we must add another element of Lenin's belief
in consciousness: his faith in organization and centralization as

rational methods of decision-making. We have seen that this too was unfounded. The party cannot be more rational than its leaders; endowing it with infallibility therefore puts theory in conflict with human behavior, as is shown by the fate of the Communist International. One conclusion which can be drawn from Lenin's theory of "uneven development" is that no generalizations can be made about the development of the revolution that are valid for all countries. An obvious application of this idea is that communist parties everywhere should be autonomous and conduct their activity on the basis of their particular situations. Many Leninists, both past and present, have drawn this conclusion. But the Leninist belief in organization and centralization makes it difficult for them to act accordingly. The Communist International has been beset by this conflict, which was resolved in favor of centralization. Founded in order to take the initiative from the moderate Marxists, who seemed ready, after World War I, to re-establish the Second International, the Communist International was from the moment of its birth subjected to the rigid discipline of democratic centralism by Lenin. In a few years, the world-wide Leninist movement had become a cumbersome machinery that not only was dominated by Russians, but also reflected purely Russian problems, preoccupations, traditions, and personality conflicts. In identifying the fate of Soviet Russia with the interests of the proletarian world revolution, Lenin helped to make the Communist International an instrument of Soviet world politics, and, in the eyes of many Leninists, he thus helped to frustrate the efforts of his own followers in many parts of the world. Russia's domination of world Leninism again and again alienated many who had joined the party with enthusiasm; and it remains one of the unresolved problems of Leninism.

Organization acquired crucial significance for Lenin because he wished to manipulate the social forces of the current moment; and his desire to manipulate arose from his pessimistic appraisal of their reliability and usefulness. Marxist theory maintained that history meant inevitable progress. But, as a practical politician, Lenin was not fully convinced of this.

Marx had believed that in the working-class movement theory and practice, reality and ideals, had merged in a unique synthesis. This unity of theory and practice, however, proved to be but a dream; the European proletariat of the mid–nineteenth century did not show itself prepared to play the role he had designated for it. For this reason, Marxism disintegrated into several rival movements, which by 1917 found themselves on opposite sides of the barricades.* The idea of the unity of theory and practice therefore suffered a strange fate. One branch of the Marxist movement abandoned it altogether. For the monism of Marx the revisionists substituted the dualism of Kant, which holds that ideas and reality, norms and facts, are irreconcilable antinomies. The inevitability of social progress was to them no longer an objective law of history, but a moral postulate. Yet they retained Marx's optimistic faith in progress. The world was bad, but man was good, and morality would conquer reality. Another group, the new radical Marxists, well represented by Rosa Luxemburg, reformulated Marx's laws to fit the world of modern imperialism and saw these laws vindicate the unity of theory and practice as a fact.

Lenin did not share the sanguine optimism of Luxemburg, nor did he wish to lapse into dualism. On the contrary, he bitterly fought those of his Bolshevik comrades who in the years after 1905 wished to integrate the Marxist movement with Kantian philosophy. It might not be amiss to connect the popularity of this empirio-criticism among many leading Bolsheviks with the mood of despair dominating the Russian intelligentsia in the period between the two Russian revolutions. Lenin, in contrast, never allowed despair to come to the surface of his consciousness. His program in these years, particularly when it was related to his idea of the Russian revolution as the spark, breathed confidence, which erupted into exuberant optimism in the revolutionary months of 1917. In the theory of imperialism, moreover, which spelt out the inevitable doom of capitalism anew, and recognized new forces of regeneration, the idea of the unity of theory and practice was resurrected.

Yet the despair and distrust lingered, though only in secret.

* For a fuller presentation of these ideas see the last four chapters of Alfred G. Meyer, *Marxism: the Unity of Theory and Practice* (Cambridge, Mass., 1954).

Under the surface, a dualistic conception of reality pervaded Leninism, in which the actual political situation was contrasted with the consciousness possessed by only a handful of professional revolutionaries. This dualism remained unrecognized because Lenin thought that he had in fact reunited theory and practice. To be sure, he had not reunited it in the working class, nor even in the "toiling masses," but in the party, the active machinery of consciousness. To the party was given the task that Marx had envisioned as being fulfilled by the working class. History, for Marx, played the role others attributed to divine forces, namely, to lead mankind to the new Eden. This faith in history, in the measure as it is based on misconceptions and unproven premises, constitutes the religious element in Marxism. Marxism, in other words, is religious because it is not fully scientific. In contrast to other religions, it is a secular religion; and the social scientist should criticize it not for being secular but for being a religion.*

Lenin, however, was a secret doubter. His faith in history being shaky, he fashioned himself an instrument to fulfill the task of the Marxist god of history: distrusting spontaneity, he turned consciousness into an organized force. A man-created instrument was thus endowed with divine infallibility. But the fetish turned out to be a false god, because the theoretical equipment with which it was endowed by Lenin was inadequate for its exalted mission. The god turned out to be all too human.

The fate of the doctrine itself has suffered at the hands of this false god is difficult to describe. Even before Lenin's death, the ambiguities of Leninism led to bitter conflicts within the party, conflicts which both before and after his death were resolved not by exhaustive argument but by political pressure from Lenin or from the party machine that succeeded him. In the subsequent struggles for power the coinage of his ideas was further and further debased, as Leninism was used as a convenient grab bag

---

* While the social scientist might tend to be critical of the religious element in Marxism and Leninism, the moralist will undoubtedly find it attractive. For the essence of this religion is the faith in salvation. To be sure, salvation does not come from God but by man's own hand. The religion of Marx is thus Promethean or, as my friend Richard De Haan says, hybristic.

of quotations by which to justify the party line of the moment. Gradually it was turned into an apologetic ideology glorifying the Soviet state, into a virtual theodicy of Stalin. It was also elevated to the status of a dogma, a holy writ untouchable for all but the leader himself. Simultaneously, its feeble and ambiguous philosophic foundations were, by higher command, made the basis for all Soviet science and thought. By the fourth decade of this century, Leninism as expressed in the litanies of Soviet pronouncements had hardened into an intellectual strait jacket of doctrines unrealistic, old-fashioned, banal, and highly conservative, a system of ideas ill-fitted to guide the actions of statesmen or revolutionaries. The strict discipline imposed on foreign communist parties by the Communist International managed to prevent the preservation and development of more acceptable elements contained in Leninism even outside the Soviet orbit, at least to a considerable extent. The consciousness on which Lenin relied to guide mankind had turned into a sorry caricature of itself. Far more than the present-day intellectual ferment taking place in the communist world is required to make it emerge in its original image.

Bibliography
Notes
Index

Bibliography

1. LENIN'S WORKS

Four editions of Lenin's works have been published in Russian, as follows:

Lenin, V. I. *Sobranie Sochinenii.* 19 vols. Moscow, 1920–1923.
——— *Sochineniia.* 30 vols. Moscow-Leningrad, 1926–1932.
——— *Sochineniia.* 30 vols. Moscow-Leningrad, 1928–1937.
——— *Sochineniia.* 35 vols. Moscow, 1941–1952.

In the first edition the material is arranged partly in topical groups, partly in chronological order. A subject index to it was published in Moscow in 1930. The second and third editions have been supposed to be identical, but there seem to exist two printings of the third edition, which differ from each other in content. Save for some sensible exceptions, the material in these editions is arranged chronologically. They are richly annotated, in marked contrast to the fourth edition, which is therefore of far smaller value to the scholar. A subject index to the second and third editions was published in Moscow in 1934.

No complete translation into a Western language exists of Lenin's works. It was apparently planned to translate the entire second edition into English, German, and French, but the task was never completed. Those volumes which have been translated should be used with great caution. I have made spot checks of several volumes of the English edition and a thorough check of volume 13, comparing it with the Russian original. I have found the English translation faulty, misleading, and therefore useless. Still, these translations ought to be cited:

Lenin, V. I. *Collected Works.* Vols. 4, 13, 18–20, 21; three of these volumes in two tomes. New York, 1927–1942.
——— *Sämtliche Werke.* Vols. 3–8, 10, 12, 13, 17–20, 25. Vienna, 1927–1934.

None of the four Russian editions exhausts the material that has come from Lenin's pen. A large mass of material that would not customarily be considered fit for publication has been gathered in a collection entitled *Leninskii Sbornik* (31 vols., Moscow, 1924–1938).

Countless editions exist of individual works by Lenin and of
selections relating to specific topics. The following anthologies may
be useful:

Lenin, V. I. *Marx-Engels-Marxism*. Published in Russian, English,
    and other languages in several editions. Moscow, 1947, 1949.
———— *Selected Works*. 2 vols. New York, 1935.
———— *Selected Works*. 12 vols. New York, 1943.
———— *Ausqewählte Werke*. 11 vols. Vienna, 1932–1938.

Finally, a number of archives both inside and outside the Soviet
Union still contain a good deal of unpublished material, particularly
letters, by Lenin.

2. BIOGRAPHIES, PORTRAITS, REMINISCENCES, PERIODICAL GUIDES

Adler, Max. *Helden der sozialen Revolution*. Berlin, 1926.
Adoratskii, V. *K voprosu o nauchnoi biografii Lenina*. Moscow, 1933.
Aldanov, Mark. *Lenin*. New York, 1922.
Bonch-Bruevich, Vladimir D. *V. I. Lenin v Rossii posle fevral'skoi
    revoliutsii do tret'eiul'skogo vooruzhennogo vystupleniia*. Moscow,
    1925.
Drahn, Ernst. *Lenin, Vladimir Illic Ul'janov; eine Bio-Biblographie*.
    Berlin, 1924.
Elizarova, A. I. *Vospominaniia ob Il'iche*. Moscow-Leningrad, 1930.
Fülöp-Miller, René. *Lenin and Gandhi*. London-New York, 1927.
Gor'ki, Maxim. *Days with Lenin*. New York, 1932.
Haimson, Leopold H. *The Russian Marxists & The Origins of
    Bolshevism*. Cambridge, Mass., 1955.
Iaroslavskii, E. E. *Zhizn' i rabota V. I. Lenina*. Moscow, 1924.
———— *Biographiia Lenina*. Moscow, 1938.
———— *Lenin: His Life and Work*. Chicago, n.d.
Ioffe, A. M. *Lenin, der kämpfende Materialist*. Vienna, 1924.
Kamenev, L. B. *Lenin i ego partiia*. Moscow, 1924.
———— *Leniniana*. 5 vols. Moscow, 1926–1930. (Guide to periodical
    articles.)
Krupskaia, N. K. *Memories of Lenin*. 2 vols. London, n.d.
Landau, Mark A. *Lenin*. New York, 1922.
Levine, I. D. *The Man Lenin*. New York, 1924.
Lunacharskii, A. V. *Lenin; ocherki*. Moscow, 1924.
Manuchar'iants, Sh. N. *Daty zhizni i deiatel'nosti Lenina 1870–1924*.
    Leningrad, 1931.
Mirsky, D. S. *Lenin*. Boston, 1931.
O Lenine; sbornik vospominanii. Moscow, 1927.
Shub, David. *Lenin: A Biography*. Garden City, 1948.
Trotsky, L. D. *Lenin*. New York, 1925.
Valentinov, N. *Vstrechi s Leninym*. New York, 1953.

Vichniac, Marc. *Lénine*. Paris, 1932.

Walter, Gérard. *Lénine*. Paris, 1950. (Excellent bibliography and perhaps the best biography of Lenin published so far in any language.)

Wolfe, B. D. *Three Who Made A Revolution*. New York, 1948.

Zetkin, Clara. *Reminiscences of Lenin*. New York, 1934.

3. WORKS ON LENINISM

Adoratsky, V. *Dialectical Materialism*. New York, 1934.

Bauer, Otto. *Bolschewismus oder Sozialdemokratie?* Vienna, 1921.

Berdyaev, N. A. *The Origins of Russian Communism*. London, 1937.

Bochenski, I. M. *Der sowjetrussische dialektische Materialismus (Diamat)*. Berne, 1950.

Bukharin, N. I. *Lenin as a Marxist*. London, 1925.

Bukharin, N. I., and E. Preobrazhensky. *The ABC of Communism*. New York, 1922.

Dan, Fedor I. *Proiskhozhdenie bol'shevizma*. New York, 1946.

Eastman, Max. *Marx and Lenin: The Science of Revolution*. London, 1926.

Gurian, Waldemar. *Bolshevism: Theory and Practice*. New York, 1932.

Haimson, L. H. *The Russian Marxists & The Origins of Bolshevism*. Cambridge, Mass., 1955.

Hill, Christopher. *Lenin and the Russian Revolution*. London, 1947.

Hunt, R. N. Carew. *The Theory and Practice of Communism*. London, 1950.

Laski, Harold J. *Communism*. London, 1932.

Leites, Nathan. *A Study of Bolshevism*. Glencoe, Ill., 1953.

Lukacs, Georg. *Geschichte und Klassenbewusstsein*. Berlin, 1923.

―――― *Lenin: Studie über den Zusammenhang seiner Gedanken*. Berlin, 1924.

Merleau-Ponty, Maurice. *Les aventures de la dialectique*. Paris, 1955.

Pannekoek, Anton. *Lenin as Philosopher*. New York, 1948.

Plamenatz, John. *German Marxism and Russian Communism*. London, 1954.

Rosenberg, Arthur. *A History of Bolshevism*. London, 1934.

Scott, Andrew M. *The Anatomy of Communism*. New York, 1951.

Somerville, John. *Soviet Philosophy*. New York, 1946.

Stalin, J. V. *Problems of Leninism*. Ed. 11. Moscow, 1941.

Treadgold, D. W. *Lenin and His Rivals*. New York, 1955.

Wetter, Gustav A. *Dialectical Materialism*. New York, 1958.

Zinov'ev, Grigorii. *Leninizm*. Leningrad, 1926.

These works should be supplemented not only by documents, such as the minutes of the congresses and conferences of the Russian

Social Democratic Labor Party, the Russian Communist Party of Bolsheviks, and the Communist International, as well as of the meetings of Soviet congresses at which Lenin participated, but also by general works on the history of the Russian social democratic movement and the history of the Russian revolution as a whole. Such an inclusive bibliography is beyond the scope of this volume.

Notes

Unless stated otherwise, all references to Lenin's works are to the second edition (Sochineniia, Moscow-Leningrad, 1926–1932, 30 vols. plus index), with English translations cited wherever possible. Instead of citing the edition each time, the notes will simply give volume and page numbers. All translations, unless stated otherwise, are by the author.

Introduction

1. The point is made effectively by Bertram D. Wolfe, *Three Who Made A Revolution* (New York, 1948).

2. These notes were first printed in vols. 9 and 12 of *Leninskii Sbornik* (Moscow-Leningrad, 1929 and 1930) in the original languages of Lenin's notes and in Russian. They were published again, this time in Russian only, under the title V. I. Lenin, *Filosofskie Tetradi* (Moscow, 1938).

3. For a discussion of these terms, see Alfred G. Meyer, *Marxism: The Unity of Theory and Practice* (Cambridge, Mass., 1954), pp. 83–89.

4. Quoted in *Leninskii Sbornik,* vol. 9, p. 144.

5. Quoted *ibid.,* p. 128.

6. In the original: "If I'm not mistaken, there is much mysticism & leeres pedantizm u Gegelia v etikh vyvodakh, no genial'na osnovnaia ideia: Vsemirnoi, vsestoronnei, *zhivoi* sviazi vsego so vsem i otrazheniia etoi sviazi — materialistisch auf den Kopf gestellter Hegel — v poniatiiakh cheloveka . . ." (*ibid.,* p. 138).

7. *Ibid.,* pp. 160–168. See also Meyer, *Marxism,* pp. 32–39; Lenin, vol. 5, pp. 17–20.

8. "What the 'Friends of the People' Are . . . ," Lenin, vol. 1, p. 105 (English translation in *What the "Friends of the People" Are and How They Fight the Social Democrats,* Moscow, 1951, pp. 110–111).

9. *Ibid.,* p. 124.

10. *Leninskii Sbornik,* vol. 12, p. 323.

11. *Ibid.,* vol. 9, pp. 212ff. See also Lenin, *Sobranie Sochinenni,* vol. 1, p. 71. For a discussion of the dialectical relation of man with nature seen as a "metabolism," see Vernon Venable, *Human Nature: The Marxist View* (New York, 1946).

12. *Leninskii Sbornik*, vol. 9, p. 8.

13. "The Economic Contents of Narodnichestvo and Its Critique in Mr. Struve's Book," Lenin, vol. 1, p. 225.

14. For a discussion of the concept of alienation, see Meyer, *Marxism, passim.*

15. Quoted in *Leninskii Sbornik*, vol. 12, p. 150.

16. *Ibid.*, vol. 9, pp. 146, 148.

17. *Ibid.*, pp. 182–184.

Chapter One. Class Consciousness

1. For a fuller discussion of the ideas presented in the following few pages, see Meyer, *Marxism: The Unity of Theory and Practice* (Cambridge, Mass., 1954).

2. Karl Marx, *The Poverty of Philosophy* (Chicago, 1910), p. 31.

3. "Friedrich Engels," Lenin, vol. 1, p. 415.

4. "The Historical Fate of the Doctrine of Karl Marx," Lenin, vol. 16, p. 331.

5. "Preface to the Collection '*Za dvatsat' let,*'" Lenin, vol. 12, p. 63.

6. "Mit der Gründlichkeit der geschichtlichen Aktion wird der Umfang der Masse zunehmen, deren Aktion sie ist" (quoted in "The Heritage We Are Renouncing," Lenin, vol. 1, p. 329).

7. "Our Next Task," Lenin, vol. 2, p. 496.

8. "No Falsehood! Our Strength Lies in Revealing the Truth!" Lenin, vol. 8, p. 242.

9. "Socialism and Religion," Lenin, vol. 8, p. 420 (translation in *Religion*, Little Lenin Library, vol. 7, New York, 1933, p. 7).

10. "A Road to Broken Promises in the Russian Social Democratic Movement," Lenin, vol. 2, pp. 552–553.

11. "What Is to Be Done?" Lenin, vol. 4, p. 384 (*Selected Works*, vol. 2, p. 54).

12. Report on the current moment made at the Fourth Conference of Trade-Union and Factory Committees, Moscow, 27 June 1918, Lenin, vol. 23, p. 82. See also his speech to the Central Executive Committee, 29 April 1918, vol. 22, p. 491.

13. *Manifesto of the Communist Party*, in Harold J. Laski, ed., *Communist Manifesto: Socialist Landmark* (London, 1948), p. 142.

14. *Ibid.*

15. What Is to Be Done?" Lenin, vol. 4, p. 384 (*Selected Works*, vol. 2, p. 54).

16. "A Road to Broken Promises," Lenin, vol. 2, pp. 534ff.

17. "Friedrich Engels," Lenin, vol. 1, pp. 410–411.

18. "Tasks of the Russian Social Democrats," Lenin, vol. 2, p. 186.

19. "Draft Platform for Our Party," Lenin, vol. 2, p. 514.

20. "Our Program," Lenin, vol. 2, pp. 491–494; "An Urgent Question," vol. 2, pp. 500–504; "Draft Platform," vol. 2, pp. 509ff.

21. The term "revolutionary by profession" is first used and explained in "What Is to Be Done?" Lenin, vol. 4, p. 446 (*Selected Works*, vol. 2, p. 126).

22. From the party platform printed in *Protokoly VIII S"ezda RKP(b)* (Protocols of the Eighth Congress of the Russian Communist Party; Moscow, 1933), p. 381.

23. *Ibid.*

24. "Tasks of the Proletariat in Our Revolution," Lenin, vol. 20, p. 130 (*Collected Works*, vol. 20, book 1, pp. 151–152).

25. "What Is to Be Done?" Lenin, vol. 4, p. 378 (*Selected Works*, vol. 2, p. 45); "One Step Forward, Two Steps Backward," Lenin, vol. 5, p. 214.

Chapter Two. The Party and the Masses

1. Karl Marx and Friedrich Engels, "Die deutsche Ideologie," in Marx and Engels, *Historisch-kritische Gesamtausgabe* (hereafter cited as *MEGA*; Frankfurt, 1927), part 1, vol. 5, p. 238.

2. "On the Results of the Congress," Lenin, vol. 9, p. 237.

3. "One of the Root Problems of the Revolution," Lenin, vol. 21, p. 142 (translation in *Collected Works*, vol. 21, p. 164). See also his speech at the Petrograd Party Conference, 25 April to 5 May 1917, vol. 20, p. 178 (*Collected Works*, vol. 20, book 1, p. 203).

4. "The Elections to the Constituent Assembly and the Dictatorship of the Proletariat," Lenin, vol. 24, p. 635.

5. "Greetings to the Italian, French, and German Communists," Lenin, vol. 24, pp. 480–481.

6. *Ibid.*

7. "On the Reorganization of the Party," Lenin, vol. 8, p. 380.

8. See for instance "The Heroes of the Bern International," Lenin, vol. 24, p. 320.

9. From a speech at the April Conference, 1917, Lenin, vol. 20, p. 246 (*Collected Works*, vol. 20, book 1, p. 278).

10. "The Childhood Disease of 'Leftism' in Communism," Lenin, vol. 25, p. 195 (*"Left Wing" Communism, An Infantile Disorder*, New York, 1940, p. 35).

11. Karl Mannheim, *Ideologie und Utopie* (Bonn, 1930), p. 95.

12. "The Dissolution of the Duma and the Tasks of the Proletariat," vol. 10, p. 18 (*Selected Works*, vol. 3, p. 383).

13. "On the Problem of a Nation-wide Revolution," Lenin, vol. 11, p. 206.

14. From a speech before soldiers' delegates, 11 November 1917, Lenin, vol. 22, p. 30.

15. "One of the Root Problems of the Revolution," Lenin, vol. 21, p. 145 (*Collected Works*, vol. 21, p. 167).

16. *Ibid.*, p. 293.

17. "Bolshevism and the 'Disintegration' of the Army," Lenin, vol. 20, p. 469 (*Collected Works*, vol. 20, book 2, p. 187).

18. This is emphasized in all of Lenin's writings around the turn of the century, especially the period of his editorship of *Iskra*. See also "The Crisis of Menshevism," Lenin, vol. 10, pp. 183–187.

19. Quoted in Sidney Hook, *From Hegel to Marx* (New York, 1936), p. 37.

20. See for instance Karl Kautsky, *Die Diktatur des Proletariats* (Vienna, 1918), p. 15.

21. See George Lukacs, *Geschichte und Klassenbewusstsein* (Berlin, 1923), p. 88.

22. "What Is to Be Done?" Lenin, vol. 4, p. 410 (*Selected Works*, vol. 2, p. 82).

23. N. K. Krupskaya, *Memories of Lenin* (London, n.d.), vol. 1, p. 129.

24. "The strength of the modern movement lies in the awakening of the masses (and chiefly the industrial proletariat) . . ." ("What Is to Be Done?" Lenin, vol. 4, p. 383; *Selected Works*, vol. 2, p. 57).

25. "Our Next Task," Lenin, vol. 2, p. 496.

26. See "The Crisis of Menshevism," Lenin, vol. 10, pp. 188, 191; "On the Reorganization of the Party," vol. 8, pp. 373, 376, 378–379 (*Selected Works*, vol. 3, pp. 456, 460–461, 463–464).

27. "Letter to Comrades About Our Organizational Tasks," Lenin, vol. 5, p. 189.

28. "On the Reorganization of the Party," Lenin, vol. 8, pp. 373, 378–379 (*Selected Works*, vol. 3, pp. 456, 463–464).

29. From a Sovnarkom report to the Fifth Soviet Congress, 5 July 1918, Lenin, vol. 23, p. 123.

30. For an application of this to collectivization and mechanization in agriculture, see "Peasants and Workers," Lenin, vol. 21, p. 112 (*Collected Works*, vol. 21, book 1, p. 133). For a thorough discussion of the press as a weapon of "moral persuasion," see the draft of an article written shortly after the October Revolution, Lenin, vol. 22, pp. 412–417.

Chapter Three. Democracy

1. "Kritik der Hegelschen Staatsphilosophie," in *MEGA*, part 1, vol. 1, half-tone 1, p. 434.

2. *Ibid.*

3. *Ibid.*, p. 435.

4. Quoted in V. I. Lenin, *The State and Revolution* (New York, 1932), p. 59 (italics added).

5. *Ibid.* (italics added).

6. Friedrich Engels, "Zur Kritik des sozial-demokratischen Programmentwurfes 1891," in Karl Marx and Friedrich Engels, *Kritiken der sozial-demokratischen Programmentwürfe* (ed. 3, Berlin [1931]), pp. 63–67.

7. Friedrich Engels' Introduction to Karl Marx, *The Class Struggles in France* (New York, 1934), p. 25.

8. *Ibid.*, p. 27.

9. *Ibid.*, pp. 26, 28–30.

10. Karl Marx, *The Class Struggles in France*, pp. 69–70.

11. Eduard Bernstein, *Die Voraussetzungen des Sozialismus und die Aufgaben der Sozialdemokratie* (Stuttgart, 1906), pp. 122, 126 (italics added).

12. Harold J. Laski, *Reflections on the Revolution of Our Time* (New York, 1947), p. 30.

13. Otto Bauer, *Bolschewismus oder Sozialdemokratie?* (Vienna, 1921), p. 109.

14. "Themes about the Dictatorship of the Proletariat," *Leninskii Sbornik*, vol. 3, p. 496.

15. "The State and Revolution: the Marxist Doctrine about the State," Lenin, vol. 21, pp. 377–378 (translation in *The State and Revolution*, New York, 1932, p. 121). In more recent years this thesis has been presented most clearly, perhaps, in Harold J. Laski, *Parliamentary Government in England* (New York, 1938).

16. "The State and Revolution," Lenin, vol. 21, p. 400 (trans., p. 152).

17. "The Proletarian Revolution and the Renegade Kautsky," Lenin, vol. 23, p. 348 (*The Proletarian Revolution and the Renegade Kautsky*, New York, 1934, p. 28).

18. Marx, *The Class Struggles in France*, p. 58.

19. First draft of "The Proletarian Revolution and the Renegade Kautsky," Lenin, vol. 23, p. 220.

20. *Kommunisticheskii Internatsional*, ed. 3, no. 1 (1 May 1919), Moscow, p. 14.

21. "Tasks of the Proletariat in Our Revolution," Lenin, vol. 20, p. 132 (*Collected Works*, vol. 20, book 1, p. 154). See also "A Caricature of Marxism," Lenin, vol. 19, p. 220 (*Collected Works*, vol. 19, p. 244).

22. "On the Tasks of the Third International; Ramsay Macdonald about the Third International," Lenin, vol. 24, p. 398. See also "The State and Revolution," vol. 21; "The Proletarian Revolution and the Renegade Kautsky," vol. 23.

23. "The Elections to the Constituent Assembly and the Dictatorship of the Proletariat," Lenin, vol. 24, p. 646.

24. "The Revolutionary Democratic Dictatorship of the Proletariat

and Peasantry," Lenin, vol. 7, p. 200. See also "Liberals and Clericals," vol. 16, p. 75; "Marxism and Revisionism," vol. 12, p. 187 (*Marxism and Revisionism,* New York, 1941, p. 10).

25. "Three Constitutions or Three Patterns of Government Structure," Lenin, vol. 7, p. 278.

26. "The First Victory of the Revolution," Lenin, vol. 8, p. 356.

27. "The Bourgeois Intelligentsia's Methods of Fighting Against the Workers," Lenin, vol. 17, pp. 481–482. See also Lenin's speech at the Second Congress of Trade-Unions, 21 January 1919, vol. 23, p. 484.

28. "The Revolutionary Democratic Dictatorship," Lenin, vol. 7, p. 200.

29. "The Bourgeois Intelligentsia's Methods," vol. 17, p. 482.

30. "Inflammable Material in World Politics," Lenin, vol. 12, p. 305. See also "Marxism and Revisionism," vol. 12, p. 187 (trans., p 10).

31. "Imperialism as the Highest Stage of Capitalism," Lenin, vol. 19, p. 138 (*Collected Works,* vol. 19, p. 155).

32. "Draft of a Speech on the Agrarian Question in the Second State Duma," Lenin, vol. 11, p. 103.

33. "Marxism and Reformism," Lenin, vol. 16, p. 610.

34. "Proposals Made by the C.C. of the R.S.D.R.P. to the Second Socialist Conference," Lenin, vol. 19, p. 58 (*Selected Works,* vol. 5, p. 233).

35. "Social democracy regards and makes use of reforms as a by-product of the revolutionary class warfare of the proletariat" ("How Not to Write Resolutions," Lenin, vol. 11, p. 65).

36. "Marxism and Reformism," vol. 16, p. 610.

37. "How Not to Write Resolutions," vol. 11, p. 64.

38. Friedrich Engels, *Ludwig Feuerbach und der Ausgang der klassischen deutschen Philosophie* (Stuttgart, 1895), p. 37.

39. "What the 'Friends of the People' Are . . . ," Lenin, vol. 1, pp. 178–180 (*What the "Friends of the People" Are and How They Fight the Social Democrats,* Moscow, 1951, pp. 255–260).

Chapter Four. The "Operational Code"

1. Nathan Leites, *A Study of Bolshevism* (Glencoe, Ill., 1953); *The Operational Code of the Politburo* (New York, 1951).

2. "Workers' and Bourgeois Democracy," Lenin, vol. 7, p. 65.

3. "Successes and Difficulties of the Soviet Regime," Lenin, vol. 24, pp. 56ff.

4. Leon Trotsky, *Arbeit, Disziplin, und Ordnung werden die Sowjetmacht retten,* pamphlet (Berlin-Basel, 1918), p. 11.

Chapter Five. Democratic Centralism

1. Lenin used the term for the first time in 1906. See "Tactical Platform for the Unification Congress of the RSDRS," Lenin, vol. 9, p. 50.

2. See, for instance, "Party Organization and Party Literature," Lenin, vol. 8, p. 389 *et passim*.

3. "Draft Platform for Our Party," Lenin, vol. 2, p. 510.

4. See "Freedom of Criticism and Unity of Action," Lenin, vol. 9, *passim;* "The Fight Against Cadet-Mongering Social Democrats and Party Discipline," vol. 10, p. 166.

5. Lenin, vol. 14, p. 100 (translation in *Selected Works*, vol. 4, p. 23).

6. "Two Methods of Disputing and Fighting," Lenin, vol. 17, p. 73.

7. *Protokoly VIII S"ezda RKP(b)* (Protocols of the Eighth Congress of the Russian Communist Party; Moscow, 1933), p. 324.

8. From the resolution on organization written by the Eighth Party Congress, *Protokoly VIII S"ezda RKP(b)*, p. 414.

9. Par. 14 of a resolution on the role of communist parties in the proletarian revolution, *II Kongress Kommunisticheskogo Internatsionala, stenograficheskii otchet* (Second Comintern Congress, Stenographic Report; Petrograd, 1921), p. 576.

10. "What the 'Friends of the People' Are and How They Fight the Social Democrats," Lenin, vol. 1, p. 192 (English translation, Moscow, 1951, p. 107).

11. "Letter to Comrades about Our Organizational Tasks," Lenin, vol. 5, p. 184.

12. "What the 'Friends of the People' Are," p. 192 (trans., p. 109).

13. *Protokoly VIII S"ezda RKP(b)*, p. 221.

14. *Ibid.*, p. 18.

Chapter Six. The Task of the Proletariat and Its Auxiliary Forces

1. The most important of these pamphlets are "What the 'Friends of the People' Are and How They Fight the Social Democrats," Lenin, vol. 1, pp. 51–222; "The Economic Contents of Narodnichestvo and the Critique of it in the Book by Mr. Struve," vol. 1, pp. 223–362; "Some Characteristic Traits of Economic Romanticism," vol. 2, pp. 5–115; "Pearls of Narodnik Project-Making," vol. 2, pp. 227–302; "The Heritage We Are Renouncing," vol. 2, pp. 303–338.

2. "What the 'Friends of the People' Are," pp. 117ff.

3. *Ibid.*, p. 167.

4. "The Development of Capitalism in Russia," Lenin, vol. 3. See also "New Economic Movements in the Life of the Peasantry," vol. 1, pp. 1–49; "About the So-Called Problem of Markets," Lenin, *Sochineniia*, ed. 4 (Moscow, 1941), vol. 1, pp. 59–109.

5. "Tasks of the Russian Social Democrats," Lenin, vol. 2, p. 176 (translation in *Selected Works*, vol. 1, p. 501).

6. This policy is expressed most clearly in the pamphlet "The Workers' Party and the Peasantry," written in 1900, Lenin, vol. 4, pp. 100–106 (*Selected Works*, vol. 2, pp. 234–242).

7. "The Agrarian Program of Russian Social Democracy," Lenin, vol. 5, p. 120.

8. *Ibid.*

9. Par. B2 of his draft of a party platform printed in Lenin, vol. 1, p. 426 (*Selected Works,* vol. 1, p. 468).

10. For a full discussion of these demands see *ibid.,* pp. 423–445, especially par. 5, items 1–9 (*Selected Works,* vol. 1, pp. 466–494); also "Draft Program of Our Party," Lenin, vol. 2, pp. 505–528.

11. "Comments on Plekhanov's Second Draft Platform," Lenin, vol. 5, pp. 18–34.

12. "Zemstvo Persecutors and the Hannibals of Liberalism," Lenin, vol. 4, pp. 119–157 (*Selected Works,* vol. 2, pp. 205–223).

13. For a discussion of Lenin's miscalculations, and Bolshevik admission of this, see Oskar Anweiler, "Die russische Revolution von 1905," in *Jahrbücher für Geschichte Osteuropas,* vol. 3, no. 2 (München, 1955), pp. 190–191.

14. "The Autocracy and the Proletariat," Lenin, vol. 7, p. 34.

15. "New Tasks and New Forces," Lenin, vol. 7, p. 147 (*Selected Works,* vol. 3, p. 435).

16. "On Our Agrarian Program," Lenin, *Sochineniia,* ed. 4 (Moscow, 1941–1952), vol. 8, pp. 219ff.

17. "Proletariat and Peasantry," Lenin, vol. 7, p. 158.

18. "The First Victory of the Revolution," Lenin, vol. 8, pp. 352–357. This is a brilliant analysis of the course and results of the revolution, which, in the half century since it was written, has lost none of its freshness and relevancy.

19. *Ibid.* See also "Strength and Weakness of the Russian Revolution," Lenin, vol. 9, p. 185. In 1910 the leader of the Cadets, Paul Miliukov, made a statement which Lenin seized upon to illustrate this contention: "As long as there exists in Russia a legislative chamber controlling the budget, the Russian opposition will remain His Majesty's opposition, but not [an opposition] against His Majesty (quoted in "The Trip of the Tsar to Europe and that of Several Deputies of the Black Hundred Duma to England," Lenin, vol. 14, p. 114).

20. "Contribution to an Evaluation of the Russian Revolution," Lenin, vol. 12, p. 206.

21. "On the Two Lines of the Revolution," Lenin, vol. 18, p. 315 (*Collected Works,* vol. 18, pp. 360–361).

22. "The Historical Fate of the Doctrine of Karl Marx," Lenin, vol. 16, pp. 301–303.

23. "Letters from Afar," Lenin, vol. 20, p. 18 (*Collected Works,* vol. 20, book 1, p. 33).

24. *II Kongress Kommunisticheskogo Internatsionala, stenografi-*

cheskii otchet (Second Comintern Congress, Stenographic Report; Petrograd, 1921), p. 646.

25. "Some Theses," Lenin, vol. 18, p. 313 (*Collected Works*, vol. 18, p. 358). See also "The Agrarian Program of Social Democracy in the First Russian Revolution, 1905–1907," vol. 11, p. 414.

26. *Ibid.*, p. 452.

27. "A Revolution of the 1789 or the 1848 Type?" Lenin, vol. 7, pp. 181–182.

28. For a recent discussion of Stolypin's agrarian policies by an American historian very favorable to Stolypin, see Donald W. Treadgold, "Was Stolypin in Favor of Kulaks?" in *The American Slavic and East European Review*, vol. 14, no. 1, pp. 1–14.

29. For discussions of the difference between these two types of capitalism, see the following articles and pamphlets: "How Not to Write Resolutions," Lenin, vol. 11, pp. 60–63; "Strength and Weakness of the Russian Revolution," vol. 11, pp. 187–188; "The Agrarian Program of Social Democracy in the First Russian Revolution, 1905–1907," vol. 11, pp. 329–498 (several chapters of this work are translated in *Selected Works*, vol. 3, pp. 157–286); "New Agrarian Policy," vol. 12, pp. 134–137; "The Movement to the 'Left' of the Bourgeoisie and the Tasks of the Proletariat," vol. 14, pp. 61–66.

30. "New Agrarian Policy," p. 136.

31. "Platform of Revolutionary Social Democracy," Lenin, vol. 10, p. 393.

32. "The Agrarian Program of Social Democracy," vol. 11, pp. 467, 352 (*Selected Works*, vol. 3, p. 185); also "How Not to Write Resolutions," vol. 11, pp. 60–63.

33. See especially "The Agrarian Problem in Russia toward the End of the Nineteenth Century," Lenin, vol. 12, pp. 266, 269ff.

34. "Political Remarks," Lenin, vol. 12, p. 125 (italics added).

35. "On Truths That Are Old Yet Eternally New," Lenin, vol. 15, p. 196.

36. "Two Tactics of Social Democracy in the Democratic Revolution," Lenin, vol. 8, p. 49 (*Selected Works*, vol. 3, pp. 63–64).

37. "Relations with Bourgeois Parties," Lenin, vol. 11, pp. 280–281.

38. "The Aim of the Struggle of the Proletariat in Our Revolution," Lenin, vol. 14, pp. 38, 42–43.

39. "The Historical Meaning of the Intraparty Fight in Russia," Lenin, vol. 15, p. 14.

40. "The Agrarian Program of Social Democracy," vol. 11, p. 413. The parallel to Communist practice in the People's Democracies of Eastern Europe is striking.

41. *Ibid.*, p. 393.

42. *Ibid.*, p. 426 (*Selected Works*, vol. 3, p. 243).

43. "The Agrarian Problem in Russia," Lenin, vol. 12, p. 267.

44. "The Agrarian Program," vol. 11, pp. 352–356 (*Selected Works*, vol. 3, pp. 185–191).

45. See also "Review of the Agrarian Program of the Workers' Party," Lenin, vol. 9, pp. 55–58.

46. *Ibid.*, p. 72.

47. "Report about Relations to Bourgeois Parties," Lenin, vol. 11, p. 252.

48. "Two Tactics," vol. 8, pp. 62–65 (*Selected Works*, vol. 3, pp. 83–86). See also "The Aim of the Struggle of the Proletariat," vol. 14, pp. 36–51.

49. "The Proletariat and Its Allies in the Russian Revolution," Lenin, vol. 10, p. 203.

50. "Speech in the Kzhesinskaia Palais," Lenin, vol. 20, p. 80 (*Collected Works*, vol. 20, book 1, pp. 99–100). See also "The State and Revolution," vol. 21.

51. "Letters on Tactics," Lenin, vol. 20, p. 107 (*Collected Works*, vol. 20, book 1, p. 128).

52. "On the Organization of the Masses and the Choice of the Moment for Fighting," Lenin, vol. 9, p. 400. See also "The Dissolution of the Duma and the Tasks of the Proletariat," vol. 10, pp. 15–17 (*Selected Works*, vol. 3, pp. 379–383).

53. "Socialism and Anarchism," Lenin, vol. 8, p. 409. See also "Tactical Platform for the Unification Congress of the RSDRP," vol. 9, pp. 44–45; "Some Theses," vol. 18, p. 312 (*Collected Works*, vol. 18, p. 357).

54. "Draft Resolutions for the Fifth Congress of the RSDRP," Lenin, vol. 10, p. 388.

55. "A Revolutionary Army and a Revolutionary Government," Lenin, vol. 7, p. 384 (*Selected Works*, vol. 3, p. 314).

56. Quoted from an article Lenin wrote in 1906 in Oskar Anweiler, "Lenin und die Kunst des Aufstandes," *Wehrwissenschaftliche Rundschau*, no. 10 (Darmstadt, 1955).

57. "Marx About the American 'Black Partition,' " Lenin, vol. 7, pp. 223–224.

58. L. D. Trotsky, *Permanentnaia Revoliutsiia* (Berlin, 1930), p. 58.

59. "On Two Lines of the Revolution," Lenin, vol. 18, pp. 317–318 (*Collected Works*, vol. 18, pp. 362–363).

60. *Ibid.*

61. "Some Theses," Lenin, vol. 18, p. 312 (*Collected Works*, vol. 18, p. 357).

Chapter Seven. Nationalism

1. "On the Problem of the Nation-wide Revolution," Lenin, vol. 11, p. 204.

2. "The Aim of the Struggle of the Proletariat in Our Revolution," Lenin, vol. 14, p. 41.

3. *The Proletarian Revolution and the Renegade Kautsky* (New York, 1934), ch. 7.

4. This strategy of Marx and Engels is succinctly presented, with ample references, in Solomon Frank Bloom, *The World of Nations* (New York, 1941), pp. 96–97, 107–112.

5. Lenin began writing about the national question in 1903 ("The National Problem in Our Program," vol. 5, pp. 337–344). But the question became a burning one only in the second decade of the century. His writings on the national problem are therefore mostly the products of the last prewar years, 1912–1914. They include "Theses on the National Problem," vol. 16, pp. 505–513; "Critical Remarks Concerning the National Problem," vol. 17, pp. 129–159; "The National Problem," vol. 17, pp. 65–67; "On Cultural-National Autonomy," vol. 17, pp. 92–95; and "On the National Program of the RSDRP," vol. 17, pp. 116–121. The most important works on this question are, however, the latest works: "The Socialist Revolution and the Nations' Right to Self-Determination," vol. 19, pp. 35–48 (translation in *Collected Works*, vol. 19, pp. 47–60), written in 1916; and a long pamphlet written in 1914, "On the Nations' Right to Self-Determination," vol. 17, pp. 425–474, which contains a brilliant theoretical polemic against Rosa Luxemburg. Of importance also are the discussions at the Eighth Party Congress, in March 1919.

For recent authoritative treatments of the nationality problem in Leninist theory and practice, see Richard Pipes, *The Formation of the Soviet Union* (Cambridge, Mass., 1954); and E. H. Carr, *A History of Soviet Russia* (New York, 1951), vol. 1, part 3. See also Alfred G. Meyer, "The Use of the Term Culture in the Soviet Union," in A. L. Kroeber and Clyde Kluckhohn, *Culture: a Critical Review of Concepts and Definitions of Culture*, Papers of the Peabody Museum, vol. 47 (Cambridge, Mass., 1952).

6. "A Caricature of Marxism," Lenin, vol. 19, pp. 220–221 (*Collected Works*, vol. 19, pp. 244–249).

7. *Ibid.*

8. "On the Nations' Right to Self-Determination," Lenin, vol. 17, pp. 431–432.

9. First draft of the article "The Proletarian Revolution and the Renegade Kautsky," Lenin, vol. 23, pp. 223.

10. For an expression of Lenin's satisfaction over the Russian defeats in the war of 1905, see "The Fall of Port Arthur," Lenin, vol. 7, pp. 44–50.

11. *Protokoly VIII S"ezda RKP(b)* (Protocols of the Eighth Congress of the Russian Communist Party; Moscow, 1933), p. 107.

12. From a speech given on 22 November 1919, Lenin, vol. 24, p. 551.

13. From a report about foreign policy, 4 May 1918, Lenin, vol. 23, p. 15.

14. *Protokoly VIII S"ezda RKP(b)*, pp. 92–98, esp. p. 93.

15. *Ibid.*, pp. 88–89.

16. See, for instance, "Friedrich Engels," Lenin, vol. 1, pp. 415–416.

17. "Great Times," in *Kommunisticheskii Internatsional*, no. 1, ed. 3, 1 May 1919, p. 70 (italics added).

18. Lenin, vol. 23, p. 382 (*The Proletarian Revolution and the Renegade Kautsky*, p. 68).

19. "Some Theses," Lenin, vol. 18, p. 313 (*Collected Works*, vol. 18, p. 358).

20. From a speech at the Second Soviet Congress, 7–8 November 1917, Lenin, vol. 22, p. 11 (*Selected Works*, vol. 6, p. 400).

Chapter Eight. Eight Months of Revolution

1. Only passing reference can be made in this work to the events of the Russian revolution. For some of the classical accounts by observers, scholars, and direct participants, see William Henry Chamberlin, *The Russian Revolution* (New York, 1935); John Reed, *Ten Days that Shook the World* (New York, 1935); N. N. Sukhanov, *The Russian Revolution 1917* (New York, 1955); and Leon Trotsky, *History of the Russian Revolution* (New York, 1932).

2. Two letters to A. M. Kollontai, 16 and 17 March 1917, Lenin, vol. 20, pp. 1–8 (translation in *Collected Works*, vol. 20, book 1, pp. 19–23); "Draft Theses of 17 March 1917," vol. 20, pp. 9–12 (*Collected Works*, pp. 23–26); "Letters from Afar," vol. 20, pp. 13ff (*Collected Works*, pp. 27ff).

3. "Letters from Afar," p. 33 (*Collected Works*, p. 47).

4. *Ibid.*, p. 35 (trans., p. 50).

5. "Materials on the Revision of the Party Program," Lenin, vol. 20, p. 294 (*Collected Works*, vol. 20, book 1, pp. 327–328).

6. "On Diarchy," Lenin, vol. 20, pp. 94–95 (*Collected Works*, vol. 20, book 1, pp. 115–116).

7. Karl Marx, *The Civil War in France* (New York, 1940).

8. "Letters from Afar," vol. 20, pp. 46–47 (trans., vol. 20, book 1, pp. 62–63).

9. *Ibid.*, pp. 38–39 (pp. 53–55).

10. "The State and Revolution: The Marxist Doctrine of State," Lenin, vol. 21, pp. 365–455.

11. "Letters from Afar," p. 27 (pp. 40–41).

12. "On Diarchy," vol. 20, p. 95 (trans., vol. 20, book 1, p. 116).

13. *Ibid.*

14. *Ibid.*

15. "Letters from Afar," p. 39 (p. 54).

16. "Political Parties in Russia and the Tasks of the Proletariat," Lenin, vol. 20, pp. 136–144 (*Collected Works*, vol. 20, book 1, pp. 158–167).

17. "The All-Russian April Conference of the RSDRP," Lenin, vol. 20, p. 241 (*Collected Works*, vol. 20, book 1, p. 273).

18. "Letters on Tactics," Lenin, vol. 20, p. 100 (*Collected Works*, vol. 20, book 1, p. 119).

19. *Ibid.*, pp. 100–105 (pp. 119–124).

20. *Ibid.*, p. 101 (p. 120).

21. "The All-Russian April Conference," vol. 20, p. 241 (trans., vol. 20, book 1, p. 273).

22. "On Diarchy," vol. 20, pp. 95–96 (trans., vol. 20, book 1, pp. 116–117).

23. From Lenin's speech to Party Comrades after his arrival in Russia, Lenin, vol. 20, p. 80 (*Collected Works*, vol. 20, book 1, p. 99).

24. Chamberlin, vol. 1, p. 169.

25. "On Slogans," Lenin, vol. 21, p. 33 (*Collected Works*, vol. 21, book 1, p. 43).

26. *Ibid.*, p. 34 (trans., p. 44).

27. *Ibid.*, p. 38 (p. 50).

28. "The Bolsheviks Must Seize Power," Lenin, vol. 21, p. 193 (*Collected Works*, vol. 21, book 1, p. 221).

29. *Ibid.*, pp. 193–194 (trans., pp. 221–222); "Letter to the Petersburg City Conference," Lenin, vol. 21, pp. 290–292.

30. "Will the Bolsheviks Be Able to Stay in Power?" Lenin, vol. 21, pp. 246–284 (*Selected Works*, vol. 6, pp. 250–296).

31. Lenin, vol. 22, p. 582, note 21.

32. Lenin, vol. 22, p. 47.

33. *Ibid.* (italics added).

34. "Contribution to the Revision of the Party Program," Lenin, vol. 21, p. 315.

35. From a speech at the Eighth Party Congress, Lenin, vol. 24, p. 117 (italics added).

36. "Letter to American Workers," Lenin, vol. 23, p. 182. See also his speech to the March 1918 Congress of Soviets, Lenin, vol. 22, pp. 390–391.

37. From a speech at the Eighth Party Congress, Lenin, vol. 24, p. 121.

38. "Successes and Difficulties of the Soviet Regime," Lenin, vol. 24, p. 57.

39. From a report on foreign policy, Lenin, vol. 23, p. 9.

40. See Oliver Radkey's realistic appraisal of socialist revolutionary

utopianism in his article, "Chernov and Agrarian Socialism," in Ernest J. Simmons (ed.), *Continuity and Change in Russian and Soviet Social Thought* (Cambridge, Mass., 1955), pp. 69ff.

41. Friedrich Engels, letter to Weydemeyer, 12 April 1853, in Karl Marx and Friedrich Engels, *Kritiken der sozial-demokratischen Programmentwürfe* (ed. 3, Berlin, 1931), Appendix 1, p. 102.

Chapter Nine. The Leninist State in Theory and in Practice

1. L. Kritsman, *Geroicheskii period velikoi russkoi revoliutsii* (Moscow, 1925), p. 40.
2. "The Next Tasks of the Soviet Regime," Lenin, vol. 22, pp. 440–441 (translation in *Selected Works*, vol. 7, pp. 314–315).
3. "On Co-operation," Lenin, vol. 27, p. 396 (*Selected Works*, vol. 9, p. 408).
4. "The Tasks of the Proletariat in Our Revolution," Lenin, vol. 20, p. 133 (*Collected Works*, vol. 20, book 1, p. 155).
5. "The State and Revolution: The Marxist Doctrine of State," ch. 1, part 4, Lenin, vol. 21, pp. 381–382.
6. "Report on the Right to Recall," Lenin, vol. 22, p. 97.
7. "The State and Revolution," Lenin, vol. 21, pp. 422–423.
8. "The Proletarian Revolution and the Renegade Trotsky," Lenin, vol. 23, p. 393 (English edition, New York, 1934, p. 81).
9. "The Chief Tasks of Our Days," Lenin, vol. 22, p. 374.
10. *Ibid.*
11. Kritsman, pp. 39–40.
12. See Robert V. Daniels, "The State and Revolution: A Case Study in the Genesis and Transformation of Communist Ideology," in *The American Slavic and East European Review*, vol. 12, pp. 22–43.
13. For his best-known statements on this topic, see his comments on the Subbotnik movement, Lenin, vol. 24, pp. 325–349.
14. Kritsman, p. 81.
15. From a speech given on 3 November 1920, Lenin, vol. 25, p. 455.
16. "The State and Revolution," Lenin, vol. 21, p. 411.
17. *Ibid.*, p. 450.
18. "The Proletarian Revolution and the Renegade Kautsky," vol. 23, p. 341 (trans., p. 19).
19. Trotsky, *The Defence of Terrorism* (London, 1921), p. 23.
20. Speech at the Third Congress of Soviets, January 1918, Lenin, vol. 22, p. 208. See also George S. Pettee, *The Process of Revolution* (New York, 1938), pp. 136–139, who agrees with Lenin and Trotsky in principle.
21. "Greeting to Hungarian Workers," Lenin, vol. 24, p. 315.
22. "Preface to the Publication of the Speech 'On the Deception

of the People by Slogans of Liberty and Equality,'" Lenin, vol. 24, p. 311.

23. "The Next Tasks of the Soviet Regime," Lenin, vol. 22, p. 462 (*Selected Works*, vol. 7, p. 342). See also "On the Dictatorship of the Proletariat," Lenin, vol. 25, p. 5.

24. "Greeting to Hungarian Workers," vol. 24, p. 314.

25. Speech at a Moscow Provincial Party Conference, 21 November 1920, Lenin, vol. 25, p. 491.

26. "The Great Initiative: On the Heroism of the Workers Behind the Front," Lenin, vol. 24, p. 336.

27. From the Party Conference of 2–4 December 1919, Lenin, vol. 24, p. 571.

28. "From the Destruction of the Age-Old Order to the Creation of the New One," Lenin, vol. 25, p. 151.

29. "Successes and Difficulties of the Soviet Regime," Lenin, vol. 24, pp. 64–65. See also his political report to the Eleventh Party Congress.

30. From the first draft of an article, Lenin, vol. 22, p. 415. See also "How to Organize Competition," vol. 22, pp. 158–167 (*Selected Works*, vol. 9, pp. 413–422).

31. Government report to the Fifth Congress of Soviets, 5 July 1918, Lenin, vol. 23, pp. 122–123.

32. "The Next Tasks of the Soviet Regime," vol. 22, p. 454 (*Selected Works*, vol. 7, p. 332). See also his speech of 29 April 1918, vol. 22, p. 486.

33. See *Protokoly VIII S"ezda RKP(b)* (Protocols of the Eighth Party Congress; Moscow, 1933), p. 108.

34. "How to Organize Competition," vol. 22, p. 163 (*Selected Works*, vol. 9, p. 417).

35. *Protokoly VIII S"ezda RKP(b)*, p. 384, in Lenin, vol. 24, p. 166.

36. Otto Bauer, *Bolschewismus oder Sozialdemokratie?* (Vienna, 1921), p. 62.

37. "Successes and Difficulties of the Soviet Regime," Lenin, vol. 24, p. 65.

38. "Speech about the Deception of the People by Slogans of Liberty and Equality, 29 May 1919," Lenin, vol. 24, pp. 299–300.

39. From a speech to Communist metal workers, 6 March 1922, Lenin, *Sobranie Sochinenii* (Moscow, 1920–1923), vol. 18, book 2, p. 16.

40. Political report to the Eleventh Party Congress, *ibid.*, p. 43.

Chapter Ten. Socialism in One Country

1. "Theses on the Question of Concluding at Once a Separate and Annexionist Peace," Lenin, vol. 22, p. 194.

2. Lenin, *Sobranie Sochinenii* (Moscow, 1920–1923), vol. 18, book 2, p. 105.

3. Lenin's demand that the Soviet state engage in a balance-of-power game is formulated most clearly in a speech of 26 November 1920, Lenin, vol. 25, pp. 498–507.

4. "Theses on the Question of Concluding at Once a Separate and Annexionist Peace," vol. 22, p. 195.

5. *Ibid.*

6. From a speech at the Fifth Party Congress, Lenin, vol. 24, pp. 560–561.

7. "Speech on the International Situation," 8 November 1918, Lenin, vol. 23, p. 265 (italics added).

8. "Speech at the Moscow Provincial Party Conference," Lenin, vol. 25, pp. 483–484.

9. *Ibid.*

10. From a speech given on 22 November 1919, Lenin, vol. 24, p. 544.

11. *II Kongress Kommunisticheskogo Internatsionala, stenograficheskii otchet* (Second Comintern Congress, Stenographic Report; Petrograd, 1921), p. 645.

12. "Opportunism and the Collapse of the Second International," Lenin, vol. 19, p. 6.

13. "The Chief Task of Our Days," Lenin, vol. 22, p. 378.

14. "On Left-Wing Childishness and Petty Bourgeois Mentality," Lenin, vol. 22, p. 510 (translation in *Selected Works*, vol. 7, p. 357).

15. From a speech given on 23 August 1918, Lenin, vol. 23, p. 194.

16. *Ibid.*

17. From a government report of 29 March 1920 to the Eleventh Party Congress, Lenin, vol. 25, p. 93 (italics added).

Chapter Eleven. The Theory of Imperialism

1. "What the 'Friends of the People' Are and How They Fight Against the Social Democrats," Lenin, *Sobranie Sochinenii* (Moscow, 1920–1923), vol. 1, pp. 274–275.

2. Allen S. Whiting, *Soviet Policies in China, 1917–1924* (New York, 1954), p. 39. I have paraphrased Whiting's remark without distorting its meaning.

3. "Imperialism as the Highest Stage of Capitalism," Lenin, vol. 19, p. 119 (translation in *Collected Works*, vol. 19, p. 135).

4. Lenin's ideas on imperialism are found primarily in the following articles and books:

"The War in China," vol. 4, pp. 60–64 (*Collected Works*, vol. 4, book 1, pp. 59–64).

"The Fall of Port Arthur," vol. 7, pp. 44–50.

"European Capital and the Autocratic Regime," vol. 7, pp. 175–180.

"Inflammable Material in World Politics," vol. 12, pp. 304–309 (*Selected Works*, vol. 4, pp. 297–299).

"The Stuttgart International Socialist Congress," vol. 12, pp. 78–83.

"Aggressive Militarism," vol. 12, pp. 311–319 (*Selected Works*, vol. 4, pp. 324–333).

"Backward Europe and Progressive Asia," vol. 16, pp. 395–396.

"Imperialism as the Highest Stage of Capitalism," vol. 19, pp. 67–176 (*Collected Works*, vol. 19, pp. 83–198).

"A Caricature of Marxism," vol. 19, pp. 191–235 (*Collected Works*, vol. 19, pp. 214–263).

"Opportunism and the Collapse of the Second International," vol. 19, pp. 5–15 (*Collected Works*, vol. 19, pp. 15–27).

"Imperialism and the Schism of Socialism," vol. 19, pp. 301–313 (*Collected Works*, vol. 19, pp. 337–351).

Leninskii Sbornik, vols. 22, 27, 28, 29, and 30.

5. "Imperialism as the Highest Stage of Capitalism," Lenin, vol. 19, p. 118 (trans., p. 133).

6. *Ibid.*, pp. 100–101 (pp. 119–120).

7. "Imperialism and the Schism of Socialism," Lenin, vol. 19, pp. 310–311 (*Collected Works*, vol. 19, pp. 348–350).

8. "Imperialism as the Highest Stage of Capitalism," Lenin, vol. 19, pp. 156–158 (*Collected Works*, vol. 19, pp. 174–177).

9. *Ibid.*, pp. 155, 172 (trans., pp. 174, 193–194).

10. Nathan Leites, *A Study of Bolshevism* (Glencoe, Ill., 1953), brings out this pessimism very well.

11. "Imperialism as the Highest Stage of Capitalism," vol. 19, p. 118 (trans., p. 133).

12. *Ibid.*, ch. 6.

13. *Ibid.*, p. 147 (trans., p. 165).

14. *Ibid.*, pp. 149, 147–151 (pp. 167, 165–169).

15. *Ibid.*, pp. 119ff (pp. 134ff).

16. *Ibid.*, p. 122 (p. 138).

17. *Ibid.*, chapters 4 and 9.

18. "Contribution to the Revision of the Party Program," Lenin, vol. 21, pp. 310–311.

19. "All-Russian April Conference of the RSDRP," Lenin, vol. 20, p. 253 (*Collected Works*, vol. 20, book 1, p. 86).

20. *Ibid.*

21. From a speech at the Seventh Party Congress, Lenin, vol. 22, p. 318.

22. From a speech at the Third Congress of Soviets, Lenin, vol. 22, p. 218.

23. "Imperialism as the Highest Stage of Capitalism," vol. 19, p. 92 (*Collected Works,* vol. 19, p. 104).

Chapter Twelve. The Dialectics of Backwardness

1. This is stated very succinctly in the Introduction to Nicholas S. Timasheff, *The Great Retreat* (New York, 1946), and also appears to be one of the basic premises of David Shub, *Lenin: A Biography* (Garden City, N. Y., 1948).

2. Eduard Heimann, *Communism, Fascism, or Democracy?* (New York, 1938), p. 10. For an appreciation of the advantages of backwardness by a non-Marxian economist, see Alexander Gerschenkron, "Economic Backwardness in Historical Perspective," in B. Hoselitz (ed.), *The Progress of Underdeveloped Areas* (Chicago, 1952); and "The Problem of Economic Development in Russian Intellectual History of the Nineteenth Century," in Ernest J. Simmons (ed.), *Continuity and Change in Russian and Soviet Thought* (Cambridge, Mass., 1955).

3. "The International Situation and the Basic Tasks of the Comintern," in *II Kongress Kommunisticheskogo Internatsionala, stenograficheskii otchet* (Second Comintern Congress, Stenographic Report; Petrograd, 1921), p. 36.

4. Speech of 26 November 1920, Lenin, vol. 25, p. 509.

Index